Utopia
and Its
Enemies

STUDIES IN THE LIBERTARIAN
AND UTOPIAN TRADITION

UTOPIA
AND ITS
ENEMIES

George Kateb

SCHOCKEN BOOKS • NEW YORK

To my parents

"Of course, no honest person claims that
happiness is *now* a normal condition among
human beings; but perhaps it *could* be
made normal, and it is upon this question
that all serious political controversy really turns."

"Happiness is notoriously difficult to
describe, and pictures of a just and
well-ordered Society are seldom either
attractive or convincing."

George Orwell

Preface to the Paperback Edition

I used to think that the idea of a utopian way of life made sense; and, even more, that such a life was a genuine alternative to the life now lived. I am now much less confident about these assumptions. The growth of interest in utopia in the last few years forces one to look at such assumptions again. There is now a certain literalism about the matter of utopia that was lacking a little while ago. On the one hand, the creation of communes; on the other, the intensified feeling that it is the fate of the world to become a unity—these nourish as they derive from the revival of utopia. With this revival, which is not only academic or literary, utopia's practicability and desirability take on some more seriousness. In this brief preface I can merely indicate the change in me induced (in part) by the real existence of utopian aspirations.

Does the idea of a utopian way of life make sense? Should the characteristics of the perfect or near-perfect society be specified? Should a sketch of utopian men, women, and children be made? Allowing for changes in utopian people and their environment, should even a minimal account of utopia be at the same time a substantial account? I do not know how to answer these questions with certainty. But I now feel less sympathetic than

I did when I wrote *Utopia and Its Enemies* to the notion that utopia should be thought to have a positive identifiable content. Every description (not only B. F. Skinner's) and every experiment, soon turn out to be, on close examination, diminishing, confining, stultifying. The world should not be made to yield itself entirely to the imagination or practice of any individual or group. In every set of arrangements much is lost, though much may be gained. If utopia implies a fairly definite set of arrangements, if it lives on the belief that it is the best possible set, then it necessarily condemns itself to narrowness and exclusion. There are too many conceivable "bests" to permit any to establish itself in such a way as to make radical departure from it unlikely. In the past, openness to possibility spoke through the literature of utopia. It may be that the world has grown so rich in actuality and near-actuality that any effort to legislate for a whole society, in the name of utopia, impoverishes the sense of life. The very wish to compose a utopia, to set forth in detail a utopian way of life, may in fact be repressive.

I do think, however, that the first two of the three utopian ends I discuss survive the doubts I have just expressed. It is not repressive to insist that utopia be defined so as to exclude war and scarcity. It is not repressive to want war and scarcity to disappear from the globe. The minimal conditions of decency in the real world are the minimal conditions of decency in the perfect world. The world would be utopia if war and scarcity were abolished—provided, of course, it were not a Brave New World in any of its numerous peaceful and affluent variations. That much we can cling to in utopian idealism. To include more in the definition of utopia itself—to include conditioned virtue, as I have in this book—risks a terrible closure. Rather, we should think of utopia as a world in which individuals and groups had the freedom, will, energy, and talent to make and remake their lives unencumbered by insufficiency and the fear of violent death.

Does utopia, as I have reduced it, present a genuine alternative to the life now lived all over the world? More specifically, is it reasonable to suppose that a world without scarcity is within human reach? Can everybody's basic material needs be satisfied? Is the suffering now so widespread corrigible with a rational reorganization and allocation of world resources? There is as yet no answer, nothing approaching an answer, to this question. Some, like Herbert Marcuse, suppose with an unwarranted ease that the reason there is scarcity is that advanced capitalism steals, hogs, and wastes the world's resources. Scarcity will end if capitalism is replaced. Others imagine that nothing can be done to improve the world's condition in the long run; that things will get worse. Population will outstrip the means of subsistence; irrecoverable resources will be exhausted; the natural environment will first become corrupted and then unlivable. One view is magical; the other apocalyptic. It seems to me that those who are guided by the idea of utopia must courageously examine the question of whether the material basis for a world without scarcity can ever come into being. The place of conjecture in such an examination will, of course, be large. The truth may be that there can be no utopia, but there can be an apocalypse. The morality of futurist thinking would then consist in trying to ward off or delay the apocalypse, not in dreaming about perfection, or even about a world without scarcity.

GEORGE KATEB

Amherst College
December, 1971

Acknowledgments

My interest in the subject of antiutopianism was stimulated by conversations with John Hollander and Marvin Minsky, when we were all in the Society of Fellows at Harvard University, 1954–57. My greatest debt is to Professor Herbert A. Deane of Columbia University, who not only read all drafts with infinite patience, but also saved me from perpetuating a number of serious errors in general approach and attitude. That errors remain reflects only on the author. Professor Neal Wood of Columbia University read the entire essay, and helped me to clarify several matters. I wish also to acknowledge the valuable aid of Professor Earl Latham and Professor Leo Marx, both of Amherst College. They read my manuscript in various stages, and made many enlightening and helpful comments. Kai Nielsen, Thomas N. Bisson, and William E. Kennick gave me the benefit of their learning and of their friendship. Lastly, I wish to record my debt to the late Franz Neumann, without whom there would have been nothing to begin.

GEORGE KATEB

Contents

1

Introduction: Utopian Ends

and Utopian Society

i

This essay is meant to consider certain attacks—
most of them modern—which have been made on utopianism.
These attacks stem from the belief that the world sometime
soon (unbearably soon) will have at its disposal—if it wishes
to use them—the material presuppositions of a way of life commonly described as "utopian." Such a prospect, one would have
thought, would be a cause for gladness. It has not been that, at
all, but rather a signal for men of various persuasions and temperaments to devote themselves strenuously and in all sincerity
to exposing both the insufficiency of utopian ideals and the unacceptability of arrangements thought necessary to the realization of those ideals. On the face of it, it would seem absurd that
serious thinkers would seek to turn us away from what mankind, all through time, has cherished. The apparent absurdity
becomes more acute, and more engaging, when it is seen that

the motives of the antiutopians are, for the most part, unimpeachable by any humanitarian. How could it be that there are well-disposed men who, from their very benevolence, take fright at the thought of a general reign of benevolence? Surely what is involved is not cheap paradox on anyone's part, nor any spite or perversity; surely, there must be something else at work in the minds of these men.

It would be tempting to say, by way of explanation, that antiutopianism is simply a more startling manifestation of the hostility to the aspirations of both the French Enlightenment and the French Revolution that has been so conspicuous a feature of Western thought for the past century and a half. In her book *After Utopia*,[1] Judith N. Shklar has demonstrated how widespread that hostility has been, showing itself in a large number of quite disparate sensibilities. The critique of the Enlightenment and the Revolution has been carried on by romantics and existentialists, Christians of every major branch of Christianity, liberal conservatives and conservative liberals. It discloses itself, in its several component attitudes, as broadly antipolitical and antisocial, and also as antirationalist and antisecular, antihistoricist and antioptimist, antiradical and antireformist. The career of the doctrines of the French eighteenth century and the history of the French Revolution have worked together with the history of the Russian Revolution and Dictatorship, and "the revolt of the masses," to produce a profound suspicion of the whole realm of politics, and, concomitantly, a profound reluctance to entertain schemes for significant changes within that realm. The unreasoned political apathy of the citizenry of the West (which we hear so much about) is thus matched by the carefully articulated political aversion of a large number of intellectuals.

Now it is certainly the case that the attack on the French Enlightenment and the French Revolution is, at some points, an attack on utopianism, either direct or by implication. Naturally any view that was, say, antirationalist or antiradical would

---

1. Judith N. Shklar, *After Utopia* (Princeton, N.J.: Princeton University Press, 1957).

perforce be antiutopian. That much is obvious. And one could see that enough had taken place since 1789 to generate anti-rationalism and antiradicalism (together with all the other attitudes that are within Judith Shklar's purview). There may be reason for regret, but there is no reason for surprise. But it is also the case that modern antiutopianism, in all its complication, is fed from many sources that have no relation to the sentiments of romantic, Christian, and liberal reaction. Modern antiutopianism is made up, in large part but not exclusively, of ideas that would have been formulated even though there had been no French Revolution and no Russian Revolution. That is to say, modern antiutopianism cannot be seen *merely* as one form or one aspect of the larger tendency of modern antiradical thought. The Enlightenment and the French Revolution, Marxism and the Russian Revolution, possessed, of course, "utopian" characteristics; the hostility to these ideas and events would correspondingly possess antiutopian characteristics. But just as these ideas and events do not by any means exhaust utopianism, so the hostility to them does not exhaust antiutopianism. In many of its essential arguments, modern antiutopianism is coincident with the modern reaction Judith Shklar discusses, but it must be understood at least in partial independence of that reaction.

The antiutopianism that we are to take up in this essay is a crystallization of a number of ideas, attitudes, opinions, and sentiments that have existed for centuries. And it is nothing but the development of technology and the natural sciences that is responsible for the crystallization that has taken place. With this development has come the awareness that some dreams and visions of the past, dreams and visions of a life of fullness and harmony for the whole race, have now, and for the first time, acquired plausibility. They have acquired a plausibility they did not have even when Marx was announcing the promise of the industrial technology that the bourgeoisie had brought into the world. The question to be answered is, What is it about the dreams and visions of the past that made them once the repository of men's longings and make them now, for some, when nearly realizable, intolerable?[2] What could make Tantalus joyous?

ii

We have already said that on the face of it, it seems absurd that there are those who would advocate that we turn our backs on what we have always said we wanted, just as we are coming to feel that we can have it, at least in theory, after all. It could be said, in reply to this charge of apparent absurdity, that all through time there has been no real agreement on what we have wanted, that fantasies of the most amazing divergence from each other have abounded, that scheme has followed upon scheme, that each age has furnished paradise in a different mode, that there has been, in short, no uniform view on the ultimately desirable social condition of man. Add to that, that there has been not only a great variety of dreams and visions, but also, obviously, abundant opposition to almost any dream or vision one would care to cite. Why, to take just one example, criticism of Plato's Republic is nearly as old as *The Republic* itself: Plato was answered by Aristotle; and Aristotle went on, in turn, to devise his own "ideal commonwealth." Notions of perfection change, inevitably; as Margaret Mead has said, one man's dream is another man's nightmare.[3] Could it not be said that since utopianism is only one kind of speculation about ideals and since ideals are always in dispute, there should therefore be no surprise at modern antiutopianism: modern antiutopianism is nothing but a continuation of the struggle of ideal against ideal? Is it not folly to suppose that the struggle should by now have stopped?

2. Cf. the remark of Hannah Arendt: "And what else, finally, is this ideal of modern society but the age-old dream of the poor and destitute, which can have a charm of its own so long as it is a dream, but turns into a fool's paradise as soon as it is realized." (*The Human Condition*, Chicago: University of Chicago Press, 1958), p. 133.

3. Margaret Mead, "Towards More Vivid Utopias," *Science*, 126 (1957), pp. 957-961, at p. 958.

It must of course be granted to this line of argument that the history of thought is witness to a succession of utopias, of plans and blueprints and suggestions for the organization of life in every detail, to be found in fiction, verse, and treatise. There are rationalist utopias, hedonist utopias, ascetic-spiritual utopias, paradisal utopias, agrarian utopias, mechanized utopias, utopias of virtue, or craft, or play. More summarily, utopian theorists have ranged themselves on both sides in their answers to these basic questions: Shall utopia be a place of abundance or austerity? Shall utopian politics be aristocratic or democratic? Is work or leisure the right mode of existence? Is the good life one in which public involvements or private pursuits absorb the main energies of the individual? And it would appear that this assortment of solutions would indicate a total absence of any agreement among the party of utopians; and would also indicate that it would be wrong to speak of "utopianism," and pretend that it meant anything uniform. It then would follow that modern antiutopianism, if such a thing existed, must have for its enemy a specific, modern utopianism; and, naturally, the burden of apparent absurdity would be taken off the shoulders of modern antiutopianism. For the battle between utopianism and antiutopianism in modern times would simply be one more battle in the realm of ideals, and not a battle between the age-long wishes of humanity and the recalcitrance of a minority of contemporary intellectuals.

It is undeniable that the institutions and forms of life that utopian theorists have urged on men are as heterogeneous, almost, as the institutions and forms of the real world. Besides being able to say, as we did, that there have been agrarian utopias and mechanized utopias (and so on), we can also say that the very arrangements of life, big and small, vary from utopia to utopia. Prescriptions concerning marriage, property, education, art, and everything else change with the utopian planner. There are not merely differences from one to the other, there are contradictions as well. In the face of all this variety (confusion?) how could we be tempted to speak of utopianism as a continuous tradition of an essential core of ideals? The answer is that though utopias may differ in shape and texture, may differ in the means seen as necessary by the utopian to attain his ends, the ends of utopian thought may indeed be considered as remaining basically similar through time. What is more, these ideals are the true articulations of the aspirations of common humanity.

If one were to go through the Greek and Roman legends of the golden age which Lovejoy and Boas have so splendidly compiled,[4] and if one were to follow, with A. J. Carlyle,[5] the course of Christian speculation—the speculation of some of the Church Fathers, and some of the early Christian philosophers and canon lawyers—on the condition of man before the Fall, the "natural" condition of man, one would find the heart of utopianism. Then if one were to examine the great and influential utopias, the fictional accounts or straightforward descriptions of (intendedly perfect) organized communities (or larger societies); and examine the great and influential "philosophical" anthropologies and "conjectural" histories; and examine the major theories of inevitable progress in social life; and connect the legends and reflections and devisings and conjectures and prophecies, one must be struck by the close resemblances in nostalgia (when there is nostalgia) and expectation (a more modern feature); or in statements on *what ought to be,* all questions of time or likelihood aside. Not in institutional arrangements designed to house the vision of perfection is there unanimity. Nor is there unanimity on whether or not institutional arrangements of any sort whatever are required. There is something like unanimity, however, in vision—in desire or purpose.[6]

---

4. *A Documentary History of Primitivism,* ed. by Arthur O. Lovejoy et al. (Baltimore: Johns Hopkins Press, 1935).

5. R. W. Carlyle and A. J. Carlyle, *A History of Mediaeval Political Theory in the West* (6 vols., New York and Edinburgh: Blackwood, 1903–1936), Vol. 1 (1903), Chaps. 10, 11, 12, 16. See also Chaps. 3–4 for a discussion of the classical writers.

6. I do not wish to deny that the word "utopia" can be used to designate any society which someone holds to be perfect. Thus, even Sade's Sodom and O'Brien's Oceania could, in some sense, be called "utopias." It is nevertheless true, I think, that when we speak of a utopia, we generally mean an ideal society which is not an efflorescence of a diseased or playful or satirical imagination, nor a private or special dream-world, but rather one in which the welfare of all its inhabitants is the central concern, and in which the level of welfare is strikingly higher, and assumed to be more long-lasting, than that of the real world.

There would seem to be, that is to say, an image of what life in its net effect would be like, if life (social life) were perfect; and the image persists through time, and persists through a sequence of differing institutional embodiments.

How then is this image of life to be characterized? A way to begin answering this question is to see what the stories of the Golden Age and of the natural condition of man most mourn the loss of; what they put forward the most insistently as the things in life that men no longer have, probably can never again have; what they say men left behind them when the necessary cycle of ages, or the will of the gods, or the flaws of their nature forced or led them out of their original perfection.[7] Once out of perfection, once into the iron age or fallen state, men find themselves in a radically transformed situation. The imperfection is defined by the presence of authority and constraint, hierarchy and class, slavery and war, property and scarcity, labor and pain, disease and mutation. There is an inequality of power, possessions, prestige, and liberty; there is an insufficiency of pleasure and tranquillity. Sometimes all or some of these things are considered inherently evil; sometimes all or some of these things are considered morally indifferent but nevertheless imperfect contrivances that necessity or prudence dictates. In any case, these are the things that are the determining conditions of life, the setting in which men are to do what they can, remembering that it was not always as it is

---

7. It would be well to keep in mind that it is possible to understand these stories and legends as saying nothing other than that anything to be found in Eden, Arcadia, or the Golden Age is, by its very nature, unattainable outside those perfect places, never to be expected in the real world: to say that something existed in, for example, Arcadia, is *only* to say that it cannot exist in the world: Arcadia is *only* that which cannot be, that which we cannot legitimately hope for, not a land that people once inhabited and lost much to their incredible misfortune. By putting some feature of life in Arcadia, the storyteller may mean only to say of that feature that it is a permanently excluded possibility for the real world. Think also of the pejorative use of the word "utopian." As Karl Mannheim said, "The representatives of a given order will label as utopian all conceptions of existence which *from their point of view* can in principle never be realized. According to this usage, the contemporary connotation of the term 'utopian' is predominantly that of an idea which is in principle unrealizable." [*Ideology and Utopia*, trans. by L. Wirth and E. Shils (New York: Harvest Books, n.d.), p. 196.]

now, and conceding perhaps that it cannot ever be different
from what it is now. But there, somewhere in the past—real,
fictional, or conjectured—is the real life, the natural life, the
perfect life, the *sensually* flawless life, the life that we would
choose to have if we had a choice to make. We all would prefer
a life of brotherhood, equality, joy, leisure, plenty, peace, health,
and a life of permanent, unrelieved, universal *satisfaction*: is
there anyone who would not?

If we go on from these stories to the great utopias and to
the theories of inevitable progress, we would find, though not
perhaps so readily and unmistakably, the same sense of what
perfection, in its rough essentials, would be. Whether one
thinker throws off a plan for an ideal society to serve as a
touchstone or as a stimulus for betterment, or another detects
in the movement of history an irresistible tendency toward the
production of a final condition of complete desirability, the conception of what is perfect, what is the best, seems to remain
constant. The ends to be served by the ideal society, or the
ends that history is bound, one day, to serve, are similar from
thinker to thinker, even though the specific arrangements by
which these ends are to be served constantly change. The
imagination of a given thinker is inevitably dominated by the
level of technology, by the means of production, available at
the time, or thought to be implicit in the technology of the
time; consequently, the arrangements he proposes are a function
of what he sees or can, in seriousness, imagine. As a result, the
ends are served in curious ways: they may even appear not to
be served at all. Recall Karl Marx's criticism of Babeuf: "The
revolutionary literature that accompanied these first movements
of the proletariat had necessarily a reactionary character. It in-
culcated universal asceticism and social leveling in its crudest
form."[8]

But despite all this surface variety, is there not still one
fundamental notion of social perfection? Of course, the utopias
of More or Morelly or Morris are not the same in detail; each

---

8. Karl Marx and Frederick Engels, "Manifesto of the Communist
Party," in *Selected Works* (2 vols., Moscow: Foreign Language Publishing
House, 1951), Vol. I, p. 58.

places the several utopian ends in a rather different order of importance, or ignores some ends altogether, or even sacrifices some ends to others. And the resting-place of world history looks to Condorcet rather different from the way it looks to Spencer. But do not both resting-places, and others in the literature of inevitable progress, lead one to feel that most of the time when a man thinks of perfection (in these cases, perfection at the happy ending of world history) he thinks of a world permanently without strife, poverty, constraint, stultifying labor, irrational authority, sensual deprivation? Is not the term "utopianism" being properly used when it is used to denote the cluster of these and related things? Utopian societies change radically from author to author; utopian means, arrangements, institutions, change radically from author to author; but is there not a common utopianism, a fairly steady perception of what ends are worthy of being called "utopian," of the net effect of perfect social life? Are we not entitled to speak of utopianism as that system of values which places harmony at the center: harmony within the soul of each man, harmony of each man with all others, harmony of each man with society at large, as that system of values which would hold social life to be perfect if between appetite and satisfaction, between precept and inclination, between requirement and performance, there fell no Shadow? Is not this the vision of utopianism through time; is not this the substance of the longings of common humanity? Is not utopianism the moral prepossession of our race? Does not antiutopianism carry, therefore, at least a burden of *surprise*?

iii

Still, we cannot go back into the Garden, backward in time to the Golden Age. Christianity does not put man, at the end of time, back where he began, exactly as he was when he began; Socrates must leave the nonluxurious state in order to found the city of justice; Rousseau laments the loss of primitivity but sees in the ideal city-state the only possible milieu for the moral life. Modern utopianism may not have a care for Christian eschatology; it may find that in *The Republic* utopian ends are had at an intolerable cost in institutional means; it may see in the community of *The Social Contract* many of the ends of utopianism established in what is for us, now, an anachronistic institutional framework. But it endorses the progression made by Christianity (if one may be allowed to speak so imprecisely of Christianity as a whole), and by Plato and Rousseau. Disobedience took us out of the Garden; appetite led us out of the pastoral setting; avarice spelled the end of the state of nature. But by means of transgression or failure, something higher or better can be made, which will be like that which was at the beginning, but not exactly like it: there is to be harmony, order, repose, and joy, but of a new kind. There is no return to nature or to childlike innocence. Modern utopianism continues along these lines.

There is to be contrivance where there once was an easy and untaught spontaneity; there is to be knowledge where there once was ignorance; there is to be morality where there once was innocence; there is to be community where there once was anarchy; there is to be civilization where there once was rawness. There is to be harmony in modern utopia, as there was harmony in the old natural conditions; but harmony on a higher level. Perfection now presupposes complication. It is unthinkable that the cluster of utopian ends could, as a cluster, have permanent existence outside a society organized for their sake.[9] This is where modern utopianism begins; this is where the books central to modern utopianism begin: books like Edward Bellamy's *Looking Backward* (1888), William Morris's *News from Nowhere* (1890), H. G. Wells' *A Modern Utopia* (1905), Lenin's

---

9. It would be foolish to deny that *some* of the utopian ends have been or can be achieved in some countries of the world, at least for a time. A few places have abundance; there are temporary arrangements for peace; there can be isolated experiments in "behavioral engineering" and the good life. One could even imagine a world welfare-state, with national rivalries abolished and the fruits of a rational industrial system rationally distributed. Such a development would be tremendous. But many of the morally greatest problems would remain untouched. For the whole range of utopian ends to be achieved, and achieved fully, permanently, and universally, a deliberately utopian world society is the *sine qua non*.

State and Revolution (1917), Freud's *Civilization and Its Discontents* (1930), B. F. Skinner's *Walden Two* (1948), and Herbert Marcuse's *Eros and Civilization* (1955). Eden and the Golden Age are always there in the back of the mind; they are the indispensable preliminary sketch; they prefigure, though they are transformed; they give modern utopianism its words: peace, abundance, leisure, equality, consonance of men and their environment—while modern utopianism proceeds to alter somewhat the signification of some of these words and to alter completely the setting in which these words have their reality. Modern utopianism presumes that the iron age is not *necessarily* permanent; and that the golden age is not that which the social life of perfection restores untransmuted. As Saint-Simon said in 1814,

The imagination of poets has placed the golden age in the cradle of the human race. It was the age of iron they should have banished there. The golden age is not behind us, but in front of us. It is the perfection of social order. Our fathers have not seen it; our children will arrive there one day, and it is for us to clear the way for them.[10]

Thus, at the very start, we must see that modern utopianism has severed its connections with primitivity, ignorance, and innocence; in sum, with nature (though there are some who claim that even a modern utopianism cannot dissociate itself from a condition like ignorance or innocence). Not because nature never was what the stories say it was (of course, it was not: "sylvan meant savage"[11]) but because even an idealized state of nature (whether "nature" is mountain, plain, forest, or sequestered

---

10. Quoted by J. B. Bury, *The Idea of Progress* (1920) (New York: Dover, 1955), p. 282. Cf. Norman Cohn, *The Pursuit of the Millennium* (London: Secker & Warburg, 1957), p. 209: "When did people cease to think of a society without distinctions of status or wealth simply as a Golden Age irrecoverably lost in the distant past, and begin to think of it instead as preordained for the immediate future? So far as can be judged from the available sources, this new social myth came into being in the turbulent years around 1380." Also Mannheim, *Ideology and Utopia, op. cit.,* pp. 211-212: "The decisive turning-point in modern history was, from the point of view of our problem, the moment in which chiliasm joined forces with the active demands of the oppressed strata of society." Mannheim refers to the Hussites, and to the Anabaptists under Thomas Münzer.

11. See W. H. Auden's thought-provoking poem "Woods" in *The Shield of Achilles* (New York: Random House, 1955), pp. 14-16.

island) no longer answers to our sense of reality or to our expectations of reality. Such a disavowal may be seized upon as a mark of corruption, as a certain indication of our perpetual exile from perfection: perfection must *literally* be natural, it may be thought. But to think thus is to reject what human artifice and invention are now capable of.

We also wish to emphasize the independence of modern utopianism from any connection with theories of inevitable progress. The pre-eminent feeling of modern utopianism is surely not optimism; just the reverse. It is so easy to show the deep faults of any view which claims that the events of history, taken together, constitute a single process, each stage of which is a preparation for the next stage, with all stages working (clearly or mysteriously, consciously or unconsciously) to produce a conclusion, and a happy one, at that. The enterprise of the philosophy of the history (to be distinguished from theories of social change) is discredited. And those who wish to attack utopianism cannot be allowed to think they have done so when they have merely shown the folly of historical determinism.

Besides nature and inevitable progress, there is a third element in the utopian tradition, whose irrelevance for modern utopianism we wish to stress. That element is—to use a clumsy word—communitarianism. As Negley and Patrick put it: "Cabet's *Icaria* represents the epitome of the communitarian ideal in utopian literature. Henceforth . . . it was to become rapidly and increasingly apparent that the utopian community was so unrealistic that it could provide no more than a setting for fantasy or satire."[12] Early in his major utopian work, H. G. Wells says, "No less than a planet will serve the purpose of a modern utopia."[13] It is important to mention this consideration here because, as in the case of nature and inevitable progress, it is easy to pour scorn on modern utopianism for connections it no longer has. Truly, what could be more depressing than the series of attempts to set up utopian communities in America

---

12. Glenn Negley and J. Max Patrick, *The Quest for Utopia* (New York: H. Schuman, 1952), p. 582.
13. H. G. Wells, *A Modern Utopia* (1905) (London: Nelson, n.d.), p. 21.

in the nineteenth century? The coexistence of a community dedicated to an ideal of perfection and the great outside world could lead to nothing but a sense of isolation and strain in that community. Even to those living in the community, the quality of life inside had to be marked by artificiality and a feeling of *confinement*. The noble experiment had to conclude in a corrupting spiritual pride. The retreat from reality could not help attracting people who were merely eccentric; utopias could not help becoming havens for neurotics; the life lived could not help being meager in texture and lacking in complexity. For all these reasons, these utopian communities can excite contempt; but this contempt must not be allowed to extend to modern utopianism, which does not conceive of a world apart from the world.[14] The aim of modern utopianism is not to construct what Northrop Frye has called a "prison-paradise."

iv

In an essay called "Democracy, Socialism and Theocracy," Nicholas Berdyaev said, ". . . it is possible that a new age is already beginning, in which cultured and intelligent people will dream of ways to avoid ideal states and to get back to a society that is less 'perfect' and more free."[15] (Aldous Huxley used this and other sentences from Berdyaev's essay as the epigraph for *Brave New World*, 1932.) This utterance could be taken as the essence of modern antiutopianism. In the kind of people it sets in potential opposition to "perfection," and in the value which it plays off against perfection—namely, freedom—this sentence

---

14. Though B. F. Skinner's *Walden Two* (New York: Macmillan, 1948) is about a small community separated from the outside world, not all of Skinner's ideals depend on the existence of a small community. Hawthorne's novel, *The Blithedale Romance* (1852) (paperback edition, New York: W. W. Norton, 1958), gives an illuminating account of the trials of living in a communitarian utopia, though that is not the author's main intent. See also Everett Webber, *Escape to Utopia* (New York: Hastings, 1958).

15. Nicholas Berdyaev, "Democracy, Socialism and Theocracy" in *The End of Our Time*, trans. by Donald Attwater (London: Sheed, 1933), p. 188.

displays its author's unexceptionable humanism. It also gives unmistakable indication of the true nature of the battle between modern utopianism and modern antiutopianism. Arrayed against utopianism are not only sinister interests, malice, sadism, despair, or a hatred of politics or reform, but also, and (for us) more importantly, good intentions. In the case of Berdyaev, modern utopianism—that is, the desire to renew creation, restore the faded glory, cancel the Adamic curse, make the earth heaven; and to do this by political means[16]—is seen as a positive threat to something worth while, something even more worth while than the things that no one, including the antiutopians, would deny to be good, truly good, in some way. That utopianism is thought to exclude something of *a temporal sort* that is valuable would be surprising enough; but that utopianism *defeats* something of a temporal sort which is valuable is a matter of the greatest interest. And as we widen our study of antiutopianism, as we hope to do, we shall see that there are other valuable things held excluded or defeated by modern utopianism. (We shall also find that antiutopianism, when it speaks through other mouths than that of Berdyaev, is not so obviously well-intentioned. Again, it is not a matter of sinister interests or sinister motives, but rather of a special kind of estheticism which does not always seem to be on the right side of the line dividing ethics and esthetics. To put it loosely, it uses an esthetic criterion where one would expect to find an ethical one, and hence seems to do injury to the requirements of justice. The main part of antiutopianism is moral and well-intentioned; but we must here mention that there is a sector of it which raises special problems.)

There is not, for the most part, skepticism about the capacity of modern technology and natural science to execute the most

---

16. Or, as a mordant Frenchman puts it: ". . . concilier l'éternel présent et l'histoire, les délices de l'âge d'or et les ambitions prométhéennes, ou pour recourir à la terminologie biblique, de refaire l'Eden avec les moyens de la chute, en permettant ainsi au nouvel Adam de connaître les avantages de l'ancien. N'est-ce point là essayer de reviser la Création?" [E. M. Cioran, *Histoire et utopie* (Paris: Gallimard, 1960), p. 174.] Cioran laments the decline of utopian thinking, while insisting that life cannot —indeed, should not—become utopian.

vaulting ambitions of utopianism; on the contrary, there is a dread it will. When Alexander Gray says, ". . . no Utopia has ever been described in which any sane man would on any conditions consent to live, if he could possibly escape,"[17] a modern utopian could not help feeling that when allowance was made for Gray's ebullience—not to put too fine a point on it—Gray was speaking the truth. But the utopian would wish to return again and again to the difference that modern technology and natural science make; he would wish to believe that it was only in the past that utopian perfection, victimized by an undeveloped technology, required that life be deficient in variety and poor to the senses, and that the price of harmony turned out to be almost everything. The kind of antiutopianism represented by Gray can be found in the camp of utopianism itself, as early as Karl Marx. Modern utopianism does not look to the construction of a gray, lifeless, and austere society; and its most interesting enemies are those who take it for granted that the form of a modern utopia need not bear much resemblance to any of the utopias devised in the past by idealist or perfectionist thinkers.

Gray's comment does, however, bring to our attention one of the major aspects of modern antiutopianism: its contention that even though there is the wherewithal to avoid an ascetic utopia, there nevertheless are dangers inherent in the very idea of any society organized to achieve even minimal social goals, and *a fortiori*, of any society organized to achieve long-lasting utopian goals on a world-wide scale. We have so far mentioned only the opposition to utopian ends: now, we must extend the notion of modern antiutopianism to include opposition to the means— that is, the social and political arrangements—needed to secure those ends. Of course, a modern utopia would have some *quantum* of organization, no matter how far it was made to move in the direction of the Spencerian-Marxist self-regulating society. This antiutopianism of the means presents a formidable mass of arguments, as we hope to show; moreover, it does not bear the burden of unexpectedness, of apparent absurdity, that we have imputed to the antiutopianism of the ends. The heart of the

17. Alexander Gray, *The Socialist Tradition, Moses to Lenin* (London: Longmans, Green, 1946), p. 62.

position in regard to the means is that utopian order involves inevitably the *permanent* rule of experts and for that very reason is open to serious moral and practical objections. It may be that utopian ends are good ends, and it may also be that the physical means are on hand to secure them. But in the course of things, other, nonutopian, ends (for utopianism does not hold within itself all good things) will be sacrified. Even though a modern utopian society would leave undisturbed such cherished institutions as the family, which in the past it was willing to give up in the name of efficiency, harmony, or cohesion, any utopian society—any society deliberately organized to maintain the traditional utopian ends (in their modern form)—would exact a terrible cost, the death of democratic politics. And that cost would be too much to pay, even for utopian ends.

To all the foregoing must be added one more link in the chain of the antiutopianism of the means. It is the most obvious of all the considerations under discussion: how does the utopian society come into being, in the first place? In theory, the ends to which utopian society devotes itself may be superb, and the means adequate and unobjectionable. But there the world stands in all its imperfection, but in all its reality: it cannot be wished away. What is to be the agency of transformation? And at what cost will it try to do what it thinks must be done?

In any event, the attempt will necessitate two things: the use of violence to overturn the established order, and the *temporary* rule of a revolutionary elite to replace the old order with the new. Both these things are open to moral and practical objections of the most serious sort. Especially important are two of the objections. There is, first, the view that the use of violence either corrupts those who use it and thus renders them unfit to undertake utopian reforms, or engenders counterviolence and thus forces on the revolutionaries measures which must prevent the later realization of utopian reforms. There is, second, the view that though the revolution and the revolutionaries may morally and physically survive the use of violence, and though a position may be reached from which an elite can begin the work of utopian reform, that elite must necessarily fail in its task. The rule of the elite would be the rule of bureaucratic planners; and bureaucratic planners could never work in such a way as to attain utopian ends. Indeed, bureaucratic rule would mean the loss of utopian and nonutopian ends alike. The upshot of all these objections is that all hope must be abandoned for realizing the cluster of utopian ends, fully, universally, and permanently, by means of a world-society dedicated to them. Let these ends come into being singly, sporadically, now here, now there, and without the illusion of permanence. Let them arise from the efforts of gradual and peaceful reformers, working within the traditional framework of national politics.

These, then, are the constituent parts of the antiutopianism of the means. Together with the critique of the traditional ends of utopianism, they are the substance of modern antiutopianism, the subject of this essay.

v

Imagine a society in which all conflicts of conscience and conflicts of interest were abolished, a society in which all the obstacles to a decent life for all men had been removed, all the hindrances hindered, a society in which the resourcefulness of modern technology was put in the unfettered service of lessening labor and increasing and enriching leisure, a society in which the advances in biological and psychological science were used to correct the work of nature and improve the species, a society in which peace, abundance, and virtue permanently and universally obtained. Such a society answers to the traditional ends of utopianism, at the same time that it bodies them forth in ways undreamt of by the tradition. Such a society not only presupposes a technology that could, for the first time, make utopianism something more than a hopeless and recurrent nostalgia, but also amplifies and elevates those things which utopianism, in its vision of perfection, has always stood for. Such a society is what we shall mean by modern utopianism.

Standing against this aspiration are numerous attitudes and assertions, of different quality and claims to inclusiveness. Some of these attitudes and assertions are thought to be of enough weight, each by itself, to lead us to reject modern utopianism completely; some are meant not so much to turn men away from utopianism as to get them to see its costs in theory and lament them. Antiutopianism can be broken down into the three following imperatives, each one of which is couched in general, summary terms:

1. Give up the vision of utopianism, though it may be a worthy vision, because there is no way to go from the real world to utopia; or if there is a way, it could be none other than the way of violence; and that is either too costly or too unreliable.

2. Give up the vision of utopianism, though it may be a worthy vision, because there is no way to insure the maintenance of its ends without an oppressive political regime.

3. Give up the vision of utopianism because the vision consists of ideals (assumed as permanent and universal) that are unacceptable; or though acceptable in the abstract, are, in fact, destructive of other, perhaps more worthy, ideals.

Some of the writers we shall consider are explicit in their antiutopianism (for any of the three main reasons listed above); while some of them say things which are only implicitly or indirectly antiutopian, but which are easily made part of an explicit antiutopian argument. When there is no writer to be found who expresses a relevant antiutopian sentiment, we shall put forth the needed argument: for the sake of completeness, we shall say what could be said but has not yet been said. We shall discuss at length some antiutopian arguments; others we shall merely mention.

We shall deal with two sorts of antiutopian attitudes. Some have been articulated in the past, but are still applicable today, because modern utopianism retains a number of values from its past, unaltered. (For example, Hegel's attack on Kant's hope for perpetual peace.) Some have been articulated only recently, and in direct answer to modern utopianism. These latter attitudes could have been elicited only in a time of advancing technology and scientific and psychological knowledge. (But the advances have also served to revive and encourage the former attitudes.)

It must also be said that there can be discussions of violence, planning, the rule of experts, anarchism, machine technology, perpetual peace, guaranteed abundance, equality, and conditioned virtue, without specific reference to a utopian society. The real world has shared, and now shares, some of the characteristics of an imaginary utopian society; and some of the arguments we take up are attacks, first of all, on things in the real world. But these attacks can simply be extended to utopia. It stands to reason that the prospect of a utopian society would make more intense certain feelings which have been aroused by near-utopian or quasi-utopian features of reality. Whereas parts of the world have achieved or can achieve some utopian ends partially and temporarily, a utopian society, in idea, is devoted to a full, genuine, permanent, universal, and simultaneous attainment of all utopian ends. Utopia carries (certain) tendencies to their conclusions. Thus, attacks made, for example, on peace or abundance in the real world would apply with greater force to utopia, and are called by us "antiutopian," even though these attacks were not originally made with a utopian society in mind. One of our tasks in this essay is precisely to show the relevance of these attacks to modern utopianism.

It must finally be said that one could not find a single text which contained the entire range of antiutopian sentiment: opposition to the use of violence and dictatorship for utopian ends, opposition to the rule of a technical elite, opposition to all the utopian ends.[18] Karl Popper's *The Open Society and Its Enemies* would probably be the most inclusive book, as regards the means needed to attain power and to commence the work of reorganizing society in accordance with the utopian plan. Some of Nietzsche's writing on the value of suffering and inequality would probably be the most inclusive critique of utopian ends. Taken together, E. M. Forster's short story, "The Machine Stops,"

---

18. Indeed, such a text would have to contain inconsistencies: some writers are antiutopian because of their opposition to the use of violence for political ends, while some writers are antiutopian because of the utopian commitment to perpetual peace. I do not assume that "antiutopianism" is the name of a single doctrine, coherent or incoherent. I describe a thinker or an argument as antiutopian whenever he or it attacks some aspect of the utopian endeavor, or the modern utopian ideal-society. Of course, some thinkers accept certain aspects of utopianism, while rejecting others.

Eugene Zamiatin's novel *We*, and Aldous Huxley's novel *Brave New World*, contain almost every fear that utopian ends arouse. These works show utopian ends when carried too far and try to expose some dangerous implications of utopian thought. They do not indict utopian ends as such. Joseph Wood Krutch's *The Measure of Man* would probably have to be considered the most inclusive critique of utopian psychology.

In this essay, we shall not confine ourselves to a description of the various antiutopian positions. We shall attempt an evaluation of those positions in the name of modern utopianism. We shall answer antiutopianism—again—with arguments that have been, *and* could be, made. Our bias is utopian; our hope is that utopianism can survive its critics; our ambition is to help it survive its critics by suggesting revisions of and improvements in (at least) some of the utopian arguments. Some of these revisions, in fact, will be in the form of borrowings from antiutopianism itself.

We undertake to discuss in this essay only two of "the means needed to maintain utopia in being": government, and mechanization; and only three utopian ends: perpetual peace, guaranteed abundance, and conditioned virtue. Obviously, there are other ends which could be discussed: for example, leisure, and work. There are also other means: utopian ends must be served by many institutional means besides government, and mechanization; and can be served in many different ways without hurt to those ends. We have chosen to talk about government and mechanization in utopia, and about peace, abundance, and effortless virtue because a wide range of antiutopian arguments refer to these features of utopian society. These are the essential features, including as they do the political form, the economic basis, and the major qualities of the social life, of modern utopia. Our concern is not to give a blueprint for a specific utopian society, with all its institutions and values set down.

Let us then try to see and assess what has been, or could be, said to discredit modern utopianism.

2

Attaining Utopia

i

Rarely has anyone made light of the problem of founding a new social order, whether the purpose of the founders was to effect a radical departure from prevailing practices or, more modestly, to set up a society largely dependent on the traditions of established societies. The difficulties are immense whether there is an already existing society on the site of the intended new order or there is a new land to be redeemed. The difficulties are immense whether there is general acquiescence in the reformist endeavor or active opposition to it. Indeed, the difficulties are so immense that utopian writers have either ignored them or faced up to them so directly as to give fright to their readers. When Alexander Gray says, "But the weakness of all Utopias is necessarily that they dodge the real difficulty of how to transform this present world into something better,"[1] we may change his "all" to "most" and agree with the sentence. (It is certainly true that much the greater number of utopias in literature have arisen in virgin lands or have emerged on the

---

1. Alexander Gray, *The Socialist Tradition, Moses to Lenin* (London: Longmans, Green, 1946), p. 62.

ruins of a convenient war. These seem to be the most promising conditions.) The utopia is generally introduced to the reader as a going concern, with all the confusion of the early days behind it, or simply presented without any reference to its origins.[2] The question of transition to utopia is thus avoided as unanswerable.

For us today, there are no more virgin lands on earth: if utopia is to come, it must come as a replacement of systems (not one system but many systems) already in being. There is no longer the possibility of utopia abiding in solitary innocence: the rest of the world stands ready to impinge, and if utopia can be utopia only without threats to its life, and without a military establishment meant to meet those threats, the whole world must be utopia for any part of it to be. "Two utopias 'twere in one/To have utopia alone"[3]; and for utopia to be alone it must be sole, it must be coextensive with the world. This is in modern times a necessary condition for utopianism; and it is, in theory, a satis-fiable condition: technology permits the dream of a world community.

"Ridiculous," however, is too weak a word to describe the idea of a world-utopia when made to face the real world with its political cleavages and dominant interests. A modern utopian would want to be realistic, and being such, he could not con-ceive of any way by which, after great exertion or small, the world stood ready to become utopia.

What must concern us here, however, is the attitude that, being antiutopian because of the moral and practical difficulties it sees in the path of attaining utopia, expresses itself timelessly and abstractly, irrespective of the specific difficulties at any given

----

2. In his antiutopian essay, Ralf Dahrendorf observes quite tartly, ". . . Utopias do not grow out of familiar reality following realistic pat-terns of development. For most authors, utopias have but a nebulous past and no future; they are suddenly there, and there to stay, suspended in mid-time or, rather, somewhere beyond the ordinary notions of time." See "Out of Utopia: Toward a Reorientation of Sociological Analysis," *The American Journal of Sociology*, LXIV (Sept. 1958), pp. 115-127, at p. 116.

3. We have reworked some lines from Andrew Marvell's poem, "The Garden," in *Poems*, ed. by Hugh Macdonald (Cambridge, Mass.: Harvard University Press, 1952), stanza VIII:

> Two Paradises 'twere in one
> To live in Paradise alone.

time. According to this view, utopianism, when it takes action, must be inextricably enwound with immorality and ignorance of the facts of political behavior. We shall take up this view only to show that at least some parts of the charge against utopianism cannot, in theory, be as easily sustained as sometimes thought. The following discussion is perforce artificial: to use a better word, it is "academic." But we engage in it in order to see what finally and in fairness utopianism must concede to its opponents, in the field of abstract argumentation; and also to take some of the sting out of the charge of evasiveness that is so commonly directed at any kind of utopian discussion.

To speak of "attaining utopia" is to mean two things: first, to reach a position from which it would be possible to begin the work of organizing society according to the perfectionist plan; and second, the actual work of organizing society according to the perfectionist plan. And in those few cases where utopian writers have answered the question of how to attain utopia, their answers have been appalling. The answers have involved, of course, force and violence, and dictatorship. Force and violence have been seen as necessary to reach a position from which it would be possible to begin the work of organizing society; dictatorship has been seen as necessary to the actual work of organizing society. These are the only alternatives to magic as the means to change the world into utopia.

Starting with the highest ends, the utopian seizes upon the most repulsive means: he begins in charity and ends in terror. For a utopian who is not willing to follow Hegel and soothe his scruples by invoking history and its supposedly higher morality, or for a utopian who is not willing to follow Marx and simply assume without further ado that history is there to be served and that any act done in its service is *eo ipso* moral, the strain induced by the problem of means and ends must be intolerable. Hegel intended his philosophy of history to be a theodicy and therefore showed that he thought that real evil had gone into the making of what he saw as harmony: evil so gross as had to be accounted for. Marx preached the necessity for violence and dictatorship, but so awful did the present strike him, and so sweet the future, that it went, for him, without saying, that anything done to bring on what the future held within itself was the right thing to do: "right" had no other meaning. But if either variant of historicism is rejected as empirically false or morally condemnable or both, then the larger cluster of perplexities accompanying the use of dirty means for clean ends, bad means for good ends, immediately forces itself upon the reluctant utopian.

ii

Speaking generally, we could say that there were three main kinds of opposition to the enterprise of trying, by means of force and violence, to reach a position from which it would be possible to begin the work of organizing society according to the perfectionist plan. These three kinds are: first, that which comes from moral absolutism in various forms; second, that which comes from a revised utilitarian theory of the relation between good and evil; and third, that which comes from a mixture of moral and practical considerations that is essentially commonsense in nature. The stages on the way from reality to utopia are the stages of any successful revolution. And because these stages would involve terrorism, conspiracy, *coup d'état*, general strike, guerrilla warfare, street fighting, pitched battle, singly or in some combination, they would involve the taking of life, coercion, treachery, lying, destruction, uprooting, the infliction of many kinds of physical and psychological pain and suffering on opponents and innocents alike. That is to say, revolution necessitates what war always and normal politics sometimes necessitate. And against this cost in evil, moral absolutism, revised utilitarianism, and common sense rebel.

In addition, we may say that the main kind of opposition to the actual work of organizing society according to the perfectionist plan is essentially common-sense in nature. Large-scale organizational efforts necessitate planning by a central elite. Common sense says that such planning cannot succeed precisely because of the immensity of the undertaking.

It is, of course, the Russian experience—revolution and its aftermath—that has promoted a good deal of thought in recent times on the moral and practical cost of revolutionary and radical reformist activity; though, naturally, this thought derived, in many cases, from ancient speculation. We shall refer to both recent thought and ancient speculation, and take into account arguments that are specifically directed to action done for utopian ends and arguments directed to action done for general political ends (including, necessarily, utopian ones).

iii

Let us treat first of the opposition to revolution. To begin with the arguments of a morally absolutist sort: there is the position which Socrates defends in the *Crito*.[4] There, Socrates says that it is impermissible for a man in his dealings with others to do certain things under any conditions whatever. Socrates does not specify those things, but speaks most broadly about doing wrong, injury, evil. At first sight, it would seem that Socrates would include within wrongdoing all the things necessary for almost all political activity, and most certainly for political activity connected with attaining utopia. But it is unclear to what extent this moral absolutism is to be extended into the realm of politics from the realm of men's private dealings with each other. It would seem that in the unjust state, the just man could reasonably decide to abstain from politics: Socrates himself says, in the *Apology*,[5] that he sought to remain in his private station because there alone could he fight for the right. In *The Republic*, however, the just man is the ruler in the just state. The just man avoids all wrongdoing in his private dealings (if the word "private" still has any meaning for a member of the ruling class of the just state); but the just man is a warrior in his youth, and will do all things needful, including lying,

---

4. Plato, *Crito*, 48-49. See also Plato, *The Republic*, 334-335.
5. Plato, *Apology*, 31-32. See also *Gorgias*, 525-526; and *The Republic*, 496.

to preserve the existence of the just state. That is to say, the just man will take life and act in ways that, if they were done for private gain, would be immoral and hence impermissible. (It is unclear what, if anything, a citizen of an imperfect state is morally prevented from doing for his state.) Thus, the absolutism of Socrates (in the *Crito* and *The Republic*) applies with full force only to private morals. It is impossible, therefore, to invoke the sanction of Socrates for the claim that traditionally the doctrine of moral absolutism is applicable to the domain of politics, and hence can be made to show the absolute impermissibility of immoral acts for utopian ends. At the same time, it must be said that there is no provision in the thought of Socrates for the commission of immoral acts to overthrow any imperfect state and replace it by the perfect one. Perfection must await the happy time when a king is also a philosopher. (In his own voice, in the *Seventh Epistle*, Plato says, "But force against his native land he should not use in order to bring about a change of constitution, when it is not possible for the best constitution to be introduced without driving men into exile or putting them to death; he should keep quiet and offer up prayers for his own welfare and for that of his country."[6]) But it must be stressed that it is love of the mother country (which possesses Socrates in the *Crito*, and which Plato voices in the *Seventh Epistle;* and despair of success, on the part of Plato), not moral absolutism, that leads Socrates and Plato to renounce revolution for utopian ends.

Again, in the case of the absolutist strand in Christian teaching, the application of its prohibitions to the realm of politics is not usual. Luther and Calvin gave specific attention to the connection between the Sermon on the Mount and political life, and both were willing to suspend the absolutist imperatives of the Sermon on the Mount for the sake of something resembling the public good. They did not let the precepts of the Sermon interfere with the conduct of politics, much as Socrates and Plato did not let the precepts of the *Crito* interfere with the conduct of

----

6. Plato, Letter VII (330e), in *The Platonic Epistles*, trans. by J. Harward (Cambridge: Cambridge University Press, 1932), pp. 123-124. However, in *The Republic*, 540-541, and in *The Statesman*, 308-309, Plato grants the permissibility of coercion and exile.

politics (clearly in reference to the just state, and probably in reference to any state). Luther refused to have the doctrine of abstention from all wrongdoing guide the workings of secular authority:

. . . a man who would venture to govern an entire country or the world with the Gospel would be like a shepherd who should place in one fold wolves, lions, eagles, and sheep together and let them mingle with one another and say, Help yourselves, and be good and peaceful among yourselves; the fold is open, there is plenty of food; have no fear of dogs and clubs. The sheep, forsooth, would keep the peace and would allow themselves to be fed and governed in peace, but they would not live long; nor would any beast keep from molesting another.[7]

In their private dealings, Christians would behave as Christians with each other, perhaps even with those who were only nominally Christians. But the good Christian, the Christian who believed in not returning evil for evil, would take advantage of the resistance to evil undertaken in his, and all men's behalf by the state, and would also make any contribution, including the profession of soldiery, that the state required for its purposes. When Luther inveighed against revolution, it was not on absolutist grounds, but rather because "the powers that be are

---

7. Martin Luther, *Secular Authority: To What Extent It Should Be Obeyed* (1523) in *Works of Martin Luther* (Philadelphia: A. J. Holman, 1930), Vol. III, p. 237. For other discussions by Luther of resistance to evil, and of the use of force and violence in private and public dealings, see *The Sermon on the Mount*, trans. and ed. by Jaroslav Pelikan in *Luther's Works* (St. Louis: Concordia Publishing House, 1956), Vol. 21, pp. 105-129; and *Whether Soldiers, Too, Can Be Saved* (1526) in *Works of Martin Luther* (Philadelphia: A. J. Holman, 1931), Vol. V. The sharp distinction between private obedience to the precepts of the Sermon on the Mount and public obedience to the precepts of political necessity was also present, of course, in the thought of St. Augustine. See, for example, *The City of God* (New York: The Modern Library, 1950), I, 21, and XIX, 17; and John Neville Figgis, *The Political Aspects of St. Augustine's 'City of God'* (London: Longmans, Green, 1921), Chap. III. For a full discussion by St. Augustine of the precepts of the Sermon on the Mount concerning resistance to evil, the scope of their application, and the possibility of modifying them *even* in private dealings, see his *Commentary on the Lord's Sermon on the Mount*, trans. by Denis J. Kavanagh, in *The Fathers of the Church* (New York: Fathers of the Church, Inc., 1951), Vol. II, pp. 80–108. For a historical treatment see C. J. Friedrich, *Constitutional Reason of State* (Providence: Brown University Press, 1957).

ordained of God." This latter principle served Luther as love
of the mother-country served Socrates and Plato. Luther's ideal,
of course, would have been a condition in which states and laws
and courts and wars were absent; but fallen human nature makes
them infinitely desirable, not merely for the sake of protecting
the wicked from each other, but also for the sake of protecting
the good from the wicked: there is a limit to the liability in-
curred by the Christian for the Sermon on the Mount.[8]

For Calvin, the distinction between human conventions and
the kingdom of Christ did not lead to considering ". . . the whole
system of civil government as a polluted thing which has nothing
to do with Christian men."[9] Furthermore—and here Calvin's
difference from Luther is quite sharp—the state exists not merely
to restrain wickedness, but to organize secular and religious life
fully, correctly, and decently. Christian men would take arms,
and do all other things inherent in political activity. Even in
their private dealings with each other certain requirements of the
Sermon on the Mount could be allowed to lapse (or the lapse
could be interpreted as no lapse at all): Christian men could
engage in lawsuits, not with hate in their hearts, of course, but
out of regard for public order, God's will. All these things are to
be seen not as necessary evils, as it could be said Luther saw
them, but as things right and proper and in accordance with the
will of God. When it comes to revolution, to resistance to
tyranny, Calvin allows it to special magistrates in special circumstances; but when he preaches against it in a general way, it is
not for absolutist reasons that he does so.

And when it is remembered that there are Catholic and
Protestant and pre-Reformation theories of the right of resistance
and of the permissibility of tyrannicide, and of the just war, it
becomes clear that the moral absolutism of the Sermon on the

---

8. For a Christian rejection of this Lutheran position, see Leo Tolstoy,
The Kingdom of God Is within You, in *Works of Tolstoy*, trans. by Alymer
Maude (London: Oxford University Press, 1935), Vol. 20, pp. 286-287.

9. John Calvin, *Institutes of the Christian Religion*, trans. by John
Allen (2 vols., Philadelphia: Presbyterian Board of Christian Education,
Seventh American Edition, 1936), Vol. I, Book IV, Chap. XX ("On Civil
Government"), p. 771.

Mount has operated only as a very distant ideal, as a kind of gnawing reminder, in the course of Christian political speculation. This is not to say that no Christian has ever tried to make the Sermon on the Mount the standard to which not merely private life but political life as well had to conform. It is only to say that the pronounced tendency of the several traditions within Christianity has been to deny the political relevance of the Sermon on the Mount. What is important for our discussion is that those who wish to discredit abstractly the enterprise of initiating a revolution for political ends—perfectionist, reformist, or what not—cannot claim that Christian theology, in any of its major forms, would support their application of the absolutist prohibitions of the Sermon on the Mount to revolutionary activity.

But that does not mean that such an application cannot be made, and does not deserve to be reckoned with. In modern times, Gandhi has made the most consistent and consequential attempt to include political action within the scope of moral absolutism. Gandhi made this attempt not as a Christian but as a Hindu influenced by Christianity, that is, by the Sermon on the Mount and some of the writings of Tolstoy on the Gospels. Now the prohibitions of moral absolutism need not conclude in a doctrine of non-resistance to evil: they may only conclude in a doctrine of nonviolent and perfectly scrupulous resistance to evil, in a doctrine of passive and moral resistance to evil, in a doctrine that assumed the possibility of *innocent* political action.[10]

---

10. Though it could be maintained that it is only by allowing yourself to be victimized by evil, by loving your enemies, blessing them that curse you, doing good to them that hate you, that evil can be made to vanish from the world. If the aim is not success for one's ends but the conversion of the wrongdoer, then you must let yourself be the focus of his hatred, and trust that when the hatred is not requited nor even passively resisted, then the wrongdoer will repent. And when repentance comes, a certain quantum of evil has somehow been permanently subtracted from the world. Nemesis is satisfied, whereas even passive resistance would not have caused repentance, and the source of wrongdoing would have remained fertile. For two recent comments on this, or an analogous, position, coming from radically divergent temperaments, see B. F. Skinner, *Walden Two* (New York: Macmillan, 1948), pp. 86-87; and Hannah Arendt, *The Human Condition* (Chicago: University of Chicago Press, 1958), pp. 240-241. For a related conception, having to do with the working out of a curse, see Simone Weil, *La connaissance surnaturelle* (Paris: Gallimard, 1950), pp. 105-107. Note

It is thought that ends that people normally take to be attainable only through the commission of immoral acts, including acts of violence, can be attained by means of acts none of which contravenes the requirements of absolute moral law.

It is possible to obey the injunctions of moral absolutism: (1) out of love for all human beings, good and bad; or (2) out of a Kantian insistence on complete duty to the moral law in the name of a perfectly rational morality, irrespective of material consequences (though Kant himself did not transfer his absolutism to political life); or (3) out of a prudent wish to remain free of all wrongdoing for the sake of one's purity or one's salvation after death; or (4) out of a belief that *all* acts (not only violent acts) commonly regarded as wicked or immoral are, in the end, self-defeating, and productive of even more mischief than what they were intended to remove or annul. Gandhi's doctrine of *ahimsa* seems to derive from all but the Kantian considerations, with considerations number (1) and (4) dominating.[11] The case of the antiabsolutist would be very easy if the third consideration were the basis for the application of moral absolutism to the realm of politics, utopian and other. For then the charge of parasitism could be levelled at the absolutists, in the manner of George Orwell[12] addressing the pacifists: they keep their purity while the dirty work from which they benefit is done for them by others: they feed off other men's sins: they abstain from evil which, if they were pressed, they

---

also her comment in *Cahiers* II (Paris: Plon, 1953), p. 135: "Quiconque prend l'épée perira par l'épée. Et quiconque ne prend pas l'épée (ou la lâche) perira sur la croix." Contrarily, it could be said that nonresistance *increases* the appetite for wrongdoing, that it works with the same effect as appeasement of an aggressor, that as George Orwell said in "Lear, Tolstoy and the Fool," "The second blow is, so to speak, part of the act of turning the other cheek." Or as John Donne put it in "The Progresse of the Soule," XXV, 1. 250, "Weaknesse invites, but silence feasts oppression."

11. For a careful discussion of Gandhi's views, see Joan V. Bondurant, *Conquest of Violence* (Princeton, N.J.: Princeton University Press, 1958). Chapters II (esp. pp. 23-26) and III are particularly relevant. See also C. F. Andrews, *Mahatma Gandhi's Ideas* (London: Allen and Unwin, 1929), Chap. 7.

12. See his essays, "Notes on Nationalism" and "Reflections on Gandhi." For an interesting pacifist attempt to answer the charge of parasitism, see Cecil John Cadoux, *Christian Pacifism Re-examined* (Oxford: Basil Blackwell, 1940), pp. 180-181.

would acknowledge to be necessary, or which they have, in their protective blindness, not seen to be necessary. As it is, the third consideration was usually kept by Gandhi in the background. What matters for our discussion is that it would be very hard indeed to find anyone who, though he claimed to be a moral absolutist, could follow in practice where Gandhi wished to take him in theory. Gandhi had the British to contend with, and his passive resistance was not met with extermination. He said, however, that even if extermination were a possibility, even if he were a potential victim of Hitler's, he still would not resort to immoral means to defend himself: he would rather die in the course of his passive resistance: he would have millions follow his lead.[13] The important thing for Gandhi was not life itself but the quality of life. And as a consequence, great loss of life could be countenanced, a greater loss of life than would be forthcoming from a nonabsolutist ethic, which would allow, for instance, the taking of the life of a guilty man to save the life of an innocent man, or the taking of a few lives to save the lives of many. There are times when Gandhi tries to show that, in the long run, the doctrine of pure means costs less in life and suffering than any doctrine of the lesser evil, but he never sounds convincing.[14] Those for whom life itself is a supreme value, or those who are convinced that immoral action may be required for attaining or maintaining moral ends, deserving ends, must renounce moral absolutism as bloody and destructive though beautiful and consistent. As Max Weber put it,

No ethics in the world can dodge the fact that in numerous instances the attainment of "good" ends is bound to the fact that one must be willing to pay the price of using morally dubious means or at least dangerous ones—and facing the possibility or even the probability of evil ramifications . . . it is *not* true that good can follow only from good and evil only from evil, but that often the opposite is true.[15]

---

13. See *The Gandhi Reader*, ed. by Homer A. Jack (Bloomington: Indiana University Press, 1956), pp. 317-324, esp. pp. 319-320. See also Louis Fischer, *Gandhi and Stalin* (New York: Harper, 1947), Chap. 5, esp. pp. 50-51.

14. For an interesting defense of this position, with specific reference to the use of violence, see Cadoux, *op. cit.*, Chap. V.

15. Max Weber, "Politics as a Vocation" in *From Max Weber: Essays in Sociology*, trans. and ed. by H. H. Gerth and C. Wright Mills (New

It is not to be concessive to the absolutist to grant that deeds which he as well as the nonabsolutist would consider evil or immoral are necessary to the conduct of all politics, including the exertion thought indispensable for attaining utopia. Your disposition to avoid evil may be weakened if you believe evil in politics is inevitable, but your ability to recognize it when you or others have caused it may be less if you believe that it is not inevitable. But once that has been said, it must also be said that moral absolutism cannot prove its claim that impure means are always self-defeating, and that these means must therefore not even be used for the "legitimate" ends of politics, the minimal ends of survival, security, and welfare. If the absolutist is willing, in turn, to grant that impure means may not invariably be self-defeating, but that nevertheless they should not be used, even to prevent the triumph of the worst oppression, then the nonabsolutist, after he has made sure that the absolutist has understood the implications of his (the absolutist's) view, can say no more, but persist in his impure ways.

The relevance of this rejoinder for utopianism is that there is nothing in moral absolutism that speaks peculiarly to utopian exertion: utopian exertion is morally of a piece with all politics in its use of impure means, and if the defenders of political activity can answer moral absolutism with the doctrine of the lesser evil, so can those who, in the abstract, defend utopian exertion. The aim of utopian exertion is, precisely, to do some evil to avoid greater evil, to do evil in order to eliminate its occurrence henceforward. If that is a condemnable wish, it is condemnable on moral grounds only by an absolutist: and we have seen that the absolutist is willing to countenance the production of greater evil in the world for the sake of keeping good men good, or out of love for bad men; but it is not condemnable on moral grounds by the nonabsolutist. The nonabsolutist can condemn the utopian only for entertaining an impossible wish. The

---

York: Oxford University Press, 1946), p. 123. See also Friedrich Meinecke, *Machiavellism,* trans. by Douglas Scott (London: Routledge, 1957), esp. pp. 1-22; Reinhold Niebuhr, *Moral Man and Immoral Society* (New York: Scribner, 1932), Chap. 9; Dorothy Fosdick, "Ethical Standards and Political Strategies," *Political Science Quarterly,* LVII (1942), pp. 214-228.

elimination of radical evil from the world is a permanent impossibility, given men as they are: the attempt to achieve utopia would be productive of more evil, in its violence and bloodiness and destructiveness, than the willingness to let things go on as they can. On these grounds, the antiutopian case appears far more convincing, and we shall shortly take it up.

iv

There is another attitude of the absolutist sort that can be interposed as a bar to utopian exertion. That is the doctrine of the sanctity of life expressed in the precept, "Never take life." Those who hold this doctrine would be willing to concede the permissibility of the use of impure means for worthwhile political ends, but stop short of taking life. Life is seen to be the pre-eminent value, and everything else must give way before it. This is surely an attractive point of view, and sympathy for it and a prima facie acceptance of it would, we should wish to say, constitute part of a civilized temperament. But on going into some of the familiar predicaments such a point of view encounters, we see that it either is made to give way in certain instances, or is held absolutely with the same bloody consequences inherent in the general position of moral absolutism.[16] And because the doctrine of the sanctity of life commands much more immediate and widespread assent than the larger position of moral absolutism, and because it is a doctrine that is, as it were, always there, tacit or spoken, we shall briefly try to show what bearing it could have, in the abstract, on utopianism.[17]

---

16. For an attack on the doctrine of the sanctity of life in the name of revolutionary exertion, see Leon Trotsky, *The Defence of Terrorism* (London: Allen and Unwin, 1921), p. 59; and the speeches by the character Ivanov in Arthur Koestler's novel, *Darkness at Noon*, trans. by Daphne Hardy (New York: Macmillan, 1941), "The Second Hearing."

17. For an excellent though brief discussion of the general issues connected with sanctity of life, see Richard Rovere, "A Matter of Life and Death," *The New Yorker*, XXXIII (Sept. 14, 1957), pp. 149-154. Rovere's essay is a review of two books: Glanville Williams, *The Sanctity of Life* (New York: Knopf, 1957), and Arthur Koestler, *Reflections on Hanging* (New York: Macmillan, 1957).

Obedience to the precept, "Never take life," is thought to count for more than all the advantages of a utopian society. Whenever a life is taken, for no matter what end, murder has been committed. But does the precept, for example, prohibit self-defense? If an adherent answers that he, and anyone holding consistently to the precept, would rather die than kill, the question then becomes, "Would you take an aggressor's life in order to save the life of someone else, an innocent person?" The answer could be, "No, the preservation of the precept is more important than the preservation of life itself; to take life even for the sake of saving the life of an innocent man is to efface the moral distinction between the guilty and the innocent by the mere fact of using the life of a human being—in this instance, a guilty human being—as a means to some end." To this position it could be answered that by abstaining the adherent had in effect taken the life of the innocent man: that, as often, abstention was a form of action. If the answer to the above question is "Yes," the next question is, "On what grounds?" If the answer is, "Life against life, the life of an innocent man is worth more than that of a guilty man," or, "If I don't take the life of an aggressor on this occasion, I shall invite further aggression in the future," then the principle of the sanctity of life has been made to calculate and recognize the claims of innocence.

The adherent to the doctrine of the sanctity of life may, however, wish to limit the area in which calculation is admissible. He may wish to say that only in the case of a man threatening murder on the spot is it allowable to take life, but that it is not allowable to take life in the form of capital punishment, or for the sake of saving other lives (as in desperate cannibalistic or life-raft situations), or for the sake of national purposes, or in the course of defensive war, or in the name of social reform, or for the sake of utopia. The utopian could respond that if he, the utopian, were allowed to take life in the struggle for utopia, it would be the last time life would ever have to be taken; that the aim of utopia is, among other things, to abolish for all time all those situations where life is taken; that outside utopia there will be endless bloodshed, innumerable instances of life being taken, and only very rarely in the name of something

morally acceptable. To which the adherent of the doctrine of
the sanctity of life could say either, "You could never guarantee
the success of your efforts," or, "Even if I were certain that
you could guarantee the success of your efforts and establish
permanent utopia, I still could not consent; let lives be taken
in the course of events: I will not *deliberately* sacrifice the life
of one man or many men; to say it again, the preservation of
the precept is more important than the preservation of life."

It is possible to condemn the taking of life in the *specific case*
of a future world-wide utopian revolution on grounds other
than the sanctity of life. A moralist could say that to take life
in such circumstances would be just like an aggressor's taking
life in his act of aggression. Most of the opponents of such a
revolution would not be tyrants or oppressors, but rather the
legitimate rulers of nation-states. And many of these rulers
(and their supporters) would not be personally and directly
responsible for the woes of the world: they would only be caught
in the necessities of power politics. Nor would they be men
guilty of any crime, or guilty of harboring any desire to take
the lives of others. Their only misfortune would be to be
opposed to the plans of the utopian revolutionaries, who are
seeking to overthrow an established order. These victims could
not even be accused of heresy: the whole rationale for per-
secuting infidels for the sake of their own heavenly salvation
or the salvation of others would have no place in the thoughts
of secular utopians. So that the usual necessities which men
cite to justify, and justify acceptably, the taking of life cannot
be cited by utopian apologists. In a strict sense, utopian revolutionaries deliberately take the lives of innocent men; and
no utilitarian calculus should be used to try to get us to forgive
what is unforgivable. Thus, the principle of the sanctity of
life can be rejected, while the principle of the sanctity of
innocent life is affirmed. And the fact that innocent lives are
often *accidentally* taken in the course of operations against
guilty men, as when civilians are killed in air raids against the
aggressor's country, offers no excuse to utopian revolutionaries.
The latter know when they begin their effort that their primary
target, their enemy, is innocent men.

The most famous extreme instance of this last position is

to be found in Alyosha Karamazov's "No" to a question put to
him by his brother Ivan:

Imagine that you are creating a fabric of human destiny with the
object of making men happy in the end, giving them peace and rest
at last, but that it was essential and inevitable to torture to death only
one tiny creature . . . and to found that edifice on its unavenged tears,
would you consent to be the architect on those conditions?[18]

Alyosha even agrees that the rest of humanity would join him
in his "No." In other words, the suffering unto death of many
in a social system that has the appearance, at least, of being at
the mercy of "vast impersonal forces," of inflicting its suffering
blindly, is preferable to having men take life—take a life—to
make the suffering stop. (Alyosha would undoubtedly have said
"No," even if the sacrificial victim were to be not "one tiny
creature" but one ordinary adult.) Life is not subject to calculation; life is not men's to take, only to give. But it could be
answered, and not only by a utopian, that unless calculation is
permitted, even where there is no guilt, unless many lives were
more sacred than a few, or some more than one, the consequences
are very bloody indeed.[19] The doctrine of the sanctity of
innocent life, no less than the doctrine of the sanctity of (all)
life, is thus a bloody doctrine; and both these doctrines never
show themselves more bloody than when they are held in the
face of the assumption of certain success for utopian aspirations.

Alyosha Karamazov's attitude is perhaps similar to the one
held by the old Bolshevik, Rubashov, hero of Koestler's *Darkness
at Noon*. In a confrontation with the Stalinist Ivanov (his first
inquisitor), Rubashov is reminded of a life he sacrificed for
the cause he once espoused, and wonders whether he is still
capable of making such a sacrifice. The idea that life is sacro-

---

18. Fyodor Dostoyevsky, *The Brothers Karamazov*, trans. by Constance
Garnett (New York: The Modern Library, 1950), Book V, Chap. IV. See
also Albert Camus, *Les justes* (Paris: Gallimard, 1950), pp. 60-66; and
Actuelles II (Paris: Gallimard, 1953), p. 22.

19. But what utopian moralist—indeed, what moralist of any kind—
could ever sanction the calculations of life and death urged by Herman
Kahn in *On Thermonuclear War* (Princeton, N.J.: Princeton University Press,
1960)? Yet it is not easy to explain clearly why Kahn's position is morally
abhorrent.

sanct; that it is not liable to arithmetic calculation; that each life is an "infinite" quality; that a man is not ". . . the quotient of one million divided by one million"; that there must be "a new kind of arithmetic based on multiplication: on the joining of a million individuals to form a new entity that, no longer an amorphous mass, will develop a consciousness and an individuality of its own" takes hold of him. Ivanov tries to destroy Rubashov's position by arguing in ways to which we have already referred. The fact that Ivanov argues as well as he does in a book devoted to discrediting his works, testifies to Koestler's genius and makes of *Darkness at Noon* one of the masterworks of political ethics in the twentieth century. Of course, it is obvious that Koestler sides with Rubashov in his struggle, even though Koestler may not accept Rubashov's position as his own. The tragedy is, however, that Koestler finally cannot manage to provide Rubashov with a coherent line of reasoning capable of refuting Ivanov's. The best Rubashov can do is to complain that Ivanov has built his case for the necessity of taking life by citing examples of sacrifices made in time of war. Rubashov says that war is "abnormal circumstances": presumably, even Rubashov's position would allow for the calculation of lives in these abnormal circumstances. But Rubashov never states the grounds for this distinction. At the end, Rubashov murmurs about "oceanic feeling": he becomes weakly mystical.

Rubashov might have saved his position from Ivanov's attack —if not to Ivanov's satisfaction, at least to that of the reader— by making a distinction between the use of violence during a revolution for idealist ends and the use of violence after the revolution has succeeded. Koestler, in staging the debate between Rubashov and Ivanov, has his characters speak in the most general way of the relation between means and ends and debate in the most general way about the sanctity of life. But it could be said that though Ivanov cannot be satisfactorily answered so long as the discussion refers solely to the use of violence to overturn an established order that is evil (or contains in it the high probability of being implicated in evil), he can be satisfactorily answered once the discussion turns to the use of violence against the very people in whose name revolution was carried out. The assumption must be that while violence may be the only method by which those who are to rebuild society can attain a position from which to commence their task, violence is not an indispensable part of the method by which that task can be consummated. Violence may *expedite* this latter task, but the argument from the sanctity of life within the limits of the strictest necessity surely prevails over any expediency. A preference for fast or sure reform over slow or uncertain reform does not fall within those limits. It is here that Rubashov should have taken his stand. If he had done so, the ordinary canons of political morality would have stood behind him; and the retreat to mysticism need not ever have taken place.

A variant of the doctrine of the sanctity of life is found in the writings of Albert Camus,[20] one of the most influential writers on the morality of violent action for utopian ends. What makes the problem so acute for Camus is a deep sense—almost a crushing sense—of human mortality, a sense of its horror and of how it makes any other consideration seem tiny in comparison. Although Camus is sensitive to the way the very precariousness of human things makes those things appear all the more valuable, death for him is the supreme enemy. Death provides the bond that joins all men; it is what they all have in common; it is what they all should hate. For a man to take a life, to inflict death, is to place himself in the enemy camp and to cooperate with what ought to be resisted, in so far as resistance is possible. Is there then no higher value than life itself for Camus? Is life to be endured under all conditions? Are there not things in life that must be defended at the cost of life itself, the life either of oneself or of a human enemy? Is violent political action, with its certainty of death for some, always impermissible?[21]

---

20. See *Les justes, op. cit.; L'homme révolté* [Paris: Gallimard, 1951; *The Rebel* (New York: Knopf, 1954)]; *Actuelles,* II, *op. cit.,* pp. 21-24.

21. It is interesting to note how Camus wrestled with the problem of taking life all through his career. In *Lettres à un ami allemand* (Paris: Gallimard, 1944), Camus argued that Frenchmen had earned the right to take German lives because of the prior *examen de conscience* Frenchmen had

Camus explicitly rejects pacifism, because it is acquiescent in the various injustices and inhumanities that men inflict on one another. That is to say, Camus recognizes that the precept, Never take life, can yield to the claims of freedom from slavery, and freedom from the state's tyranny. But the doctrine of the sanctity of life exacts concessions in return: he who takes a life must be ready to part with his own. The model revolutionary act is that of the Russian, Kaliayev, who assassinated the Grand Duke Sergei in 1905, and willingly went to his death on the gallows, feeling that the life he had taken had been paid for: the tyrant had to die, but a tyrant is a man, and he who kills a man must die. For Camus, all deaths inflicted in the course of political action that are not thus requited must be considered as murder.

The scrupulousness of this position goes beyond that of any Christian theory of the right of tyrannicide. But Camus sees no other way of insuring that the moral distinction of oppressor and oppressed be maintained; he also sees no other way of insuring that the initial commendable act of resistance to injustice not lead to activities (on the part of those who were formerly oppressed) that are as unjust as those of the old oppressors.

In Camus's view, then, the stain of blood can be wiped clean by more blood. Once again, the doctrine of the sanctity of life (as embodied in the precept, "Never take life") shows itself as bloody. Starting with an animus exactly opposite

---

undergone: the French were on the side of life and the Germans on the side of death, and the French would therefore reluctanctly take life in the name of life itself. In *La peste* [Paris: Gallimard, 1947; paperback edition, New York: Macmillan, n.d.; *The Plague* (New York: Knopf, 1948)], Camus's novel about the general problem of resistance to evil, evil took the rather convenient form of a natural phenomenon, namely plague, and thus the sharpness of the moral dilemma was completely blunted. The device of the plague works to lead one to forget that everything becomes difficult when the enemy is human: only then is resistance a moral issue. The plague, that is, is a device of evasion. Again in *L'état de siège* (Paris: Gallimard, 1948), totalitarianism is embodied in the person of a character named La Peste, and once more, the moral problem of resistance is kept at a distance. When finally Camus directly took up the problem of taking life for moral or revolutionary or utopian ends, in "Persecutés–Persecuteurs" (1948), it was to adumbrate the position more fully expounded in *L'homme révolté, op. cit.*

to the old retributory doctrine of a life for a life—Camus has written eloquently against capital punishment—Camus's theory reaches the same practical conclusion. The doctrine of the sanctity of life increases the number of deaths. Besides that, it makes any utopian action impossible: the battalions would constantly be losing their numbers through surrender, so that the moral law could be fulfilled. (Sometimes Camus speaks as if *the mere risk of death* is price enough for him who takes the life of an oppressor; but that does not seem to be the main tendency of his writing.) Organized and sustained action, with success in mind, is placed out of reach: success becomes a shame. The perpetuation of the established order would seem to be guaranteed: rebellion whether for utopian purposes, or for something less, is to take its moral superiority as compensation enough for its inevitable failure.

The quandaries that a concern for life can lead to are terrible; and writers like Camus make us see how really terrible these quandaries are; without these writers, the world's callousness would even be greater. We must be forcefully reminded that the maxim, Never treat any man merely as a means, induces its greatest tension when the taking of life is judged to be the means to some political end. Finally, however, anyone who has thought that sometime in the flow of events, life *had* to be taken, whether in the waging of war for national purposes, or in civil strife, or in revolution, or for the sake of utopia—for the issue of the sanctity of life touches not only utopian politics, but all politics—can only respond with some kind of rough calculation, a gruesome adding and subtracting of existences; and then leave every man to his conscience. Presumably, the utopian who was sure of success would carry the lightest conscience, for his aim is precisely to take life now so as to produce a condition where it would never again be taken. And the utopian need not be alone in saying that a flexible calculating humanitarianism is likely to cost less blood than the doctrine of the sanctity of life in its absolutist form.

v

The trouble, then, with any moral prohibition that is made absolute is that it can lead to the most awfully destructive consequences, consequences more destructive, in some cases, than those of acts done in full knowledge that they are undesirable acts, although they are done nevertheless. The absolutists would not grant the propriety of the doctrine of the lesser evil. It is precisely in the name of the doctrine of the lesser evil, however, that an attack on utopian exertion, in the abstract, has been made. In his celebrated book *The Open Society and Its Enemies,* and elsewhere,[22] Karl Popper has tried to show the moral unacceptability of all efforts directed at the violent removal of the existing order in order to replace it by a perfectionist one.

For Popper, pain is the major category (as death was for Camus), so that the avoidance of pain must always take precedence over the search for pleasure. Popper holds that " . . . there is, from the ethical point of view, no symmetry between suffering and happiness, or between pain and pleasure . . . from the moral point of view, pain cannot be outweighed by pleasure, and especially not one man's pain by another man's pleasure."[23] And " . . . the best of ends do not as such justify bad means, but the attempt to avoid worse results may justify actions which are in themselves producing bad results."[24] If then utopia is considered as a condition of "pleasure," Popper would say that on no account could pain be inflicted to achieve it.[25] There are several difficulties in this position.

----

22. See Karl Popper, *The Open Society and Its Enemies* (Princton, N.J.: Princeton University Press, 1950), p. 155; note 6 to Chap. 5 (pp. 508-509); note 2 to Chap. 9 (pp. 570-571); note 6 to Chap. 9 (pp. 573-574). See also Popper's "Utopia and Violence," *The Hibbert Journal,* XLVI (1947-1948), pp. 109-116.

23. Popper, *The Open Society and Its Enemies, op. cit.,* pp. 570-571.

24. *Ibid.,* p. 574.

25. A much more extreme version of Popper's idea can be found in the writings of Simone Weil. Popper says, Never do evil except to avoid greater evil; Simone Weil says, Do not act at all except to avoid evil. So convinced

It is clear that the hedonic calculus would always require that some pain be inflicted or undergone in order to avoid a greater pain, now or in the future. Probably most people would also agree that the removal of the suffering of some should come before the increase of the well-being of any. For example, in a situation in which some people lived meagerly though tolerably well, and some lived wretchedly, the first task of the reformer would be to relieve the wretchedness even if that meant that the condition of those who lived meagerly were to remain unimproved. The first aim should be to rescue everyone from radical evil. Popper would probably consent to the reform even though it meant that the wretched were benefited at the expense of their somewhat more fortunate neighbors. On the basis of this example, it could be said that, within limits, there was no symmetry between "pleasure" and "pain." What is disputable, however, is the *unqualified* assertion that pleasure cannot be measured against pain, that no pleasure, be it ever so great, can compensate for any pain, be it ever so small. Of course, neither the satisfaction of one man's whim, nor even his ecstasy, would be worth the torture or misery of another man. There are, in short, *some* pains or evils not to be compensated for by any sort of pleasure or satisfaction: this revision of the calculus seems sensible. But is it so obvious that there would not be situations in which much pleasure should be gained at the cost of some pain, a new advantage at the cost of some hardship?

These comments are, however, incidental to the utopian argument. The utopian apologist would try to show that it was precisely by Popper's own version of the hedonic calculus that the case for utopia was at its strongest. A utopian possessed

---

is Simone Weil that all action tends to the production of evil, that no action is free from the possibility of bringing harm into the world, that she wished to have action done only when accompanied by a sense of its necessity, and she sees the necessity to act only when evil threatens. Such an attitude naturally favors the *status quo*. One could also say, on the basis of Simone Weil's views, that the purer the ends (and what could be purer than utopian ends?) the more emphatically should the temptation to realize them be avoided, for otherwise the discrepancy between aspiration and the inevitably sordid attainment would show at its greatest and hence at its most humiliating. See Simone Weil, *Cahiers* I (Paris: Plon, 1951), pp. 90-91.

of a sense of the inevitable recurrence of wars and the permanent existence of numerous social and economic evils outside utopia, could say, as he said to the absolutist, that if he were allowed to inflict pain now, he would insure that violence and pain would never again be; that the essence of his strategy and calculation was to trade a comparatively small amount of present evil for the very purpose of avoiding the greater evils that are bound to keep on happening outside utopia. He could say that *before everything else*, utopia signified the permanent absence of radical evil, and that the eradication of such evil was its initial motivation. To represent utopia otherwise is to misrepresent it. He is not letting blood flow for the sake of cake; he is not imposing suffering now in order to "maximize pleasure," though he surely aspires to the maximization of pleasure as a secondary goal—a goal he refuses, unlike Popper, to regard as contemptible.[26] (Popper goes so far as to say that "the principle 'Maximize happiness,' in contrast, seems to be apt to produce a benevolent dictatorship.")[27] The *absolutist* would refuse this calculation; *but on the assumption of success for the efforts to attain utopia*, Popper could not. Aware that a Marxist could make an argument somewhat like this one, Popper asks, " . . . can we condemn one generation to suffer for the sake of later generations?"[28] But by refusing to do some evil to prevent greater evil, has not Popper departed from the very principle he set up?

---

26. Compare the statement of John Stuart Mill in *Utilitarianism*: "Neither pains nor pleasures are homogeneous, and pain is always heterogeneous with pleasure." (New York and London: American Everyman's Library, 1950, p. 13.) For a position very close to Popper's, see Stephen Toulmin, *An Examination of the Place of Reason in Ethics* (Cambridge: Cambridge University Press, 1950). Toulmin says (p. 160): "The notions of 'obligation,' 'right,' 'justice,' 'duty,' and 'ethics' apply in the first place where our actions or institutions may lead to avoidable misery for others; but it is a natural and familiar extension to use them also where the issue concerns the chance of deeper happiness for others, and even for ourselves." Toulmin insists on his claim that to make happiness an ethical concern is to *extend* the commitments of ethical action. (See pp. 159-160.) See also R. N. Smart, "Negative Utilitarianism," *Mind*, LXVII (1958), pp. 542-543. There is a historical discussion of the primacy accorded the prevention of pain over the promotion of pleasure in Sheldon Wolin, *Politics and Vision* (Boston: Little, Brown, 1960), pp. 325-331.

27. Popper, *The Open Society and Its Enemies, op. cit.*, n. 6, p. 508.
28. *Ibid.*, p. 574.

And for no very readily discoverable reason? And surely it is never a question of sacrificing a *whole* generation. Futhermore, how is the sacrifice of (part of) one generation for all later ones different in principle from sacrificing parts of one generation to another part, as has happened and will continue to happen outside utopia?[29]

vi

Everything depends, then, on the degree to which a utopian activist could assure the success of his efforts. If he could, the moral arguments used against him either fall or are seen to give somewhat less cause for disturbance to his conscience than to the conscience of any other political man. But when he encounters those common-sense arguments which try to show that it is wrong to think that success for any violent venture could ever be guaranteed, he must yield. It is not absolute morality, nor the antiutopian ethics of Camus and Popper that provide the insuperable obstacles to utopian exertion, but rather a series of unpretentious practical-moral considerations. If antiutopianism makes its stand on these grounds, it would seem to be unbeatable.

The antiutopian case, here as in the foregoing, is a matter of means and ends. But in the arguments we have already examined, the dualism was that of immoral means and moral ends. In the common-sense arguments we are to examine now, the dualism is inadequate means and all-inclusive ends. The heart of the matter is that the means that must be employed are treacherous and unreliable: violent revolution defeats the purposes for which it was undertaken. This is not only a generality of common-sense, but a commonplace. Harold Laski, in *A Grammar of Politics*, said, "Revolutions do not achieve the direct end at which they aim; and the weapons of which they

29. For a discussion of the claims of one generation on another, in relation to nuclear warfare and surrender, see the opposing articles: Bertrand Russell, "Freedom to Survive," and Sidney Hook, "Bertrand Russell Retreats," in *The New Leader*, LXI (July 7-14, 1958), pp. 23-28.

are driven to make use destroy by their character the prospects they have in view."[30] Simone Weil said, "La guerre révolutionnaire est le tombeau de la révolution. . . ."[31] The opinion that George Orwell attributes to Arthur Koestler informs Orwell's own *Animal Farm*:

If one writes about the Moscow trials one must answer the question, "Why did the accused confess?" and which answer one makes is a political decision. Koestler answers, in effect, "Because these people had been rotted by the Revolution which they served," and in doing so he comes near to claiming that revolutions are of their nature bad. . . . Revolution, Koestler seems to say, is a corrupting process. . . . It is not merely that "power corrupts": so also do the ways of attaining power. Therefore, all efforts to regenerate society by *violent means* lead to the cellars of the Ogpu.[32]

In his bitterly anti-Soviet novel, *The Burned Bramble*, Manès Sperber has the character Professor Stetten say, "Victory in war is problematical enough; in a revolution it just doesn't exist. The alleged victory automatically creates new conditions which reduce it to nothing. Every revolutionary movement reaches its zenith before its success. That success is the beginning of the counterrevolution which naturally starts off under revolutionary banners."[33] These utterances are just a sampling.

It would seem that the use of violence as a means for any end whatever raises in its acutest form the primitive problem of how the means may interfere with the ends they are supposed to accomplish.[34] Now to talk as if means and ends were different species of things, discrete and isolable, is, as many have pointed

---

30. Quoted in Herbert A. Deane, *The Political Ideas of Harold J. Laski* (New York: Columbia University Press, 1955), p. 137. See also pp. 71-73 of Deane's book for a discussion of Laski's early views. See also John Dewey, *Liberalism and Social Action* (New York: G. P. Putnam's Sons, 1935), pp. 76-80.

31. Simone Weil, "Réflexions sur la guerre" in *Écrits historiques et politiques* (Paris: Gallimard, 1960), p. 236.

32. George Orwell, "Arthur Koestler," in *Critical Essays* (London: Secker and Warburg, 1946), pp. 136-137.

33. Manès Sperber, *The Burned Bramble*, trans. by Constantine Fitzgibbon (New York: Doubleday, 1951), p. 116.

34. One of the most interesting discussions of this problem in recent times is to be found in Simone Weil, "Réflexions sur les causes de la liberté et de l'oppression sociale," in *Oppression et liberté* (Paris: Gallimard, 1955), pp. 57-162. See p. 146.

out, terribly imprecise.[35] But crude as the distinction is, it has its uses: to speak, for example, of violence as the means to the end of a utopian society is *simpliste* but intelligible.

What is at issue in this problem of means and ends is not mere inefficiency—say, the inefficiency of a man who uses a plow horse instead of a tractor—and how inefficient means can circumscribe the ends sought. Rather, attention is directed to occurrences of the sort in which "the means become ends in themselves," as the saying goes, and divert energy and attention wholly or partly from the ends; even, perhaps, making what were formerly ends into subservient means; or the means produce unexpected effects that require a consonant modification of the end or ends; or the means produce unexpected effects that may coexist with the achieved end or ends and be even as troublesome as, or more troublesome than, what the means were originally employed to remedy. These net results are possible whether the means are actions, institutions, or instruments and implements: the usage is loose and covers much; but there is a common understanding that means may defeat or interfere with ends. It is also part of this common view that violence makes its users especially vulnerable to all the deflections and distractions that attach to any action. If predicting the consequences of action, most generally, is a mad pursuit, predicting the consequences of violent action would seem hopeless.

Utopian exertion, when it is the subject of attack, is generally taken to have the form of a consummated revolution. When the Russian Revolution is taken as the revolution which, in its morphology, most resembles what a revolution for utopian ends would have to be, four rough stages can be distinguished: conspiracy, the seizure of power, the consolidation of power, and the replacement of the existing social order by a new one. And by using the Russian Revolution as *the* model in his discourse, the antiutopian chooses that revolution which presents all these stages, and in their absolutely most repulsive form.

---

35. See, for example, Popper, *The Open Society and Its Enemies, op. cit.*, p. 573.

For, in the Russian example, the *donnée* was a brutal ruling class controlling a brutalized mass, in an immense and backward country. Conspiracy, merely to be initiated, had to possess, from the start, those characteristics that must mark an all but hopeless enterprise: an extreme of frenzy and hatred, a despair that easily turns into nihilism, and an appetite for destruction that seems to be much larger than the appetite for creation. The conspiracy had to take its shape from its opposition, the secret police. The masses of men, having no dream of change, had to strike the conspirators as inert matter, to be ignored or used, but not consulted or relied on. Power had to be seized by a few men, and seized when the existing social order was falling apart, at a time of war and dislocation. The irony was that the very conditions that made seizure of power possible—war, weakness, dislocation—made the consolidation of power necessarily coercive. Also, hostility was nearly omnipresent, and where there was no hostility there was apathy or stupidity instead. The very men attracted to make a revolution under these circumstances could be trusted to engage in the most ruthless internal struggle, once power had been seized, and pretext was never lacking for intimidation and ferocity. And the transition from one order to another was, in Russia, the transition from one order to its opposite; not an alteration but a transformation; the break with the past had to be painful, even if the motives of those in power were faultless.

This is an old story, but a story that can always serve to inhibit the revolutionary impulse, and to the degree that modern antiutopianism derives from the Russian experience, it is, of course, this sequence which accounts for it. A recital of this sequence is, by itself, the strongest possible way of putting forward the case of antiutopianism of the means. And in reserve is the French Revolution, with its regicide, terror, Thermidor, and Napoleonic conquest; and the great voice of Burke saying (even before regicide, terror, and Thermidor) how in every revolution there was something of evil, how "Criminal means once tolerated are soon preferred . . . Justifying perfidy and murder for public benefit, public benefit would soon become the

pretext and perfidy and murder the end . . . ,"[36] and how " . . .
by hating vices too much, they [the revolutionaries] come to
love men too little."[37]

In sum, each stage of revolution is thought to be filled with
perils for the ultimate aim of all that endeavor: each stage holds
within itself innumerable occasions for the ends to be com-
promised, forgotten, betrayed, or rendered permanently unreachable. The French Revolution died at the stage of consolidation; the Russian Revolution irretrievably lost the possibility of
achieving its ends at the stage of consolidation. Every revolution
consumes the dreams which set it in motion. It is not that
every recourse to arms is bound to fail of its goal: that would
be absurd; it is that whenever the goal is an idealist and radical
reform of an existing society, the recourse to arms (and all that
leads up to it and all that comes after it) will insure that the
idealism will fail, or materialize in a diminished or mottled way.
Revolution will be conquered by counterrevolution, or use the
power it has managed to keep for other than idealist ends. It has
its choice of failures. (If the way to heaven must be through
hell, you may finally find that the "heaven" you have reached
seems heaven only because of the hell that has gone before it,
and may be no better than where you began, and that real
heaven is yet to be reached; and never through violence.) It
is not that only evil men would try to make a revolution; it
is that making a revolution makes men evil. And most important
of all, the consequences of a use of violence cannot be trammeled
up, they cannot be predicted in full: a revolutionary could never
guarantee the success of his efforts, and hence the risk involved
in his efforts would never be worth taking.

In answer to this onslaught, he who wished to defend utopian
exertion, in the abstract, could try to say that in the case of

---

36. Edmund Burke, *Reflections on the Revolution in France* (New
York and London: Everyman's Library, 1955), p. 79.

37. *Ibid.*, p. 167. For a fair-minded discussion of reigns of terror, see
Crane Brinton, *The Anatomy of Revolution* (New York: Vintage Books,
1957), Chap. 7, esp. pp. 208-214. The model liberal attitude toward revolutionary violence, most generally, is that of R. R. Palmer in *The Age of the
Democratic Revolution,* Vol. I (Princeton, N.J.: Princeton University Press,
1959). See pp. 10-11.

the Russian Revolution all the earlier Marxist preconditions of revolution were lacking ('and these, in essence, are the ideal preconditions of revolution). There was no mass agreement that what existed simply could not be suffered to exist any longer; no mass agreement on what the alternative should be; no mass agreement on the methods needed to attain the alternative; no mass belief that it was indeed materially possible to construct the desired alternative; and there was next to nothing in the existing order that even remotely resembled, even in outline, any feature of the desired alternative. Perhaps such preconditions must always be lacking. In any event, Marxism in Russia had to be Leninism, and Leninism had to become Stalinism (at best, Stalinism without a few of its excesses); and at the very beginning, there had to be Bakunins and Nechaevs. The Marxist theory of revolution as the work of a class-conscious and oppressed body of workers, responding to their oppression in a uniform way and entertaining a uniform sense of a better life in the future, gave way to the Leninist theory of revolution as the effort of a small number of professional revolutionaries. The Marxist theory of the dictatorship of the proletariat, in which there is full democracy for the proletariat combined with dictatorial repression of its few enemies, gave way to the practice of the dictatorship of the party over the proletariat and all other classes in society. The Marxist theory of socialism, in which hours of labor alone determine compensation, gave way to the theory of socialism, in which the nature of the work and the quality of the performance determine compensation.

But must every idealist revolution pass through the same trajectory, and fail, and, apparently, fail in the same way? Is there an ineluctable "natural history of revolution," as Lyford P. Edwards tried to show; is every great idealist revolution doomed to conform to the same pattern, as Crane Brinton tried to show?[38] Must not allowance be made for the way in which

---

38. Though Edwards stresses the fact that his generalizations are not based on a large number of cases. See Lyford P. Edwards, *The Natural History of Revolution* (Chicago: University of Chicago Press, 1927), pp. 210-211.

social conditions on the eve of revolution may affect the course of revolution? Let it be granted that revolution must always be the affair of a minority[39] and that therefore coercion and manipulation remain necessary ingredients of any revolution. Still, it stands to reason that a revolution taking place in a country at peace will have a different history from a revolution taking place in a country beset by war or other chaos, that a revolution taking place in a technologically advanced country will have a different history from a revolution taking place in a technologically backward country, that a revolution taking place in a country with a tradition of bourgeois civility and respect for individual liberties will have a different history from a revolution taking place in a country lacking that tradition. Must violence infect a movement at its source, so that whatever follows its use must exhibit ineffaceable traces of that infection? Are not the "variables" that influence the result different from situation to situation; and if they are, could not at least some of the horrors of past revolutions be avoided, on the supposition of foresight? Must utopianism be identified with failure, must its connection with terror and repression be taken as everlasting?

Naturally, in so far as utopianism is thought to require violence as its instrument, it cannot lose its connection with terror and repression: it is hopeless to conceive that any radical movement would ever command the loyalties of nearly everyone concerned (that is, of those whose interests are not threatened by utopianism). Again, naturally, the consequences of any use of violence could never be predicted, and hence, success could never be guaranteed. And, again, naturally, as

---

39. The moral issues raised by the consideration that utopian exertion would certainly violate the majority-principle, and represent the imposition of a political order by a minority, are very grave, needless to say. Unfortunately, the utopian apologist must always defend himself by saying that the enlightened minority knows better than the majority what is good for the majority, the majority is too lazy or too much the prisoner of the *status quo* to know where its real interest lies. In time, hopefully, the majority will come to see that the minority was right; and, in time, majority-rule can be restored. This utopian position is ugly in itself, and is liable to the most awful perversions. But what more is there that can be said?

long as a radical movement requires and engenders *enthusiasm*,[40] there will be excess. So much must be conceded by an utopian apologist. What the utopian apologist could possibly feel did not need conceding is that the period after the consolidation of power must perpetually remain a period of terror and repression wherein no steps can be taken to realize the ends for which the entire sequence of awful events was initiated in the first place. On the basis of the Russian experience itself (the experience most damaging to the general utopian position), could it not be maintained, with some plausibility, that the next decades may show the Russian regime making good some of the claims of Soviet Marxism? The speculation of scholars in the field of Russian studies on this possibility must be of the most intense interest to the student of utopianism.[41]

There are several questions of particular interest. First, are purge, terror, intimidation, and coercion unremovable features of the Soviet system; or if they vanish, will it be merely because

---

40. See the brief but concentrated discussion by Isaiah Berlin in his essay, "The Silence in Russian Culture," *Foreign Affairs*, XXXVI (1957), pp. 1-24, esp. pp. 15ff.

41. See, for example, Julian Towster, *Political Power in the U.S.S.R., 1917-1947* (New York: Oxford University Press, 1948), Chap. 14; George F. Kennan, "America and the Russian Future," in *American Diplomacy* (Chicago: University of Chicago Press, 1951); W. W. Rostow, *The Dynamics of Russian Society* (New York: Norton, 1952), Chap. 15; Merle Fainsod, *How Russia Is Ruled* (Cambridge, Mass.: Harvard University Press, 1953), Chaps. 4, 17; Karl W. Deutsch, "Cracks in the Monolith: Possibilities and Patterns of Disintegration in Totalitarian Systems," in *Totalitarianism*, ed. by Carl J. Friedrich (Cambridge, Mass.: Harvard University Press, 1954), pp. 308-333; Barrington Moore, *Terror and Progress USSR* (Cambridge, Mass.: Harvard University Press, 1954), Chaps. 6, 7; Barrington Moore, *Soviet Politics—The Dilemma of Power* (Cambridge, Mass.: Harvard University Press, 1956), Chap. 18; Zbigniew Brzezinski, *The Permanent Purge* (Cambridge, Mass.: Harvard University Press, 1956), esp. Chap. 10; Isaac Deutscher, *Russia in Transition* (New York: Coward-McCann, 1957), pp. 3-32; Herbert Marcuse, *Soviet Marxism* (New York: Columbia University Press, 1958), *passim;* Alex Inkeles and Raymond A. Bauer, *The Soviet Citizen* (Cambridge, Mass.: Harvard University Press, 1959), Chap. 16; Philip Mosely, "Soviet Myths and Realities," *Foreign Affairs*, 39 (April, 1960), pp. 341-354; W. Laqueur and L. Labedz, eds., *The Future of Communist Society* (New York: Praeger, 1962), *passim.* Also see the analysis of Russian aspirations for the future by Elliot R. Goodman, *The Soviet Design for a World State* (New York: Columbia University Press, 1960), Chap. XIII.

the stultification and herdlike acquiescence of the Russian people will make them unnecessary? Second, to what extent will Russian society embody values any liberal can recognize as his own: can it be that out of conspiracy, revolution, terror, and coercion, something fully humane can develop without foreign intercession or domestic upheaval? Third, if a welfare state within the framework of the rule of law does emerge, will it in turn be smoothly transformed into the stateless, classless and libertarian society (at least classless and libertarian society) which is, in essence, the utopian society? The intent behind these questions is simple: it is to allow for the possibility that though revolution may corrupt those who make it, those who follow may still be able to salvage the original purposes of the revolution; it is to allow for the possibility that the Russian Revolution—the revolution carried out with the worst possible initial handicaps for idealism—may appear to future observers as something somewhat different from a cruel and bloody failure and just another example of the replacement of one selfish oligarchy by another; it is to indulge in "taking the long view."

We must acknowledge that there is a wide gap between a humane welfare state and a society in which the fullest aims of modern utopianism are realized. Included within these aims are (a) the eradication of all traces of political authority and (b) the flowering of human individuality in a milieu of full freedom of thought and behavior. And it may be that just as Lenin and Stalin, in response to Russian conditions, departed from the Marxist theory of revolution and reformation in all stages leading up to the last, so Soviet Marxism may have to depart from orthodox Marxism in the last stage, as well. That is to say, it may be that the attainment of a genuinely libertarian society is permanently foreclosed. But if that is the case, where does the explanation lie? Is the reason for the (assumed) dismal ending of Marxism in Russia the initial use of violence and coercion? Or is it rather that revolution in a technologically backward country in which there was, at best, a weak, incipient tradition of bourgeois civility and respect for individual liberties, could never bring about a genuinely libertarian society? After all, there are few libertarian precedents in pre-Soviet Russia

on which future Russians can draw; there is little in Soviet life
that can prepare either the Soviet leaders or people merely to
understand the full meaning of Marxist—and utopian—humanism,
even if the problems of production, the exigencies of world
politics, and the prevailing characteristics of party dictatorship
were some day to cease offering obstacles to that humanism.

In summary, we say that considerations adduced by those
wishing to show that violent means always fail idealist ends
are overwhelmingly impressive and lead, understandably, to
the recommendation to renounce the utopian vision. There are,
of course, certain reservations a utopian apologist can have
about the *absoluteness* with which the antiutopian puts his
considerations forward; there are certain consolations the utopian
apologist can extract from the fact that the antiutopian has
built his case on a limited range of historical experience. But
the common sense at the heart of the antiutopian position does
seem, after all, unanswerable.

vii

It must be noted that of the four stages of revolution and
radical reform, two have dominated the political imagination:
the stages of conspiracy and the consolidation of power. It
would seem that these two stages present the gravest perils
to revolutionary ideals and the most fecund source of corruption
for revolutionaries. When moralists—novelists and dramatists—
take up the revolutionary theme, they are usually drawn to
these two stages; they find in them occasions of the sharpest
and most revealing predicaments of means and ends; and ample
illustration of the saying of a poet that "revolution is the affair of
logical lunatics."

One's image of conspiracy cannot help being permanently
influenced by Dostoyevsky's *The Possessed*;[42] and what Dostoyevsky says is confirmed by Conrad and, in a way, by Sartre

---

42. Fyodor Dostoyevsky, *The Possessed*, translated by Constance Garnett
(New York: Macmillan, n.d.).

in *Dirty Hands*.[43] It is true that Dostoyevsky's novel seized on
the most extreme tendencies of conspiracy; indeed Dostoyevsky
was possessed by the possessed. Yet his caricature is just that: a
caricature but roughly true. The scandal of Bakunin's *Cathecism*
exceeds anything in Dostoyevsky's novel; while Malraux, who
was sympathetic to radical revolution when he wrote *Man's
Hope*, could still have one of his revolutionary characters,
Ximenes, say: "All that estranges you from your fellow-men is
bound to link you up more closely with your party."[44]

Similarly, one's image of the period of consolidation can,
with justice, take its leading features from Georg Büchner's
Danton's Death and Arthur Koestler's *Darkness at Noon*. The
reign of virtue and -enthusiasm and the time of purges are
treated dramatically and convincingly in these two works.
When one thinks of revolution one probably thinks first of terror
and purge, and what one thinks stands to be enormously influenced by Büchner and Koestler, and remain influenced after
the historical records are read.

viii

The last stage of utopian exertion, the replacement of the
old social order by a new one, is naturally the subject of much
less speculation. History gives few examples of really complete
and thoroughgoing alterations of a society, affecting all or most
of the basic traditions and practices in existence, consciously
introduced, carried out in a short time and after violent revolution. The neatest story of total change is that of Lycurgus,
but there was no revolution which preceded his reforms, and
he worked (if he existed at all) with a small city-state. The

---

43. There are numerous antirevolutionary sentiments in another play
by Sartre, *The Devil and the Good Lord*, printed in *The Devil and the
Good Lord, and Two Other Plays*, trans. by Kitty Black (New York: Knopf,
1960).

44. André Malraux, *Man's Hope*, trans. by Stuart Gilbert and Alastair
Macdonald (New York: The Modern Library, 1938), p. 408. The entire
conversation between Ximenes and Manuel is of great interest (pp. 407-
409).

notorious advice given by Socrates to philosopher-kings, namely to banish all people over ten years of age from the land in which the perfect state is to be erected, points up the immensity of the problem of transition.[45] It is a problem much attended to by Lenin in *State and Revolution,* and his gloss on some of Marx's comments (in *The Critique of the Gotha Program*) is emphatic: " . . . as a matter of fact, remnants of the old surviving in the new confront us in life at every step, both in nature and in society."[46]

The utopian dream would be to have a clean slate: not to banish those over ten, but to be given infants from the start. But even in that case, difficulty remains. The utopian reformers are themselves products of preutopia: the old remains to infect or at least affect the new.[47]

For Karl Popper, the fact that history gives so little example of the systematic modeling of a society is enough reason for believing that remodeling would never proceed according to plan.[48] Without any of Burke's piety ("The very idea of the

---

45. Plato, *The Republic,* 540. Recall also the words of Aristotle: ". . . there is quite as much trouble in the reformation of an old constitution as in the establishment of a new one, just as to unlearn is as hard as to learn." *Politics,* trans. by Benjamin Jowett (New York: The Modern Library, 1942), 1289a. Rousseau even goes beyond Aristotle: ". . . Legislation is made difficult less by what it is necessary to build up than by what has to be destroyed." [*The Social Contract and Discourses,* trans. and ed. by G. D. H. Cole (New York: American Everyman's Edition, 1950), p. 49.] Note the words of the poet, Richard Wilbur: "But a heaven is easier made of nothing at all/ Than the earth regained." ["Juggler," in *Ceremony and Other Poems* (New York: Harcourt Brace, n.d.), p. 18.]

46. V. I. Lenin, *The State and Revolution* (1917) in *Selected Works,* (2 Vols., London: Foreign Languages Publishing House, 1947), Vol. II, p. 208.

47. See, for example, Skinner, *Walden Two, op. cit.,* pp. 207-208.

48. Popper, *The Open Society and Its Enemies, op. cit.,* Chap. 9. For the much more sanguine view of a man whose political and economic preferences were much like Popper's, see Joseph A. Schumpeter, *Capitalism, Socialism and Democracy* (1942) (third edition, New York: Harper, 1950), pp. 219-231. There, Schumpeter speaks about the specific matter of going from capitalism to socialism. For a non-soviet discussion of issues related to the transition from socialism to communism, see Walter Lippmann, *The Good Society* (1937) (New York: Grosset's Universal Library, 1956), pp. 70-71; and Herbert Marcuse, *Soviet Marxism* (New York: Columbia University Press, 1958), pp. 121, 127, 151, 153. For strong statements of the view that a great disparity between blue-

fabrication of a new government is enough to fill us with disgust and horror"[49]), without very much attention to the specific problem of how traces of the old order remain to complicate the establishment of the new, and without specific reference in this context to the complicating consequences of violent revolution for the problem of transition, Popper still maintains that each step taken to attain a society that answered to the prescriptions laid down for it in advance would invariably modify those prescriptions: the net result will always be unexpected. Such are the limits of human foresight, and such is the complexity of social life, that every step forward is also a half-step sideward, even in the best circumstances. (These comments of Popper on social control apply to the transition from old to new, not to the maintenance of a planned society in a constant form. These problems are related but not identical.) Popper insists, that is, that we do not know enough to achieve the major social changes we plan for. We can perhaps change one thing at a time, but nothing very great at any time, and surely not everything all at once. There will generally be opposition to change; measures taken to suppress opposition affect the ultimate ends; even without opposition, life is too much for the radical reformer, especially when his reforms encompass something larger than a city-state. The upshot is that no utopian exertion could ever be acceptable, because it

---

print and end-result is certain, whether or not violence precedes reform see, for example, Hans J. Morgenthau, *Scientific Man vs. Power Politics* (Chicago: University of Chicago Press, 1946), pp. 145-152; Michael Oakeshott, "Scientific Politics" (a review of Morgenthau's *Scientific Man vs. Power Politics*), *The Cambridge Journal*, I (1947-1948), pp. 247-258, esp. pp. 255-256; Karl Popper, *The Open Society and Its Enemies, op. cit.*, Chap. 9; Karl Popper, *The Poverty of Historicism* (Boston: Beacon Press, 1957), esp. Chaps. II and III; Friedrich A. Hayek, *The Counter-Revolution of Science* (Glencoe, Ill.: The Free Press, 1952), Chaps. 8-10. See also, note 20 in Chap. 3 of this book, below.

49. Edmund Burke, *Reflections on the Revolution in France, op. cit.*, p. 29. For a recent restatement of this position, see Michael Oakeshott, "Political Education," in *Philosophy, Politics and Society*, ed. by Peter Laslett (Oxford: Basil Blackwell, 1956). For cogent criticisms of Oakeshott's doctrine of "intimations," see J. C. Rees, "Professor Oakeshott on Political Education," *Mind*, LXII (1953), pp. 68-74; and S. I. Benn and R. S. Peters, *Social Principles and the Democratic State* (London: Allen and Unwin, 1959), pp. 312-318.

could never claim to be able to do with society what it wants; it will shatter the peace and regularity of a society only to substitute no one knows what. The huge gamble utopianism takes in the name of perfection is foolhardy in the extreme: it could never redeem its promises. Social reality would prove too refractory.

The utopian apologist would have to acknowledge the force of these arguments; but again he could wonder whether the case presented is not too absolute, too abstract, too heedless of time and place. And, again, he would be compelled to scrutinize the experience of the Soviet Union. Does that experience bear out Popper's contentions? Clearly, the Soviets followed a winding road to socialism in the 1920's and 1930's; but what is to be said about the Russian course since the Second World War? What is at issue here is not so much the nature and aims of the change, as the degree to which Soviet achievement answers to Soviet intention. And to take the Russian experience is to make the case as hard as it can be made for the utopian, for the obvious reason that where Russia started was so different from where Russia is supposed to finish. It is no mitigation to say that Soviet brutality compensated for Russian backwardness. Indeed such consideration makes it even less promising, on the face of it, for the utopian apologist: the use of force is held to be either inherently unpredictable because it is disruptive and sets in motion the passions of fear, hatred, and revenge, or inevitably destructive of the ends for which it is used, or both. Such a belief about the use of force is central to the antiutopian position. If the Soviets turn out to have taken in hand an immense society which bore little likeness to the intended order, and then set up the order that was intended, and done so despite zigzagging, despite coercion of the masses, and despite the constant tendency to terror within the state and party apparatus, then Popper's generalizations would stand in need of rather serious qualification; and at one of its points, the antiutopian case would have been weakened.

Of course slow change is better than rapid change: it is less painful and more certain. In the spirit of Burke, but with

measure (that is, in the spirit of Montesquieu), and in awareness of the potency of modern technology, Dahl and Lindblom,
in their book, *Politics, Economics and Welfare,* have listed the
reasons why slow and piecemeal change is preferable.[50] Their
reasons, like Popper's, are of a general nature, but rather more
telling. And their reasons are more telling, in part, because there
is nothing doctrinaire in their approach. "Incrementalism [Dahl
and Lindblom's name for gradual change] should not be confused with a simple commitment to the idea that gradual change
is always preferable to rapid change. The greater the degree
of scientific knowledge available about a given instrumental
goal, and provided people are reasonably confident about their
preferences, the larger is the increment of change that can be
rationally made. . . ."[51] The authors stress, with Popper, the
uncertainty attaching to the outcome of all large-scale action,
but go on to make a solider case by noting that a blueprint is
at best a sketch, the details of which are filled in by experience;
and once filled in, these details—actually the substance of the
blueprint—may, in truth, turn out to be so different from what
was expected as to be unwanted. Also, as effects of the great
change are felt, new wants may be generated that were not
even imagined at the beginning; but these wants cannot now
be satisfied, because great change is much less easily reversible
than moderate change, and the blueprint cannot accommodate
novelty. There is, in short, a tremendous difference between
vaguely imagining what life ought to be and experiencing the
life that has been made in accordance with the promptings of
the imagination. Let there be, then, caution, flexibility, pause:
let reality catch up with the imagination.

The good sense of such reasoning is undeniable. But there
are times, all the same, when rapid and radical change can be
seen to be the only alternative to chaos. And to allow that this
kind of change is not, in the abstract, inevitably doomed to
failure—as Dahl and Lindblom indeed allow, though they

50. Robert A. Dahl and Charles E. Lindblom, *Politics, Economics
and Welfare* (New York: Harper, 1953), pp. 82-88.
    51. *Ibid.,* p. 84.

dislike utopianism—is all that the utopian apologist would want.

Our discussion has assumed that in the period of transition, control over society will be in the hands of those who made the revolution, and that the task of making the world over will proceed, if necessary, undemocratically, and despite whatever opposition there may be. That is, the revolutionaries will stand to utopian society as Plato's Statesman stands to his imaginary ideal state. Now, if there are antiutopian arguments that are directed to showing that systematically carrying out radical social change according to a preconceived plan must necessarily fail because of the irreducible complexity of social life, there are other antiutopian arguments that are directed at showing that such an enterprise could succeed but only at the cost of making society lose all its texture and variety. And such a cost would be too high even for utopia. The heart of the argument is that measures will be taken in the period of transition that could never thereafter be undone, and that these measures could have no tendency but to level, and to produce the most dispiriting uniformity.

There are those who feel that a world-wide (or indeed any very large-scale) reordering of social life could not be had without regimentation and the curbing of certain traits of human nature to the point of its stultification, without an immense and overbearing bureaucracy and the bureaucratization of life itself, without a cultivated obtuseness to the particular and the eccentric and an active hostility to regional differences in customs and language, without worship of the Machine and the extension of mechanization and automation to all aspects of life, without the elevation of stability and efficiency into the prime virtues of social existence, without a flat, monotonous equalitarian uniformity and an unnatural geometric regularity, without producing a condition in which there are "no more invisible means of support, no more invisible motives, no more invisible anything,"[52] without seeing to it that ". . . la simplication des types humains . . . compense la com-

---

52. Robert Frost, "The Constant Symbol" in *The Poems of Robert Frost* (New York: The Modern Library, 1946), pp. xv-xxiv, at p. xvii.

plication des organismes collectifs,"[53] without, in short, converting the world into one vast barracks, post office, or insect colony. Taking the world in hand and directing it from a single center must lead to the extinction of certain cherished elements of society as we now know it. If the world is seen as one political entity to be reconstructed in conformity to one plan and by one group of men, the problems of employment, resources, consumption, population, and regional differences, on the one hand, and education, culture, and the demands of equality on the other, would be so immense that the planners, inevitably, would seek to impose the most bureaucratically efficient and convenient solutions.

It is not so much a question of malice or self-interest on the part of the planners.[54] Quite simply, the enormousness of

53. Paul Valéry, "Propos sur le progrès" (1929), in *Regards sur le monde actuel* (Paris: Gallimard, 1945), p. 167.

54. However, what Robert Michels said of socialist party leaders could perhaps be extended to all bureaucratic leaders: "Thus, from a means, organization becomes an end. To the institutions and qualities which at the outset were destined simply to ensure the good working of the party machine (subordination, the harmonious cooperation of individual members, hierarchical relationships, discretion, propriety of conduct), a greater importance comes ultimately to be attached than to the productivity of the machine. Henceforward the sole preoccupation is to avoid anything which may clog the machinery." [Robert Michels, *Political Parties* (1915), trans. by Eden and Cedar Paul (New York: Dover Publications Reprint, 1959.] This view of Michels' is harsher than the one we formulate above, but far more controlled and reasonable than the view of planners and bureaucrats found in Herbert Spencer, "The Coming Slavery," in *The Man versus the State* (1884) (Caldwell, Idaho: Caxton, 1940); Friedrich A. Hayek, *The Road to Serfdom* (Chicago: University of Chicago Press, 1944); Ludwig von Mises, *Bureaucracy* (New Haven: Yale University Press, 1944). The latter authors carry their arguments to absurd lengths. For an early and very suggestive sketch of the bureaucratic mentality, see Walter Bagehot, *The English Constitution* (1867) (London: Oxford World's Classics, 1928), pp. 171-174. There is also some interesting writing on bureaucrats in the last pages of Mill's *On Liberty* (New York: Everyman's Library, 1950). Mill says: "For the governors are as much the slaves of their organization and discipline as the governed are of the governors." (p. 226.) See also Karl Mannheim, *Ideology and Utopia*, translated by Louis Wirth and Edward Shils (New York: Harvest Books, n.d.), pp. 118-119; Fritz Morstein Marx, *The Administrative State* (Chicago: University of Chicago Press, 1957), Chap. 6. For a discussion of the various images of the bureaucrat, and of the various shortcomings of bureaucratic mentality and procedure, see Robert A. Dahl and Charles E.

the venture would dictate that the readiest answers be given; and in the process, all the consequences listed above must needs come about. Bureaucrats notoriously consult their own ease of rule, transform human beings into numbers and file folders, eliminate all deviations and particularities from their consideration, and give dissimilar problems a standard solution. All bureaucratic arrangements tend to approach the condition of an army: Prussianism and Socialism are, ideally, never far apart.

Even granted that the bureaucrats who form utopia would be more enlightened and solicitous of the good of those they rule than bureaucrats generally are, they still would fall into the bureaucratic pattern of disposing the affairs of men. If the whole world were theirs to arrange and compose, their task would strike them as so vast that they would quite understandably take the easiest way in all difficulties. And the easiest way is the way of uniformity. They will want to grant a decent life for all; but they will find that it is least vexatious to assume that what is a decent life for some men—perhaps, most men—would be a decent life for all. Efficiency would recommend that some image of the average man guide the planners in their deliberations; efficiency would recommend that all areas of the globe become as like to each other as possible. The equanimity of the rulers would be disturbed by the needs of unaverage people. If everything is the managers' to give, they will give uniformly (mass-produced goods, lacking in taste and intricacy) and withhold the means required to nourish untypical inclinations and desires or accomodate regional peculiarities; and all that did not conform to bureaucratic expectations would perish. As Tocqueville said, ". . . Every central government worships uniformity: uniformity relieves it from inquiry into an infinity of details, which must be attended to if rules have to be adapted to different men, instead of

Lindblom, *Politics, Economics and Welfare, op. cit.,* pp. 247-261. For a brief but fine treatment of the bureaucratic mentality in a recent work, see Edward C. Banfield, *Political Influence* (New York: The Free Press, 1961), pp. 330-331. Finally, consult Martin Kessler, "Power and the Perfect State," *Political Science Quarterly,* LXXII (1957), pp. 565-577.

indiscriminately subjecting all men to the same rule. . . ."[55]
Working on the convenient assumption that all men are the
same, the planners would eventually *make* all men the same.
And the system would gather such momentum that it could
never be peacefully modified: uniformity would be perpetual:
the very possibility of conceiving heterogeneity would have
been lost, and nothing could bring it back.

In the words of Walter Lippmann,

For in so far as men embrace the belief that the coercive power of the
state shall plan, shape, and direct their economy, they commit themselves to the suppression of the contrariness arising from the diversity
of human interests and purposes. They cannot escape it. If a society
is to be planned, its population must conform to the plan; if it is to
have an official purpose, there must be no private purposes that conflict with it.[56]

In the words of Isaiah Berlin,

The entire trend of such an order is to reduce all issues to technical
problems of lesser or greater complexity, in particular the problem of
how to survive a condition in which the individual's psychological or
economic capacities are harnessed to producing the maximum of un-
clouded social contentment; and this in its turn depends upon the
suppression of whatever in him might raise doubt or assert itself
against the single all-embracing, all-clarifying, all-satisfying plan.[57]

The tendency of these attitudes would be to recommend that
the world, *as a whole,* be left alone, even though it strikes the
utopian thinker as chaotic. Let each part of the world attain
its social and economic salvation in its own way and in conformity with its regional character, even at the cost of slow or
imperfect attainment of that salvation. The wish to impose
universal salvation from the top must be abandoned.

It would be safe to say that one of the most pervasive antiutopian fears is that in utopia, similar people would lead identical
lives in the midst of indistinguishable surroundings; and that

55. Alexis de Tocqueville, *Democracy in America,* trans. by Henry
Reeve, ed. by Francis Bowen (2 Vols., Cambridge: Sever, 1862), Vol. II, p.
363.

56. Lippmann, *The Good Society, op. cit.,* p. 51.

57. Isaiah Berlin, "Political Ideas in the Twentieth Century," *Foreign
Affairs,* XXVIII (1950), p. 376.

out of a "rage for order" or a passion for equality, or simply
because it is impossible to have both central control and allowance for the free play of consumers' tastes and preferences,[58]
the planners would finally produce a society in which people
came to resemble interchangeable parts; from man to man and
generation to generation, the human race would show no more
differentiation than any animal species. What would happen to
" . . . the diversity which goes with a multiplicity of social
groups, and the diversity resulting from human spontaneity and
empiricism"[59] if all the world were the shaping-clay of even
the best artisans? It will not do for the utopian apologist to
dismiss the foregoing charges with the word "estheticism."
Of course, the complaint about uniformity is partly esthetic;
and, of course, the complaint is sometimes made by men who
would not balk at having diversity even if it meant that
serious inequities would be the accompaniment. That is to say,
there are times when conservative social thinkers (for example,
Tocqueville in *Democracy in America* and T. S. Eliot in *Notes
towards the Definition of Culture*) assume that for there to
be diversity, there must be social classes and gradations; and
that the existence of social classes, hierarchically arranged, is
a small price to pay for that diversity. They do not appear to
be able to conceive a diversity amidst equality. It seems that
there can be diversity only if there are disparate styles of life
emanating from " . . . all trades, their gear and tackle and
trim"; only if there are different levels of wealth, hardship,
power, and education; different kinds of life-experience. Inevitably, suffering and benefit would be unequal. The conservative stress is not on individual variety, but rather on *class* variety,

---

58. For a statement of this position, see, for example, Lippmann, *The
Good Society, op. cit.*, Chap. VI; *Collectivist Economic Planning*, ed. by
F. A. von Hayek (London: Routledge, 1935). For an attack on this position,
see Barbara Wootton, *Freedom under Planning* (Chapel Hill: University of
North Carolina Press, 1945); Karl Mannheim, *Freedom, Power and Democratic Planning* (New York: Oxford University Press, 1950), pp. 29-37, 281-
284. For a survey of arguments made against planning, see Judith N.
Shklar, *After Utopia* (Princeton, N.J.: Princeton University Press, 1957),
pp. 245-256.

59. J. L. Talmon, *The Origins of Totalitarian Democracy* (Boston: Beacon
Press, 1952), p. 250.

or on the variety of *roles*, from saint to beggar; not character,
but spectacle. And the spectacle must be fed by inequality and
by distance between social classes. If the division of labor were
attenuated by economic equality, abundant leisure for all, a
universally high level of education, and a spirit of fraternity,
the spectacle would, it is felt, be gravely threatened. (This is
not to say that when conservatives have defended inequality,
their only reasons have been esthetic ones. They have thought
that the only *efficient* society is a class society.) It must be
added that even where the stress *is* on individual variety rather
than on class variety, as in J. S. Mill's *On Liberty*, some regard
is paid to disparate styles of *group* life. Inspired by both
Humboldt and Tocqueville, Mill attacks "the Chinese ideal of
making all people alike" by praising the time when " . . . different
ranks, different neighborhoods, different trades and professions,
lived in what might be called different worlds . . . " Mill believed
that a "variety of situations" is a necessary condition ". . . of
human development, because it is necessary to render people
unlike one another." For a minute, Mill forgets the social cost
of his views: he ignores the fact that a "variety of situations" then
meant a great variety in well-being as well, a great variety in
happiness and rationality; that, in short, variety cost inequality.

But who indeed could contemplate, with satisfaction, a whole
world with just one architecture, one cuisine, one language,
one kind of amusement and play, one system of manners, one
code of behavior, one outlook on life, one *way* of life? Who
could feel that a world community with those features was
the best utopia a modern utopia could be? It is not merely that
the eye must eat and can eat only if surface contrasts abound—
contrasts between many kinds of good; perhaps, even, between
good and bad and indifferent. It is also that the mind must learn,
and can learn only by difference and variety. One wants to feel
free to go about the world and encounter all kinds of things; one
wants the Chinese to be Chinese. To think of the world in its
almost holy complication of human experience changed over
into one homogeneous entity, even the most glittering and
efficient and beautiful, is more depressing than can be said.
It is not that any utopian could scorn the political thinkers

whose utopias issue in uniformity. He must respect the motives of men like Morelly and Babeuf, who, in the name of equality, and on the assumption of scarcity, and out of a belief that, after all, a life of austerity could perhaps be, in the end, man's happiest life, could endorse a uniformitarian society: there is nothing contemptible here: Morelly and Babeuf did not write in the spirit of Dostoyevsky's Shigalov or Grand Inquisitor, whatever may be alleged. But there is no doubt that the utopias of Morelly and Babeuf and others partake of something like a common Spartanism, unwarlike as they are. And modern utopianism is nearly unanimous in its desire to avoid Spartanism: it is neither Stoic nor Puritan: it does not generally find in abundance an obstacle to happiness; and though it is, by and large, equalitarian, it does not assume scarcity: it rather assumes that it is possible to have a variety of equally excellent things. So that everything that leads thinkers like Morelly and Babeuf to devise their social plans is missing from modern utopianism. Uniformity is thus not seen as the inevitable result of *moral* considerations. The question is, Is uniformity the inevitable result of bureaucratic practicalities? Despite the petulance with which the complaint about uniformity is sometimes voiced, and the whimsical attachment to the moldy and the rusty, the crooked and the inefficient, which is sometimes indulged in, and, what is worse, the ethical heedlessness which is often flickeringly present, the question must trouble the soberest utopian.

A utopian apologist could ask, however, whether in modern times uniformity is necessarily implied by the nature of the activities undertaken in this hypothetical period of transition by a single central group. Could it not be said that the bureaucratic tendency to uniformity is at its most threatening if, at the beginning of the period of transition, the area to be reconstructed everywhere presented a similar (and low-level) material condition? For then the planners would probably try to elevate that condition by rapidly applying the same measures throughout the area, and conclude, perhaps, by making it uniform. Or if the area in which utopian society were to be established were small, the utopian planners would find it easier to indulge their temptation to make all things new; and they could conceivably finish by making all things alike, and rationalize their doings by thinking that a real community was simply a great family or fraternity and that it was therefore natural to have all things alike. But if, instead, the area to be reconstructed were the world and hence no community in any genuine sense, and if, instead, at the beginning, the world presented—as surely it must —the sharpest differences in both levels and kinds of well-being from country to country and region to region, there would be no reason to suppose that what was good would be destroyed while the bad was being corrected. That would only profoundly complicate the work to be done. The aim would be, of course, universal welfare; to put all the world, as it were, on the same footing. That aim, though, would not require—indeed, it would be hurt by—undoing the work of the centuries. No modern utopian begins with the belief that whatever is, is wrong, and that whatever would continue to exist in utopia would have to be looked on as a useless vestige or as an anomaly, or as an ineradicable shortcoming. Even in Marxist-Leninist theory much of the old survives in the new to the *advantage* of the new. If it is granted that there is a planner's tendency in the direction of uniformity, the vast world is there in its viscosity to offer a salutary resistance to that tendency. There are dangers; but there is no warrant for claiming that, in modern times in a world society, in a period of technological potency, the period of transition is doomed to eventuate in a uniform world doomed to remain forever uniform.

ix

We have tried to say that the strictly moral antiutopian arguments concerning the means needed to attain utopia are sympathetic but not peculiarly burdensome to the utopian apologist, and are also counter to the general moral foundation—such as it is—of all political endeavor. In addition, we have tried to say that the common-sense view of the use of violence, though remorselessly pedestrian, is really what any utopian apologist would probably find it impossible to counter: as usual, common sense must have its way: success for utopian exertion could never be guaranteed. We now wish to add (or reiterate) however, that, when all is said and done, the most impressive argument against utopianism, on the ground of what is needed to establish a utopian society, is the real world as it is. When Laski's comment, "The Marxian [*sc.* Leninist] view of a secretly armed minority assuming power at a single stroke is unthinkable in the modern state,"[60] is remembered, and when it is also remembered that a utopian would want a simultaneous coming to power of the utopian party all over the world, the utopian dream is lost.

If the utopian apologists were willing to dare common sense, and still feel that, in the abstract, exertion need not unalterably defile his ideals, he would, at the last, be brought up short by the realization that the configuration of circumstances needed to make thought of any exertion plausible has next to no chance of occurring. But, more than that, the conditions under which the transition from preutopia to utopia could be accomplished at the smallest short-term cost to utopian ends are out of the range of possibility altogether.

---

60. Harold J. Laski, *Karl Marx* (London: Allen and Unwin, 1921), pp. 39-40.

3

Maintaining Utopia

i

If there are some for whom the sequence beginning in conspiracy and ending in the attempt to change the world into utopia would be full of insuperable difficulties of a moral and practical kind, there are others for whom the enterprise of keeping utopian ends in being would be full of difficulties of the same kind. If, for the sake of argument, it were granted that utopian ends could somehow survive this sequence and be inaugurated, the most serious questions could still be asked in regard to the measures taken to preserve those ends. The means-end problem is thus moved into utopia itself. There is a whole family of arguments that have been made or could be made to show that the utopian vision must be abandoned either because the vision simply cannot be embodied for any length of time, or because the vision cannot be embodied without a frightful cost. And the arguments center on the nature and duties of rule in utopian society.

ii

Traditionally, utopian order has been conceived as the result of continuous control exercised by a class of rulers peculiarly fitted to rule; or as the result of direct democracy in a community of equal citizens; or as the spontaneous or easily coordinated result of regular, routine, and harmonious operations carried out by a basically equal and undifferentiated population habitually doing all things needful for the functioning of a system which stood in no need of governance.[1] In all cases, the details are invariably only sketched in: there is always a good deal of trust on the part of the utopian theorist that the friction in the perfect system is minimal, that there is nothing in human nature or the outside world that stands in the way of sustained perfection, that the system can be made to work. But the important point is that rule is not left to chance workings of heredity or political competition or to the politics of representative government. Rule is either so demanding as to necessitate that it be in the hands of the best; or so elementary—transformed as it is into the merest superintendence—that it lies in the capacity of all to exercise it, such as it is; or is simply rendered otiose. The author of Federalist Paper No. 51 said, "If men were angels, no government would be necessary. If angels were to govern men, neither external nor internal controls on government would be necessary." Utopian theorists have assumed either that a few men were (or could be made) close enough to angels to be entrusted unchecked with the great power required by the perfect social order; or that the great mass of men were (or could be made) close enough to angels, and hence would live in such a way that the coercive tasks of government could lapse: the noncoercive tasks of government would be almost within the competence of children, or would be automatically fulfilled by the smooth operation of the division of labor. Whether the figured utopia has been a city-state, or a nation-state, or the whole world, utopian theorists seem to have thought, pretty much, that these were the sole arrangements in accord with perfection. For example, in Plato's city-state there is aristocracy,

---

1. In *Proposed Roads to Freedom* (London: G. Allen, 1918), Bertrand Russell discusses, from a modern utopian point of view, the comparative merits of state socialism, anarchism, and syndicalism (as well as discussing labor, leisure and art in an ideal society). His discussion, sometimes explicitly, and sometimes by extension, is generally relevant to the concerns of this section.

in Morelly's city-state there is direct democracy; in Saint-Simon's nation-state there is aristocracy, in William Morris's nation-state there is a democratic anarchy; in H. G. Wells's world community there is aristocracy, in the Marxist world community there is a democratic anarchy. Utopia, very roughly, then, is marked by the rule of savants,[2] by the rule of all, or by the absence of any genuine species of rule.

The prevailing assumption among utopian writers is that, in modern times, if utopian ends are to exist fully and unambiguously, and over long periods of time, they will require a world society in which the most advanced techniques of production, administration, communication, and education would be used. The question is what place, if any, rule will have in such a society and what sort of rule it will be.

Now it would be safe to say that when utopia in the past has had the features of a hierarchical society, a society with a wide gap between rulers and ruled, it was because the claims of efficiency were felt as imperative. That is to say, the removal of all the major kinds of social malaise was thought to require the sacrifice of the spirit of equalitarianism; and hopefully, the condition of society produced by the existence of a strict hierarchical arrangement would compensate for the sacrifice. One would want to say that utopian theorists have usually sacrificed equality with regret: its loss was a necessary evil; and they

---

2. In the preachings of Shigalov (in *The Possessed*), and in The Legend of the Grand Inquisitor (in *The Brothers Karamazov*), Dostoyevsky presents a brilliant and shocking parody of utopian elitism. In a few pages, Dostoyevsky expresses the great fears shared by many antiutopian writers: fears aroused by the idea of a painless society cared for by a Jesuitical few. Dostoyevsky's descriptions are as useful as they are unfair: they provide the therapy of caricature. Huxley's *Brave New World* (New York: Harper, 1932) brings the theme up to date; but when we say that Huxley's book does not, in essentials, go beyond Dostoyevsky, we do not mean to denigrate Huxley's achievement. For a saner, though similar, critique of elitism see Alexis de Tocqueville, *Democracy in America*, trans. by Henry Reeve, ed. by Francis Bowen (Cambridge: Sever, 1862), Vol. II, Book IV, Chapter VI. Tocqueville is, of course, concerned with a future democratic society, not with utopia; but his words can easily be extended to apply to utopianism. The moral perils of benevolent authority are beautifully suggested.

sacrificed it not out of a passion for efficiency-for-efficiency's-sake, out of a fiendish taste for engineering, but out of the conviction that for the best to be made out of a hard world, the most had to be made out of the human resources available; hence the rule of the best. It is, after all, to the greatest good of the whole that all of Plato's prescriptions in *The Republic*[3] are avowedly directed. Given an immature technology, hierarchy is an understandable way to achieve harmony. It is, of course, not the only way: the technology of Morelly's utopia, for instance, is every bit as primitive as that of Plato's or Aristotle's utopia, and yet Morelly designed a society with the most regular rotation in rule, while rule was not really rule but only watchfulness. But the price Morelly paid for his democracy was utter uniformity, a flat texture of life, and the abolition of all activities that were not within the capacity of a very undeveloped human nature. (Perhaps Morelly did not even see that he was paying a price: he believed his society was natural, and for him the natural, the simple, and the ascetic were synonymous.) We do not wish to say that every hierarchical utopia was hierarchical merely because of an immature technology; efficiency is not the only reason why the just or the virtuous or the wise should rule: it was not only the intelligence of the just or the virtuous or the wise that, say, Plato and Aristotle wanted to see in full sway. For Plato, under the conditions of any technology, the just should rule, because only the just, disliking to wield power, could be trusted to wield it, and because only the just had knowledge of that which provided the supreme illumination for all action, namely, the Good. For Aristotle, virtue could be displayed in its fullness only in the activities included within rule. But these considerations aside, when we come to study the utopias of old, and are struck by their anthill quality, it would be only fair to keep in mind how utopian theorists struggled with material limitations, with scarcity. (Though it has been said that it would have been better not to think of harmony if the price for it were either Plato's or Morelly's, that they gave up too much to get what they got.)

---

3. Plato, *The Republic*, 420, 519-20.

iii

Surely, however, the pure utopian aspiration is anarchism
when it can be had; though not any more the anarchism of
Eden[4] or Arcadia or Locke's state of nature. The underlying
view is that not merely coercion but authority as well—even
the most benign, rational and democratic authority fails to com-
port with human dignity. The modern utopian dream is of a
community of equals in which each man enforces on himself the
moral law, and no other law is needed, superior intelligence and
ability are not translated into leadership or control, and not
only absence of conflicts of interest, but, beyond that, an
incredibly sophisticated technology, leaves no need even for
managerial regulation, discretion, and adjudication, but permits, instead, a spontaneous harmony. The Lockian (and ancient) presupposition for a moral condition of anarchism was
universal rusticity; the modern presupposition is an inexhaustibly
versatile technology. The aim now would be a society in which,
because the means of production were such as to make abundance
easy, and because the techniques of education were such as to
make all men good men, and because the processes of production were such as to be nearly self-regulating, governance could
be replaced by a kind of superintendence within everyone's
reach, or even disappear altogether. The aim now is to make
men more capacious and at the same time, make the system more
nearly independent of human capacity: human energies are
to be simultaneously enlarged and directed away from politics
and put to other uses. There are those, however, who maintain,
in effect, that such a dream is impossible, and that if any sort
of utopia is to be had, it must be had in the image of Plato's or
Comte's: democratic anarchism, *especially* a modern techno-

---

4. Though we must remember that just as there is hierarchy in heaven,
so, according to St. Thomas Aquinas, there was unequal authority before
the Fall. See Dino Bigongiari, Introduction to *The Political Ideas of St.
Thomas Aquinas* (New York: Hafner, 1953), pp. xii-xiii. Also, there is
unequal authority in the Golden Age as described by Plato in *The Laws,*
IV, 713.

logical version of it, is unthinkable. When Marxists say that the state can eventually wither away, they are foolishly wrong not merely because men in power never cede their power, but also, and primarily, because men in power are always needed. The material and psychological conditions for democratic anarchism are permanently unattainable.

In modern times, Marxism has done the most to press the view that the stateless society was the ultimately desirable social condition and to feed the hope that it will one day be reached. The peculiar power of Marxism on this subject comes from the great trust it lodges in the power of technology to produce a society in which the processes of production (*ipso facto* the processes of governance) do not monopolize, as they do in a syndicalist or guild-socialist society, the time, the cares, the talents, the energies, of those who labor. Marxism claims, in effect, that the price of statelessness need not be everyone's unremitting devotion to economic (hence political) affairs, nor a decentralized and perhaps inhibited machine technology, nor a confining parochialism. The most opulent and centralized technology can coexist with anarchy: for Lenin, the democracy of workers' controls over production and administration gives way to a condition in which organization of almost every sort vanishes: "the more complete [the] democracy, the nearer the moment approaches when it becomes unnecessary."[5] Socialism, which in the ritualist theory of *State and Revolution* bears some resemblance to syndicalism and some to guild socialism, is to be replaced by communism.

For the time when Lenin wrote *State and Revolution* (1917), these phrases could not help having an air of the wildest implausibility; and it would be fair to say that Lenin could write as he did only because he was imprisoned by the Marxist contention that governance was inherently and almost exclusively coercive, (coercive of everyone's wickedness and coercive also of the exploited in behalf of the exploiters), and that when the causes of coercion were removed the causes of governance were simultaneously removed. If Lenin had had a different theory of

---

5. V. I. Lenin, *The State and Revolution*, in *Selected Works* (Moscow: Foreign Languages Publishing House, 1947), Vol. II, p. 210.

politics and the state, he would not have prophesied statelessness; for there was nothing in the means of production, as they then were, even in the most advanced capitalist countries, that could have led a man free of theoretical preconceptions to imagine that anarchism and the fullest technology could coexist.[6] There was nothing in the means of production even to lead a man to imagine that soviets and modern technology could coexist. Thorstein Veblen, in *The Engineers and the Price System* (1921) could make a believable case for technocracy as the method of governance appropriate for a developed technology; syndicalists and guild socialists could make a believable case for direct workers' controls, but their view of technology was static or retrograde. In 1917, technology was both too complex and not yet complex enough to vindicate Lenin's vision of eventual statelessness. The control offered by corporate capitalism or by state socialism could alone suffice. Eduard Bernstein had enough balance to see that (given the level of technology that Bernstein knew) some kind of political apparatus was necessary, even in the classless society of communism.[7] What Lenin did

---

6. Cf. J. L. Talmon, *Political Messianism, The Romantic Phase* (London: Secker and Warburg, 1960), p. 508.

7. See Peter Gay, *The Dilemma of Democratic Socialism* (New York: Columbia University Press, 1952), pp. 243-244, 300-301. Compare the remark of Robert Michels in *Political Parties,* trans. by Eden and Cedar Paul (New York: Dover, 1959), p. 383, (the date is 1915): "It is none the less true that social wealth cannot be satisfactorily administered in any other manner than by the creation of an extensive bureaucracy. In this way we are led by an inevitable logic to the flat denial of the possibility of a state without classes." In a short piece written in 1873, "On Authority" [Karl Marx and Frederick Engels, *Selected Works in Two Volumes* (Moscow: Foreign Languages Publishing House, 1951), Vol. I], Engels attacked the view that all authority could ever disappear, even from the most advanced society. In Engels' opinion, the industrial means of production were such as to require permanently a locus of authority, within each factory, prepared to make decisions of an economic sort. These would be decisions connected with the operation of the individual factory; and no matter how those decisions would be made—by workers' delegates, or by a majority vote—something resembling authority and subordination had to continue. Engels was willing to grant that political authority could vanish: ". . . public functions will lose their political character and be transformed into the simple administrative functions of watching over the

not, could not, foresee was that by the middle of the twentieth century, the beginnings of automation and the development of computing machines, could, for the first time, give some unintentional and *post facto* authenticity to the Marxist vision. So that what began as a scholastic deduction from Marxist principles, unrelated to anything in the real world, could, in truth, years later, and at last, acquire *some* measure of credibility. It is, of course, still too soon to say exactly *what* measure of credibility: there are now only the faintest foreshadowings of the things automation and cybernetics and nuclear energy are capable of.[8] If the utopian apologist is to continue to hold to anarchism as the one condition that is in accord with perfection; if he is to continue to hold that not merely the absence of coercion but the absence of authority, as well, is required for human dignity; if he is to continue to hold that any exercise of political discretion is morally injurious to those over whom it is exercised, it must be to what Norbert Wiener has called "the second industrial revolution" that he must look to find the material support for his aspirations. And if that revolution cannot provide the material support, nothing now imaginable can.

---

true interests of society" (p. 577). This is a considerably more realistic position than that of Lenin, given the state of technology both men were familiar with. But it is not realistic enough; for, given the state of technology both men were familiar with, it was far-fetched to think that all authority could be reduced to decisions concerning the way each factory should be run. Even if all the coercive aspects of authority had become dispensable, there still remained immense decisions of a broadly political sort to be made, which would affect all society.

These decisions demanded an ability beyond that of most workers, and the decisions would have to relate to ends as well as to means. A different kind of authority, political authority, was needed, in addition to the kind Engels said was needed, when technology was as it was then; the kind of authority Engels said was always needed may one day, not too far in the future, not be needed any longer. The question is whether or not political authority will still be needed, no matter how automation and cybernetics and the rest of technology develop.

8. See Norbert Wiener, *The Human Use of Human Beings* (New York: Doubleday Anchor Books, second edition revised 1954), Chap. X; Barrington Moore, *Political Power and Social Theory* (Cambridge, Mass.: Harvard University Press, 1958). Moore's whole volume is of great interest to the student of utopianism.

vi

At this point, it is open to the antiutopian to maintain, quite reasonably, that the dream of vanished authority is hopeless. He could say, first of all, that if the so-called second industrial revolution contains some promise of a kind of self-regulating economic system, that promise is so vague that even the most modest speculation about it, at the present time, must be rejected. To use automation and all the rest as an integral part of current discussion of utopianism—indeed, as an integral part of the defense of utopianism—is, really, not to be any the less unrealistic than Lenin in 1917, and Marx before him. Promises have a way of not being kept; and to bank on technology, even a technology most marvelously projected into the future, to solve the problem of authority is simply to evade that problem—a problem as important as any. But suppose it were granted, though there is no good reason to do so, that technology could develop into something that would seem to accommodate anarchism at some distant date in the future; and suppose it were granted that the coercive duties of government could be rendered unnecessary by a universal and flawless virtue (though it must be remembered that where the regulation of morality is entrusted to the community as a whole without the aid of the police, the most overbearing and oppressive inquisitiveness and conformism can ensue);[9] it must still be said that as usual, utopian theory has left out of account what any species of anarchism always leaves out—the element of change. It may be fine to think of a world in which authority, the rule of some over others, no longer has any reason for being, but such a thought,

---

9. See the very sensible words of George Orwell on this subject in his essay on Swift, "Politics vs. Literature," in *Shooting an Elephant* (New York: Harcourt, Brace, 1950), pp. 65-66. What must be remembered is that when it is hard to be virtuous the reign of virtue will be either a reign of terror or a condition of constant vigilance, "vigilantism." When it is easy to be good, when virtue is nearly effortless, the complexion of this problem changes. Much depends, therefore, on whether or not the promise of scientific psychology to make virtue less difficult can be redeemed. (See below, Chap. 6.)

if it suits anything, suits only a condition of petrifaction. But so so long as change is to be expected, change coming from a variety of sources, there must be something like a government to deal with it. There will be the constant need for the making of decisions; and the decisions, surely, will involve more than the mere substitution of one industrial process for another, in the name of efficiency. That is to say, decisions will continue to have to be made concerning ends or values as well as means or instrumentalities. Any advance in technical proficiency could necessitate a change in the whole social structure; at the least, a change in means could provide the opportunity for a change in ends, whether or not that change was finally decided on. Even in periods of technological stability, there is no reason to think that whim, fancy, taste, belief, opinion would remain fixed, or that human interests and aspirations would remain undisturbed by changes naturally forthcoming in the realms of fashion, art, and social and philosophical speculation. Some mechanism for assimilating and accommodating change is a permanent necessity; therefore, some *quantum* of authority stands forever indispensable. In a vast and populous social system—in utopian theory, the entire globe is taken as the social system—utopian anarchism (or its alternative, direct democracy) can appear only as a daydream or as the most ridiculous archaism; universal rusticity is indeed the only allowable presupposition for the former condition and a small and simple society for the latter. Is it not ironic that even Marxism, so attuned to change and to technology as a source of change, could still prophesy a final and static resting place for humanity where technology —which Marxists, at least as well as anyone else, should know to be inherently restless—will be central?

Such a line of criticism is not any the less powerful for being obvious. There was a time, perhaps, when such criticism would have struck a utopian theorist as missing the real point: he took for granted that his was a scheme calculated to achieve perfection, calculated to include within itself the whole aggregate of values traditionally desired by the mass of men through time. How can a man who thinks he has finally attained an understanding of social perfection and of the institutional arrangements

necessary for it, allow for change, in ends or means? The very
idea of utopianism precludes thought of alteration. It is a fact
that designers of utopias, generally, even of those utopias wherein
authority has a crucial position, have not imagined that it was
incumbent on them to provide their utopias with a mechanism
for accommodating change. If change was reckoned on, it was
—as in the case of Plato and Rousseau—the decay they felt all
human things were subject to. There is no sense of change as a
normal process of growth. The underlying assumption is that if
the best social and economic and cultural institutions have once
been achieved, any change in them would, by definition, be a
change for the worse. Plato's fear of change in styles and
fashions, habits and manners, is the standard utopian attitude;
and this fear extends to the smallest aspects of life: in fact, no
aspect of life is innocent of potential subversion. Utopias possessed not only order, but fixity; and a sympathetic student of
utopias could feel that the dread of disorder informing them was
sometimes allowed to influence too much. Human appetites were
taken as immutable; human knowledge was taken as completed;
human techniques and artifacts were taken as stable. Censorship
is a notorious feature of many utopias; and the rationale for
the censorship is always the view that the arts are mere orna-
ment or, at best, devices for indoctrination, while philosophy,
left to itself, is just an unending sequence of errors. So delicate
was the equilibrium of imaginary utopian societies, that there
was very little that did not seem ready to upset it. It is easy, of
course, to condemn the entire tradition of utopianism for the
fact that it appeared so unremorseful about what it was prepared
to give up in the name of a continuous social harmony. It is not
always clear, however, what (aside from the great matter of
censorship) there was in the various utopias, given the world
as it was, that needed apology. It must be an open question,
even for defenders of the open society, whether almost any
utopia was not, by and large, preferable to the real conditions
that called forth the utopian response.[10] But in *modern* times

10. For a critical, yet genuinely sympathetic, discussion of "the closed
society," see Bertrand de Jouvenel, *Sovereignty,* trans. by J. F. Huntington (Chicago: University of Chicago Press, 1957), Chap. 8.

(let the insistence on modernity be taken as vulgar), utopianism does, after all, have to ponder the question of change, as H. G. Wells rightly remarked in his *A Modern Utopia*. (But Wells's utopia itself, though accompanied by the celebration of change, really has little institutional allowance for it.) The emphasis is on the word "modern" mainly because of the nature of the technology we now have: for all the cant about the horrors of "progress," a failure to see that the advances in the biological and physical and psychological sciences carry with them implications for human betterment as well as the threat that they will be put to evil uses can be nothing but mischievous. Change, at least to a certain extent, must be allowed for, not because change is in itself good, but because change can, after all, in modern times, be for the better. And to allow for change forcibly opens up, once more, the problem of how it is to be institutionally assimilated, the problem of how decisions of value are to be made and implemented.

Yet we cannot rule out the possibility that some could feel that the Marxist vision of statelessness could be salvaged by the traditional utopian device of calling a halt to developments in certain kinds of research and technology. It could be maintained that so desirable was a society in which the need for authority had fallen away, that it would be worth the sacrifice in technical advance. Whenever, in the past, utopian theorists have made that choice, they have condemned the intended residents of their societies to "universal asceticism and social leveling in its crudest form" (as Marx said of Babeuf's schemes). It is conceivable that sometime in the near future, however, technology could reach such a stage, that to prevent it from going further would not condemn the world to asceticism and leveling, but, on the contrary, guarantee the world a life of material abundance. If, at the same time, automation fulfilled its present promise, the hope for a nearly self-regulating economic system would thus have some chance; and with it, the possibility of a society without government. Marx was peculiarly anxious to avoid any utopian speculation that did not wait on the course of history to bring forth into the world all that history held within itself: he feared that the result of such speculation would be to produce an abortive society. He did not see that, in modern times, all utopian speculation that concludes in the vision of a stateless society must, in some sense, be abortive, that the cost of democratic anarchy is, among other things, technological stability. The only difference that modern technology makes—and it is a huge difference—is that a stabilized technology need not mean asceticism and leveling. It may, of course, mean that the most amazing discoveries and applications are foreclosed; but a life of virtuous scarcity is not entailed. A modern utopia could thus be in some respects what past utopians have been in most respects: static, but, though a modern utopia would have technological fixity in common with most of the utopias that exist in the history of political thought, it would differ from them in that its fixed technology would be compatible with abundance, variety, and periodic novelty, with a life of sensual fullness and of energy and motion.

v

In the abstract, then, and with all technical details left aside, it is possible to imagine that it would be open for people, one day, to decide whether arresting technological development, though at a high level, was an acceptable price to pay for securing other values; primarily, the value of a life without politics. The dangers of such a decision are immense: the dangers of truncation are always immense. It is unnerving to think of holding utopia fast in the prison of a predetermined range of possibilities, no matter how large that range is. To some degree, features of all utopian designs are inspired by the desire to make life the opposite of what it is at the time the utopian design is put forward, to correct the errors of the real world, and fulfill the longings of the oppressed and the deprived. The evil of the world thus conditions or sets limits to the workings of the utopian imagination; it forces on the imagination certain anxieties and concerns to which utopian generations no longer would respond. As a result, procedures and institutions the preutopian mind thought permanently indispensable could become, once established, outmoded and constricting. Besides, a utopian society, after a while, would have potentialities of which one never conceived. To concede that this could happen, and to take seriously, from the start, the problem of change in utopia, constitutes, in part, the morality of utopian speculation in modern times. (Notice that we here assume the *permanent* commitment of a utopian society to certain basic values: peace, abundance, equality, conditioned virtue, and so on. What we are allowing, in theory, is change in means (techniques, practices, customs) and in lesser ends (tastes, fashions, pleasures, manners). Presumably, the *net effect* of social life in a utopian society would be in constant conformity with the long tradition of utopianism.) But it would seem to be clear that something will have to be given up for something else; that, even in (any presently conceivable) utopia, all good things cannot be concurrently had. And the question always is, "Is the net result a large enough gain?"

vi

An antiutopian could assert, in spite of all we have so far said, that even on the assumption of technological fixity, those technical "details" we have so easily left aside would be so complex, the problems of production, distribution, and shifting patterns of consumption would be so intricate, that the notion of a (nearly) self-regulating economy still defies any sense of reality. This assertion could very well be true; but it is not necessarily true, and only time will tell whether it is true or not; there cannot now be any very intelligent debate on the subject, there can only be hopes voiced and hopes derided. A utopian apologist, however, could assert, in return, that the problems of production, distribution, and shifting consumption are problems that could be left to technicians without the feeling that what was being left to them were decisions of value, acts of discretion and authority. In a more elaborate sense, the technicians could be regarded as machine-tenders, discharging one of the numerous functions necessary for the continuous existence of utopian society; and their functions, though demanding a special knowledge, would carry few if any of the usual attributes of rule. To allow for a corps of technicians to "keep the economic machine going," to follow to the letter the mandate given them by utopian society, is not, in theory, to depart from anarchism.

An antiutopian could go on to assert that the decision to rest content with a stable technology exacted a cost not only in technical improvements and material progress, but also in something at least as important; some would say, in something much more important. That cost would be in the advance of knowledge. It is not easy to imagine that contributions to the store of human knowledge would continue to be made if all hope of seeing those contributions applied in the life of society were extinct. It could be said that the nobility of our race consisted in knowing ever more, and any society that had a vested interest in ignorance was intolerable; any society that did not feel an overriding obligation to truth was corrupt. Add to that the fact that contributions to the store of human experience are made whenever an increase in knowledge forces on men the need to respond and adapt, and thus change the way they live and the way in which they conceive of life. What is at stake here is not the responses and adaptations that strife, poverty, and insecurity elicit, valuable though they are: in talking to a utopian apologist, the antiutopian could leave those aside, and still make his case, make it, even, more forcefully. To believe that the record of human life could be enriched without suffering; to hold it possible, that is, to accommodate rationally a developing technology of infinite promise, and thus permit the human race to display itself variously through time in a changing social system (which could remain just through all its changes); to hold this possible, and disallow it in the name of anarchism, is to cheat humanity of something inestimably valuable. In the opinion of this writer, there is no satisfactory answer that a defender of utopian anarchism could give to this criticism.

vii

Suppose, then, that it were decided that, on balance, technological stability was too extravagant a price to pay for democratic anarchism, and suppose, also, that it were conceded (as it obviously must be conceded) that technological change could not take place amidst a condition in which choices and decisions emerged spontaneously and unmediatedly from the mass of people the world over and were then enforced. It would follow that the necessity for some kind of politics has been granted, that one of the great utopian ideas, anarchism, would have to give way, and government reluctantly accepted as a necessary evil, as the lesser evil. The question then becomes, What sort of government can a modern utopian suggest as consonant with his idealism? A definite answer to these questions clearly cannot be made without reference to the general form society would have in utopia, to the utopian way of life and the institutions meant to house that way of life. The aim of this essay, however, is not to examine the details of any utopian society to be found in the literature of utopianism, nor to contrive a utopia for the occasion. This may sound evasive, but we cannot range so far afield and still serve our purpose. The aim rather is to deal, in so far as it is possible, with utopian ends abstracted from particular institutional embodiments, on the assumption that any utopian end can be served by several different practices or routines or patterns of activity. We shall deal with the question of government, therefore, only in the most general way.

The ends we have all along taken as utopian are peace, abundance, leisure, equality, untroubled virtue. We have seen, so far, that one aspect of equality is not reconcilable with unhindered technological advance: the possibility of economic change makes some kind of political apparatus necessary and hence rules out anarchism. If, then, change is to be allowed, though it means the death of anarchism, what political arrangement would best promote a full and harmonious life for all men? Can it be some form of direct democracy? Or must it be representative government? Or, worse still, must a modern utopian, in a common utopian manner, endorse some kind of aristocracy?

It would be strange to champion aristocracy in a modern utopia which presupposed a high level of universal education, and a high level of virtue among the mass of men, and which, at the same time, presupposed that many of the traditional tasks of politics—such as resolution of domestic conflicts, preservation of inequalities, the management of foreign policy, and the waging of war—had disappeared. It could nevertheless be done, if the defenders of aristocracy could somehow show that both the exercise of rule *and* an evaluation of its workings required a special kind of knowledge or a special kind of virtue, or both, within the reach of only a few men. The only claim on which a few could base their pretension to rule in utopia is superior wisdom of one kind or another. Claims of greater wealth, strength or courage, or of better birth or appearance, or of larger interest, would be out of place. Necessary to the aristocratic position is the demonstration that *even* the evaluation of the workings of rule is beyond the competence of most men, beyond the competence, in effect, of the men over whom rule is being exercised. A democrat can concede (and still remain a democrat) that rule may demand an intelligence, or capaciousness, or dispassionateness, or experience, or knowledge, that is greater than the average. But then the democrat must go on to say that, for all that, the ordinary citizen is worthy enough to choose between rival aspirants to power and to understand the bases on which the aspirants establish their claim to rule. And the democrat must add that the wishes, or desires, or values of the ordinary citizen possess a dignity equal to that of the wishes, desires, or values of his elected rulers; indeed, the assumption is that there will be a rough agreement between rulers and ruled on the underlying moral principles of their common society. The defender of aristocracy is interested in maintaining the reverse of these assertions; and the classic exposition of the aristocratic position is, of course, Plato's. In rough outline, Plato's contention is that rule requires a certain kind of wisdom, which only a few men can have. Therefore, the workings of rule cannot even be so much as examined and judged by the great mass of men. The great mass of men, however, need not worry that power will be abused by the wise, or that any interest but the common interest will be pursued by the wise, for the wise would rather not rule; and, also, to be wise, one must first be temperate, that is, one must have learned how to govern one's appetites and inborn fierceness. In the case of the wise, then, their virtue is the check on their power; and their power, because they are wise, must be absolute. The greatest general good can ensue only if the wise rule, and rule absolutely.

Now, the great perplexity about Plato's position is that the wisdom of which he speaks as indispensable to rule is not merely statecraft or political science; it is not merely a compound of high intelligence, common sense, worldly experience, a knowledge of history and human nature, and a flexible acceptance of the ordinary morality informing the society in which the political man operates; it is not merely the mental equipment which, say, Machiavelli, Bacon, Montesquieu, and Burke, in their roughly similar ways, wish political men to have. It includes something else: an apprehension of something literally metaphysical, which apprehension enables the philosopher to see the things of the world better than those who can see *only* the things of the world.[11] For seeing the light, the philosopher, the man of wisdom, can see in darkness better than those who have no light but darkness. The only man capable of dealing with the things of this world, which are imperfect, is the man who knows that these things are imperfect and also knows what perfection is. The only man capable of dealing with the things of this world, which are mortal and protean, is the man who knows that these things are mortal and protean and also knows that which is eternal and fixed in its qualities. The only uncorrupt involvement with the things of this world is that of the man whose knowledge of the Good allows him to look at that which is not the Good from a distance, with detachment, and with something better in his head. The point Plato wishes to make is that, given (what Plato takes to be) the best natural endowment, together with (what Plato takes to be) the best

---

11. Plato, *The Republic*, 520.

course of instruction, all men so endowed and so instructed (and they could be only a few) could not help coming to the same view as to what Goodness was, and hence as to what would be good in all earthly matters. The philosopher will *know* Goodness itself, and therefore know what to do in all realms of life, including the political. Knowledge of Goodness is higher than justice and the moral virtues, and ideally commands them and all other things. The difficulty at the heart of Plato's position is to understand what could possibly be meant by "knowing" Goodness or the Good.

It may be true that all people with the natural endowment described by Plato, and instructed in the way Plato recommends, will come to a uniform conception of perfection, and uniform ideas on how political life is to be organized. What Plato apparently omits from consideration, however, is that to attain to such a conception of perfection is not to attain to more knowledge or to a higher degree of knowledge, but to decide to accept a certain standard of value. Calling something "good" is not simply a matter of seeing; it is a matter of seeing *and* judging—let the seeing be literal or metaphorical. In the case of a knife or of a road the judgment is automatic: there are rules governing the application of the word "good" to these things: there are conventional assessments of knives and roads.[12] Certain facts about, say, a knife entail the judgment that it is a good knife. But in the case of goodness itself, what rules could possibly apply? What rules could possibly govern the application of the word "good" to a view or vision of the world. Judgment cannot be automatic here: this is, above all others, the realm of dispute and uncertainty. Hence, the most Plato can claim is that a man of a certain natural endowment refined by a certain course of instruction will come to *prefer* a certain general standard, or, more grandly, a certain view or vision of the world which arranges all the things of the world in a graded order. It may very well be that the general standard or grand view accepted, chosen, preferred, by Plato's philosopher can, if acted on, produce a society in which the

---

12. See Philippa Foot, "Goodness and Choice," *The Aristotelian Society, Supplementary Volume XXXV* (London, 1961), pp. 45-60.

greatest possible amount of social happiness is realized. But the fact remains that what is involved *is* a standard or a view; and, as such, must be liable to articulation, open to acceptance or rejection, capable of being recognized when it is or is not in force. Plato wishes to avoid having it appear that knowledge of the Good is finally *choice* of a standard or acceptance of a view, the preference of one group of men as against the preference of some other group of men; Plato wishes to avoid having to say that one set of values is better than another. And to avoid this appearance, Plato tries to suggest that what the philosopher does is not learn and then choose, but only learn something that very few others could learn. To make a judgment concerning a whole pattern of relations, some amount of knowledge is always necessary; but no amount of knowledge, by itself, ever entails such a judgment; no matter how well grounded in knowledge, a judgment of this sort remains a judgment. Surely, ethical philosophy since the time of G. E. Moore's writing on "the naturalistic fallacy" has unassailably established this point. It is a matter of the most intense interest why a man holds the opinions he does, on ethical and esthetic matters; and the fuller and more reasoned the support for an opinion, the more persuasive a listener should find it. Plato, however, locates the source for his political preferences in some remote sphere, access to which is by means of a course of study that seems as divorced from political life as any could be; and, at the same time, tries to disguise the fact that what he has done is to state a preference (specifically, a preference for the political system of *The Republic*, which is supposed to be in accord with the Good). Any defense of a system of government in which power was held unchecked and unscrutinized by the citizenry must have the general form of Plato's defense; and if Plato's defense fails, all others like it must also fail. We should want to say, then, that though some men would make better men of state than others, the reason that they would could not be of a metaphysical sort. If wisdom is to be a desirable characteristic of a man of state, that wisdom must be practical wisdom, the wisdom endorsed by Machiavelli, Bacon, and others.

viii

The importance of trying to show the deficiencies of the classic aristocratic theory is, naturally, to clear the way for some kind of democratic system of government in utopian society. For, though some of the reasons for supporting democracy outside utopia would be irrelevant in utopia, other reasons are valid both inside and outside utopia, reasons of a moral and practical sort.

To take up the possibility of direct democracy, it would be well to notice why, from the utopian point of view, the politics of direct democracy is less desirable than anarchism, the absence of all politics. (Recall Lenin's ranking of anarchism over democracy in the fifth chapter of *State and Revolution.*) The plain fact is that the existence of any political system is a sure indication of the existence, in turn, of division of opinion. And where there is division of opinion, there must inevitably be generated discontent, even if the finest civility and spirit of tolerance are present. It is hard to find room for discontent in utopia, in the abstract.

Now, there are two kinds of direct democracy which can be suggested. The first kind is Aristotelian, and looks to rotation in rule. The second kind is Rousseauist, and looks to the direct participation of every man in the making of laws, while leaving to a permanent executive power the enforcement and implementation of laws.

The Aristotelian kind presupposes, among other things, first, that the political community is small enough to allow every adult, after he has reached a certain age, to claim his right to become a statesman or ruler for a time, sharing authority with others; and second, that the exercise of authority, the performance of the tasks of statesmanship, is an indispensable part of the range of activities included within virtuous behavior. A world utopian society makes satisfaction of the first presupposition impossible. More important, the nature of utopian politics makes satisfaction of the second presupposition impossible: the conflicts and tensions, the balancings and weighings, which bring the qualities of statesmanship into play are missing from utopian political life. Thus, a practical consideration forces us to rule out the Aristotelian kind of direct democracy; and a moral consideration permits us not to lament the necessity of ruling it out.

When we come to Rousseau's theory of direct democracy, we are closer to home. Let us recapitulate the relevant portions of this theory.

1. To be a person, one must be a moral agent, a creature of rights and duties, of expectations and obligations, a being who deals with other beings in regular ways and according to certain rational principles. Persons—as distinct from presocial men in a state of nature dominated by impulses and appetites—enter into moral relations with one another.

2. A significant part of the web of moral relations which exist between persons is made up of political relations. Included therefore within the very idea of person is the role of citizenship. The fortunes of people are tied up with each other in such a way that political decisions greatly affect the tenor of even everyday life. Politics permeates much of social life.

3. Political decisions seek primarily to preserve, specifically to preserve the civil rights of everyone in society. These rights are life, liberty, and property. The preservation of these rights— the supreme benefits of society—sometimes may require sacrifices; for example, in the form of the payment of taxes or the discharge of military duty. The premises are that each man has a stake in the continued existence of society—that is, that he is such as to treasure his life and his liberties, and that he has some property he wants protected; that he is willing to respect the rights of others, as others respect his; and that he is also willing to make the sacrifices needed to preserve his rights and the rights of others. Political decisions therefore must be just or fair, as the case may be. Furthermore, the concept of the common good is meaningful. The common good is justice, the protection of each man in his own, the preservation of the *status quo*. The fact that most men are farmers, that every farmer owns land, and that there are no great differences in the sizes of holdings discourages the formation of conflicts of interests or of conflicting notions of the public interest, the common good.

4. Political decisions are expressed in laws. Laws should be just or fair, as the case may be; and laws should be obeyed.

5. To be politically moral, it is not enough to obey laws. To be a moral agent, one must take part in the deliberations which conclude in the making of laws. Laws are an expression of will; and to live by laws in the making of which one has had no part is tantamount to living according to the dictates of the will of another; hence to live very much like a slave. One cannot live very much like a slave and still be a moral agent; consequently, one cannot live very much like a slave and still be a person. Autonomy is indispensible to morality.

6. A simple economic system, and a fairly uniform mode of life among the citizens result in the infrequent need for new laws. Lawmaking is not a full-time or complex occupation.

7. The principles of justice and fairness are easily translated into statute law: refinement of understanding or of political perception is not required. And because society will be economically simple and economically static, and because training in virtue will be a prominent feature of society, there will be few obstacles to the desire of each man to be just and fair. Where principles are easily understood and easily applied to concrete cases, and where there is a will to understand correctly and to apply correctly, there should be a tendency to unanimity or near-unanimity in the political decisions embodied in law.

8. There must be a strong executive power to enforce and implement the laws, but not in any way to determine what the laws should be.

We must remember that these ideas are associated, in Rousseau's theory, with the institution of private property (primarily agrarian), with the sovereign community coexisting with other sovereign communities, with the city-state, with a preindustrial technology, with a comparatively low level of civilization, and with the assertion of human rationality over human individuality. When we therefore come to relate Rousseau's principles of direct democracy to modern utopianism, certain questions must be asked, and certain comments made.

1. In a modern utopian society, would the concepts of rights and duties still have a place? It seems odd to say that in a society

in which there was perpetual peace, guaranteed abundance, and little difficulty in being virtuous, citizens would have duties to perform and rights to claim. Conflicting desires, unfulfilled aspirations, national troubles and emergencies, and suspicion of power are all presuppositions of the language of rights and duties. Nevertheless, the fact that social change could be an aspect of life in a modern utopia means that some measure of dissatisfaction has to be taken into account. To allow for social change is to allow for the emergence of *policy;* in any given instance, decisions would have to be made on whether or not change was to be introduced, and if it was, how much of it, how fast, at the sacrifice of what, how widespread, and so on. The emergence of policy entails disagreement over policy; and disagreement over policy must bring with it dissatisfaction on the part of those in the minority. It follows that though the concepts of rights and duties may have no place in a modern utopian society, the concepts of accommodation, of deference to majority opinion, of solicitude for minority opinion, of general political civility would have a place.

2. In a modern utopian society, would it still be true that a significant part of moral relations would be political relations? Would there be need for continuous functioning of the political order? On the assumption that the coercive tasks of government would be next to none at all, and that the economy was nearly self-regulating, do the processes of government remain central to social life? The chances are that if the introduction and assimilation of innovation became the major task of the political system, the political system would shrink. And having shrunk, it would no longer be the object of weighty moral consideration which it has always been. This does not mean that it would cease being the object of moral consideration altogether.

3. As we remarked above, the language of rights and duties would seem inappropriate in a modern utopian society. The assertion of claims by people on one another, and the expectation that each has that the others will help bear the cost of keeping the system in being, do not seem to square with the traditional understanding of utopian life. The idea of utopia excludes fears that one's rights may be encroached on or that others may default

on their obligation to protect the rights of all against the outside. But it is obvious that the aim of political decisions would remain preservation. What is to be preserved is the cluster of utopian ends, and they must be preserved throughout time, whatever sorts of change are introduced into utopian society. Conceivably, then, one kind of opposition to a given innovation in utopia would come from those who thought that it betrayed the fundamental principles of utopian life, to leave aside whether or not there was opposition simply because some disliked the proposed innovation.

4. Would it not be better to say that political decisions in utopia would be expressed not only in laws, but also in administrative pronouncements?

5. Though a *just* law is not an expression of will, but a conclusion arrived at with the aid of reason and with reference to the principles of justice, personal assent to a just law (which is understood to be just) is a precondition of moral autonomy.

6. Once the fixity of the economic system is no longer taken for granted, the view that there would be infrequent need for new laws and regulations becomes untenable. But one would not expect nearly the same abundance of legislation in utopia as in any modern nation-state.

7. Is it not arguable that the task of abiding by fundamental utopian principles in the laws and regulations introducing novel institutions, procedures, and practices would not be as narrow a matter as translating the terms of the social contract into statute law? As we have said, utopian ends can be served by differing means. The range of possibility is great, though not, of course, limitless. There can be no presumption that all right-minded men should have the same opinion of a given proposal: both sides can disagree over the desirability of the proposal, and still agree that it conforms to fundamental utopian principles. On the other hand, it may be that fundamental utopian principles share with fundamental law, most generally, the quality of being inherently unamenable to automatic application. This consideration would extend even to the principles embodied in the social contract, as Rousseau describes them. Guiding principles must always be expressed in general language. General

language is always open to competing interpretations. Guiding principles are formulated at a specific point in time. Things happen in the future which were not envisaged by the original propounders of those principles. Competing views of equal plausibility on whether plans for change remain faithful to fundamental principles rightly emerge. It is true that on one subject utopianism shares an assumption with Rousseau; namely, that there will be a common desire to understand correctly and apply correctly the fundamental principles of utopianism. But the equal honesty, if not equal correctness, of opposing interpretations and applications of these principles must be granted.[13]

8. Is it not unrealistic to think that the executive power can remain innocent of involvement in lawmaking; or that the mere enforcement of laws can be free of decisive interpretation of laws?

When the articles of Rousseau's defense of direct democracy are restated for the purposes of modern utopianism they take, then, the following form:

1. To be a person, one must be a moral agent, entering into moral relations with others. These relations are governed by certain rules and regulations.

2. A part of the web of moral relations is made up of political relations. That part, while not possessed of the significance it has outside utopia, nevertheless possesses enough significance to warrant consideration of it. Political behavior, that is, still comprises a noticeable segment of the totality of moral relations.

3. The major burden political decisions must bear is conforming to the fundamental principles of utopianism.

4. Political decisions are embodied in laws and administrative regulations.

5. The moral idea of autonomy or self-determination is intrinsic to modern utopianism; and its political form is the ability of every citizen to take part in the making of the laws and regulations by which he must live.

---

13. For a review of the arguments against the belief that mandate can be automatically applied, see Glendon Schubert, *The Public Interest* (Glencoe, Ill.: The Free Press, 1960), Chap. 2.

6. The making of laws and regulations, while not an all-consuming activity, may still be a fairly frequent matter.

7. Dissatisfaction with new laws and regulations can legitimately be expected; as can be disagreement over the conformity of these new laws and regulations to fundamental utopian principles.

8. The sharp distinction between will and power, between lawmaking and law-enforcing, between legislative and executive is impossible to sustain. If there is to be an executive in continuous existence, and made up of a permanent body of small officials (even though elective), infringements on the principle of autonomy are certain.

We should wish to say that if allowance for change in utopian society is enough, by itself, to place anarchism out of reach, a political system which incorporated the principles of direct democracy, as we have revised them, would be the next best thing. It would be the political system which did the least damage to utopian idealism in its modern form. Much more than the Aristotelian version of direct democracy, the Rousseauist version speaks to modern idealism. That is why we have taken up at some length Rousseau's notions, and tried (tentatively) to extend them to a hypothetical modern utopian society. But we must conclude that, even in their revised form, the principles of direct democracy are unsuitable for any but a small sovereign community. Such a conclusion is, of course, obvious. Obvious or not, it is, however, a conclusion to be regretted. Not all the realism in the world can make it easier to forgive the world its inability to accommodate Rousseau's principles. For his principles are those which most forcibly demonstrate the connection between politics and the moral life, which most clearly associate autonomous manhood and political activity. When we have understood Rousseau's principles, it is not too much to say, we have understood the distinction between a fully acceptable political order and one that is not. And just as Rousseau (in his book on Poland) had finally to come to terms with the real world, and accept representative government, so a modern utopian, after he has abandoned both anarchism and direct democracy, must come to accept representative government. Again, just as

Rousseau advocated frequent elections to the lawmaking body, and defined the task of the representative as faithfully obeying the mandate of his constituency, so a modern utopian must think of advocating these practices.

To think of representative legislatures and elected executives and a party system as features of a utopian society is to depart from all modern utopianism.[14] In fact, writers like Wells and Bellamy specifically denounce these institutions as outmoded or as inadequate to the great task of maintaining utopia in being. (Wells in *A Modern Utopia* resorts to an aristocracy [the Samurai]; Bellamy has politics turn into administration, and the administration entrusted as a reward to those who excel in their various employments.) Underlying the general utopian aversion to modern democratic government is the view that that kind of government is fit, if it is fit for anything, only for a society in which there are conflicts of economic interest, and in which that conflict must be mediated, and no single interest or group of interests allowed to tyrannize over the rest of society. If there are no interests in utopia, if there is no conflict to be mediated, and if some kind of politics is still needed, why should a utopian endorse representative government? Apart from the fact that representative government satisfied the requirement of political self-determination more nearly than any system except direct democracy, there are other reasons to endorse it.

Very simply, it could be said that the great traditional defenses of representative government have been:

1. Society inevitably contains a competition of material interests, and since every man knows his own interest best and knows what is needed to protect it, and since every interest has an equal claim at least to be heard, every man should have a voice in the deliberations that resolve that competition.

2. The great mass of men can be trusted to have at least a rough understanding of the public interest, and therefore their

---

14. But Karl Mannheim said, "Whatever criticism may be leveled against representative government its outstanding virtues are bound to make it the point of departure for any social organization safeguarding freedom." [*Freedom, Power and Democratic Planning* (New York: Oxford University Press, 1950), p. 149.]

views concerning the public interest deserve to be heard and heeded.

3. Power tends to corrupt,[15] and unless those who hold power are made to stand for election and feel their tenure to be precarious, and unless they must face competition for public office, their inclination to ignore or sacrifice the interests of society and pursue their own interests instead is strengthened greatly.

4. An open political system allows for the comparatively easy formation of temporary majorities on various issues. No majority is permitted to be permanent; no majority policy is allowed to become frozen. Channels are left clear for undoing any arrangement. The political system responds sensitively to the changing aspirations of masses of people.

5. Since government is to be the source of some of the blessings of life in civil society, the only way to avoid the enervation of paternalism is to have the recipients of those blessings able to look on government as their agent or servant, and have the members of government in both its legislative and executive branches hold their positions on the sufferance of the citizenry. Add to these arguments the fact that democratic systems of

---

15. When we say (with Lord Acton) that "power tends to corrupt" we can mean among other things:

1—Making decisions with the constant expectation of having those decisions carried out—having one's way—discretion—tends to corrupt;

2—Being set above men in dignity—being set apart from men in prestige —eminence—tends to corrupt;

3—Having at one's disposal strength of any sort, with the expectation of successfully using that strength, tends to corrupt.

By "tends to corrupt" we can mean: tends to result in arrogance, insensibility, a loss of the sense of the purpose for which discretion, eminence, or strength exists, as well as in the more blatant vices of selfishness or cruelty. Precariousness of tenure and limited scope to one's authority help to mitigate the ravages of discretion and eminence. These procedures help to keep good men good; nothing more. Naturally, no procedure, by itself, affects strength: only inner virtue or outer counterforce does that. For the corrupting effects of discretion and eminence, see Lord Acton's letter to Mandell Creighton, dated April 5, 1887, in John Emerich Dalberg Acton, *Essays on Freedom and Power*, ed. by Gertrude Himmelfarb (New York: Meridian Books, 1955), pp. 335-336; and the splendid writing of Henry Adams in *The Education of Henry Adams* (New York: The Modern Library, 1931), pp. 147-148, 365. For the corrupting effects of strength, see the great essay by Simone Weil, "L'Iliade ou le poème de la force," (1940) in *La source grecque* (Paris: Gallimard, 1953), pp. 11–42.

government are more likely to contain the following features: open recruitment of rulers, regular transmission of power, need for only a normally human moral virtue on the part of rulers, and minimal distinctions in dignity and way of life between rulers and ruled.

In the history of political theory, the foregoing arguments and considerations have been present in various combinations and with various patterns of emphasis. The Levellers, Locke, Bentham, Madison and Hamilton, James Mill, and John Stuart Mill have each defended representative government with a different cluster of arguments taken from those listed above, and have arranged the arguments of their cluster in a different scale of importance.

It could be said that the values to which democratic government is dedicated in the abstract are included within the values meant to be served by utopian society. In essence, democratic government is dedicated to a condition approaching self-determination, and also dedicated to the avoidance of tyranny, political mystique, and the passive acceptance by the citizenry of favors bestowed on it at the pleasure of political men set above it. And if utopia is to have government, its government must, at the least, achieve what democratic government is, in theory, supposed to achieve, and avoid what democratic government is, in theory, supposed to avoid. Modern utopian idealism could not otherwise be fulfilled. It would be odd to think that a modern society was utopian if its government were separated by a wide gulf from its citizenry; surrounded by an aura of divinity; accorded servile gratitude by a citizenry accustomed to regard it as the sole source of happiness in society and hence as something to be feared and propitiated; and if its government were not hedged round by procedures aimed at minimizing the unalterable inclination of all rulers to abuse the power they hold. While it is taken for granted that the theory of democratic government was formulated with a society in mind that was different from what utopian society is intended to be, the fundamental impulses of that theory are in accord with utopianism. If, then, utopia is to have change (strange as that must sound), and if government is necessary for change, utopian government must have, at least, the differentiating characteristics of modern democratic government. Though utopian society is not presumed to have conflicts of material interests, it still must have—given the allowance for change—conflicts of value or opinion, even though those conflicts take place amidst the most marvelous civility and mutual tolerance. And once conflicts of value have been substituted for conflicts of material interest, the various defenses of democratic government we have listed above continue to hold good for utopian society.

In the utopian case, the premise is that utopian citizens all understand the fundamental principles of utopian society and want them to continue to be adhered to, whatever specific policy they may favor. The normal utopian dispute would be over which of two or more policies, all of them correctly *believed* by their respective supporters to be faithful to the fundamental principles of utopian society, is more desirable, from the point of view of taste, tradition, feelings, and so on.[16] (The operation of the majority principle in each constituency must also be taken for granted.)

It is not that democracy is intrinsically valuable, or that the game of politics is worth playing for its own sake.[17] There are those who sometimes sound as if they would prefer to invent differences between people in order to give democratic politics some *raison d'être,* rather than to have a society which could dispense with all politics, democratic or otherwise. Such a view is frivolous. Democracy exists to mediate substantive differences (of interest or of opinion) in the fairest of all possible ways, not to give a few people a chance for self-expression. Once change has been judged to be a value more important, in the abstract, than anarchism, all that change entails must be considered: some mechanism for politics becomes necessary. And for an assortment of moral and practical reasons, a mechanism that accom-

---

16. Utopian politics are to be looked at, as Tocqueville looked at American politics: ". . . [one] is at a loss whether to pity a people who take such arrant trifles in good earnest or to envy that happiness which enables a community to discuss them." (*Democracy in America, op. cit.,* Vol. I, Chap. X, p. 226.) The politics of utopia is the politics of high triviality.

17. For an opposite point of view, see the stimulating writing of Hannah Arendt in *The Human Condition* (Chicago: University of Chicago Press, 1958), Chap. V, *passim.*

modated democratic politics (most broadly defined) would be the best mechanism, the mechanism best fit for the utopian values which survived the allowance for change.

If, then, each citizen is not able to take part, in person, in the deliberations concluding in laws, then at least everything possible must be done to have the representative or delegate speak accurately for those he represents, and to have the executive obey faithfully the instructions transmitted to it by the body of representatives. It is under these conditions that the institution of representative political bodies does the least damage to the principle of moral autonomy or self-determination.

Yet once more, practical considerations arise to threaten that which is morally desirable. Let us consider first lawmaking in utopia. The view that a representative should be nothing more than the mouthpiece of (the majority in) his constituency has been severely criticized by theorists of democracy. Leaving aside the Madisonian fears of unmediated public opinion, we find that there are other obstacles to the workings of this ideal. One set of obstacles relates to the difficulties of ascertaining what, in fact, majority opinion is. In his distinguished book, *An Introduction to Democratic Theory*,[18] Henry B. Mayo has listed these difficulties, in the course of trying to discredit the idea that the task of a representative is to follow, to the letter, the mandate of (the majority in) his constituency. The objections relevant to our discussion which Mayo takes up are (in paraphrase):

1. It is next to impossible to determine the wishes of large numbers of people.

2. Elections deal with many issues; and it is rare that those who make up a majority on one issue will make up a majority on some or all other issues. One must therefore vote for a man with whom one more or less agrees, not expecting him to hold one's opinion on every issue. Mayo also asserts that there is no reason to be morally confounded by these difficulties: any realistic theory of democracy must teach that elections are to choose policy-makers, not determine policy: the great mass of people are not competent to reason carefully about policy.

It must be conceded to Mayo that, given the nature of

18. Henry B. Mayo, *An Introduction to Democratic Theory* (New York: Oxford University Press, 1960), pp. 87-88.

democratic politics in the real world, his objections are unanswerable. But 'it may be that our hypothetical utopian politics
can get around his objections. Mayo's position rests on two
certain truths: first, to make reasonable decisions of policy in
a state marked by conflicts of economic interest and by the
quest for national security in a hostile international world is
an occupation demanding of the policy-makers a wide assortment of political and intellectual gifts; and second, policy-
making is a full-time occupation owing to the complexity of a
wildly diverse society, and to the constant intrusion of the
unexpected. There are many issues; each issue is complicated;
new issues arise without warning; divisions of opinion shift from
issue to issue. However, utopian idealism looks to a more simple
species of politics: if not to the simplicity of politics in Rousseau's good society, then to a politics surely more simple than
that of democracy in the real world. In the abstract, the politics
of utopia is the politics of taste, not the politics of conflict of
interests. In the abstract, though (as we have said) utopia is
not static, utopia is not in constant flux. In the abstract, the
level of virtue and understanding of the citizen is higher than
it is in the real world. These things, taken together, may help to
remove the obstacles to the theory of representative-as-deputy
which Mayo (and others) sensibly remark. Where there are
few issues; where issues are not distressingly complicated; where
it is hard to imagine that new issues will arise in such a way
as to require immediate decision without prior consultation with
the constituency; and where division of opinion on one issue can
form and become stable without other divisions crowding in on
it or existing simultaneously with it, chances revive for the
theory of representative-as-deputy. Of course, there can be
nothing approaching certainty in talking about these hypothetical
matters, and talking about them in such a brief and abstract
way. But if our entering into this discussion makes any sense
at all, these few remarks may be of some utility.

The purpose, then, of deputies would be to register formally
the wishes of (the majority in) the various constituencies.
Naturally, they would have to serve other purposes as well.
They would have to formulate the issues before each election;

they would have to draft the legislation which embodied the new policy after each election. For this last-named purpose to be served, deputies in the majority would have to consult with those in the minority, to avoid excessive divisiveness, secure agreement that the new policy conforms to fundamental utopian principles, and prepare the way for a new consensus. And for all these purposes to be served, the vocation of (part-time) politician would have to come into being.

We must turn next to the problem of executive power in utopia. It is to be assumed, one supposes, that the executive power must remain in continuous existence. The question then becomes, Must the personnel of the executive power have permanent tenure? The answer to that question must depend, in large measure, on the degree of technical knowledge that the executive power would require to do what it is supposed to do. All along, we have been assuming that the basic reason for the existence of a political system in a modern utopian society is the need to have an institutional framework able to assimilate change. Clearly, technical knowledge, many kinds of scientific knowledge, would be necessary to the intelligent *implementation* of policy dictating change, while such technical knowledge would not be necessary for the initial act of deciding whether or not to accept a new policy, a policy introducing innovation into some aspect of utopian life.

And the technical knowledge would have to be supplemented by practical wisdom. The practical wisdom of the members of the executive would consist of the ability to understand the processes of life in utopian society and the values those processes embody; to grasp, in a general way, the material preconditions of any of those processes; to know what can and cannot be done, given the material conditions at any given time; to have a sense of the short-term vs. the long-term; to be able to form some idea—within the limits (hopefully less narrow in a utopian society) of possible social prediction—of how things would change if a suggested course of action were adopted; and to preside over any innovation popularly decided on. Practical wisdom would thus relate to details and to trends: to the institutions of utopia in their complex interdependence, and to the impact on those institutions of *conscious* innovation. It would not ever take it upon itself to innovate without consent, or to pretend that its values were better values than those of society as a whole, or of any group in it. Like the practical wisdom outside utopia, that inside utopia is, in principle, fully accountable. Its workings are fully estimable, and liable to the scrutiny of the people in whose behalf it exists. The values which can be served by it are manifold, and none of them entailed by the practical wisdom itself. The wisdom is there to be used, but cannot itself be made to justify one set of values rather than another: no wisdom can. It is clear, however, that though this practical wisdom relates only to things of this world, and though it does not pretend to give the lead to a herdlike citizenry, it still cannot be conceived of as being within the competence of every man. It, like technical knowledge, would seem to require, even in utopia, talents and habits and interests which could never be universally distributed. In utopia, some of its traditional ingredients—cunning, an overpowering sense of the limits of possible action, a readiness to expect the worst, a mind trained for emergency and sudden shifts of fortune—would not be called for; but the ingredients still needed would be, perhaps, as uncommon.

The problem then becomes to ascertain where the seat of technical knowledge and practical wisdom would be. Is it to be expected that within a system of democratic government only a bureaucracy, suitably trained and allowed permanent tenure, and recruiting its own personnel, could possibly come close to guaranteeing the constant presence of the elements of practical wisdom and technical knowledge somewhere in the system? Will it turn out that for all the moral and practical necessity for democratic government, it is possible to have the citizenry—given the average level of their competence—elect only their deputies, while leaving all really important political power to the bureaucracy? Would the power of the bureaucracy make the function of deputies trivial? What is the most that can be hoped for: that deputies can, from time to time, demand some sort of vague accounting from the bureaucracy? If that is the case, democratic government would only be a deceptive façade for the exercise of power by a small group of men whose say on things would most of the time have to be taken as authoritative; the gulf would be wide between bureaucrats and elected officials, but even wider between bureaucrats and citizenry. The point is to avoid having knowledge of any kind turn into a cause of separation between people, into a pretext for rigid hierarchy and for social manipulation. But how is that to be avoided if practical wisdom *does* presuppose something more than decency and common sense? A permanent bureaucracy, if watched over, surely need not turn into either a monster of efficiency or into a monster of inefficiency: into either a heartless organization which disciplines reality by eliminating anything in it that threatens the niceness of a pre-established pattern or into a mindless organization that cannot even discipline its own vast and intricate workings: either into Zamiatin's nightmare or Kafka's. That is to say, the contention of writers like Herbert Spencer, von Mises, and Hayek that any bureaucracy, whether it rules or aids others in ruling, must inevitably become tyrannical or anarchic is refuted by the experience of too many countries to have even prima facie plausibility. But no matter how useful and well-behaved a permanent bureaucracy can be, its mere existence threatens the principle of equality, its mere existence tends to promote mystique and paternalism. And how could we think we had utopia if we had either mystique or paternalism, and had not carried the principle of equality in social relations as far as it could be carried? In utopian society, all basic social innovation would be conscious, and initiated politically: political power would be its only instrumentality. That is why it is so necessary to have political power measure up to moral expectations.

Can some alternative be conceived? First, can practical wisdom be located somewhere else than in a permanent bureaucracy? Can it, in fact, be imagined as the unfailing possession of men elected to office, and holding office for a limited time? The answer is that the only way of getting anything like such a condition would be to have a system of regional schools, admission to which would, of course, be solely dependent on aptitude and inclination, and from which all those wishing to stand for office must have graduated. The graduates, taken together, would form a pool of candidates, prepared to share in the executive power, if chosen by lot; prepared to cede their power after a fixed time in office; and prepared to enter into other occupations than rule for most of their lives. And the indispensable accompaniments to such a political mechanism would be first, a superlatively educated citizenry; second, a large measure of automatism in the processes of production and distribution; and third, some measure of similarity in the various styles of life from region to region—though that measure could stop far short of oppressive uniformity. Second, technical knowledge could be supplied by treating scientists as temporary consultants, most of whose lives are spent not in consultation but in advancing scientific knowledge. With these conditions satisfied—and it is only the first condition that presents serious cause for doubt—there would appear to be no reason, in the abstract, why some sort of acceptable political mechanism could not exist. There would be innumerable details to be filled in, but it is not our purpose to do so here. Our only purpose is to try to say what minimally would have to be the case, if utopian ideals were not to founder on the political rock. The modern utopian aim must be to perfect *and* to diminish the political process.

ix

The discussion we have just entered into has no other aim than to acknowledge the gravity of the species of antiutopianism concerned with what is needed politically to keep utopian ends in being. In the Legend of the Grand Inquisitor, in the speeches of Shigalov in *The Possessed,* and in Aldous Huxley's *Brave New World,* we find the frightening premise that the inescapable cost for social harmony (or for the parody of social harmony) is the sharpest division of society into leaders and led, rulers and ruled: actually, into elite and herd; the frightening premise that social harmony ensues only when society is made up of angels and beasts or a few adults and many children, that the only conceivable utopian situation is one in which Prospero

lords it over Miranda and Caliban, in which magic holds innocence and ignorance in thrall. It is true that Dostoyevsky,
Huxley, and other antiutopian writers do not try to see what
could have led numerous social thinkers to espouse the solutions
they did: missing from much antiutopian literature is the simple
awareness that the passion for justice can, in a time of scarcity
and immature technology, issue in strange social designs, but
that it is, after all, the passion for justice that is at work. But it
is also true that a number of utopian theorists, taking their lead
from Plato, have seemed too ready to incur the risks of tyranny,
mystique, and paternalism, for the sake of order and contentment; and this readiness lends itself to the kind of cruel caricature that has been forthcoming. It would seem possible for
modern utopianism, however, not to turn into Shigalovism, nor
into the almost equally objectionable alternative of Spartanism.
That is—and we come back to this point yet again—scientific
technique together with advances in the study of human nature
seems to allow for the hope that abundance *and* equality, change
and control, government *and* consent, happiness *and* rationality,
privacy *and* involvement, can coexist in a utopian society. Fear
of Shigalovism and Spartanism must become part of the super-
ego of modern utopianism; the tendency of earlier utopianisms
to incline in these two directions must be remembered (with all
respect to the intentions of utopian theorists), and all care taken
to avoid any similar inclination in the future. A fundamental
task of utopian society would be to give the lie to those who
assert that freedom is irreconcilable with security[19] or planning[20]

---

19. See, for example, Bertrand de Jouvenel, *Power* (1945) trans. by
J. F. Huntington (London: The Batchworth Press, revised edition, 1952),
Chap. XVIII.

20. Attacks on bureaucracy are often accompanied by attacks on planning. See Walter Lippmann, *The Good Society* (New York: Grosset's
Universal Library, n.d.), Chaps. V-VI; Friedrich A. Hayek, *The Road to
Serfdom* (Chicago: University of Chicago Press, 1944); Ludwig von
Mises, *Bureaucracy* (New Haven: Yale University Press, 1944); Michael
Oakeshott, "Contemporary British Politics," *The Cambridge Journal,* I
(1947-1948), pp. 474-490, esp. pp. 484-485; J. Jewkes, *Ordeal by Planning* (New York: Macmillan, 1948). For a defense of planning against
its extremist enemies, see, for example, Barbara Wootton, *Freedom under*

or equality[21] or happiness[22] or "political salvation,"[23] and that
a choice between freedom and the others has to be made. It
could be said that the major supposition of modern utopianism
would have to be that scientific progress, most broadly understood, has at last reached the stage where a utopian society that
was neither Shigalovian nor Spartan—neither rigidly stratified
nor insufferably public—could plausibly be imagined. This development is what makes utopianism at the present time an
idealism that could hold within itself the idealism of other, traditionally antithetic doctrines (such as liberalism); and what
will make utopianism, in days to come, a matter worth serious
discussion, a matter (it could be said) of urgency. In the past,
material conditions forced utopianism to sacrifice freedom and
equality; in the not distant future, we can hope to see a science
and technology that will permit all utopian ends to be achieved
in conjunction. It is precisely this possibility which distinguishes
utopianism in the modern age from all previous utopianism.

X

Hard as one tries to fit politics (for the sake of change) into
utopia, the feeling could nevertheless persist that once politics
has been admitted into utopia (for whatever reason), the ser-
pent has been admitted into the garden. Once the necessity for
a political mechanism has been granted, a great deal else has
been simultaneously incorporated in the utopian scheme. For,
after all, it could be said, a political mechanism means the following things: (1) a strong chance that sooner or later men of
politics will go beyond their confines, and change into an iron

Planning; Herman Finer, *Road to Reaction* (Boston: Little, Brown, 1946).
For a survey of arguments made against planning, see Judith N. Shklar, *After
Utopia* (Princeton, N.J.: Princeton University Press, 1957), pp. 245-256.

21. See, for example, Talmon, *Political Messianism: The Romantic Phase,*
op. cit., p. 510.

22. That is the theme of The Legend of the Grand Inquisitor in
Dostoyevsky's novel *The Brothers Karamazov.*

23. See J. L. Talmon, *Utopianism and Politics* (London: Conservative
Political Centre, 1957).

oligarchy which may or may not, as it pleases, be beneficent: once allow authority of any kind, you cannot predict that it will be perpetually wielded as it is supposed to be wielded; (2) a strong chance that, whether an oligarchy develops or not, a sense of apartness from the citizenry will grow in the minds of those who take part in the processes of rule: no matter how peripheral politics becomes, no matter how limited the scope of authority, there simply is a great distinction between those who hold authority and those who do not; and this distinction is fatal to the establishment of even an attenuated version of the principle of equality; (3) a strong chance that sooner or later the political mechanism, though it works as it is supposed to work, will work in such a way as to confront large groups of people with the unpleasant need to obey regulations to which they are opposed, on penalty of suffering legally or socially. Perhaps, when all is said and done, utopia must be thought of as a place in which, irrespective of the level of technology, the pattern of life must once be determined and thereafter adhered to, without deviation. Perhaps utopia, to be utopia, cannot allow for change and whatever is needed to accommodate change; for with change comes politics, and with politics comes abuse of rule, or genuine authority, or the forcing of people to do what they do not want to do; and all of these are antagonistic to the spirit of modern utopianism. Perhaps, after all, the old utopian alternatives of rule of the few, direct democracy in a small community, and anarchism are the only alternatives. Our knowledge and our morality lead us to reject rule of the few; we see that direct democracy cannot operate outside a city-state, and hence is inapplicable to a world-utopia; we conclude that anarchism cannot exist if scientific and technical change is to continue. But then, modern utopianism must perhaps choose anarchism if it is to achieve its ends; perhaps it cannot permit change; perhaps it must exclude politics.

Perhaps this line of argument is correct: perhaps, even for modern utopianism, all good things are not concurrently realizable: values, even utopian values, may inevitably war on each other.

xi

Before leaving the subject of the antiutopianism concerned with the means needed to keep utopian ends in being, we must take note of one other cluster of arguments; and this relates to mechanization in utopia. We have all along been speaking as if machine technology were a blessing not to be quarreled with; that, as a matter of fact, it was the *sine qua non* of any utopian society in the modern world. We have seen that though technology, by its very versatility and inexhaustibility, raises the problem of politics in utopia in its most imperative form, and therefore must contribute somewhat to the uneasiness of mind of any utopian theorist, technology still is that which gives credibility to utopian speculation, that which alone makes interesting and relevant the utopian hope in the twentieth century. The fact is, however, that there have been, in our time, a large number of men who have seen in machine technology the death of a number of cherished values, the source not of good or of good primarily, but of harm.

Fear and hate of the machine are among the stalest and most pervasive emotions of modern life, and exist much of the time apart from any feeling about the desirability or undesirability of utopia.[24] Mechanization is taken as an irresistible and soul-destroying tendency. What links it to utopia is the belief that any

---

24. Two general and often intemperate attacks on the Machine can be found in Friedrich Georg Juenger, *The Failure of Technology* (1946) (Chicago: Gateway Editions, 1956); Gabriel Marcel, *Man Against Mass Society*, trans. by G. S. Fraser (Chicago: Regnery, 1952). Marcel, for example, says: ". . . I am not sure that every kind of technical progress may not entail, for the individual who takes advantage of it *without having had any share in the effort at overcoming difficulties of which such a progress is the culmination,* the payment of a heavy price, of which a certain degradation at the spiritual level is the natural expression." And: "It would be no exaggeration to say that the more progress 'humanity' as an abstraction makes towards the mastery of nature, the more actual individual men tend to become slaves of this very conquest" (pp. 40-41). The hostility of modern poets and novelists to the Machine is notorious. A typical expression can be found in William Faulkner's *A Fable* (New York: Random House, 1954), pp. 353-54.

future utopia could draw out this tendency to its bitterest conclusion by making sure that no corner of the world escaped it, and no department of life remained free from its steely touch. The Machine is seen as that which ensures the attainment of (admittedly beneficent) utopian goals, as that without which utopian hopefulness is really unthinkable; and supposedly it is in utopia that it will therefore receive its ultimate consecration. So by a progression of this sort, a loathing of the Machine can lead to a loathing of utopian aspiration. What then does this hatred of mechanization consist in?

There is first the idea, wonderfully mocked by Samuel Butler in *Erewhon*,[25] that somehow machines will develop a volition of their own, independent of that of men their makers, and come eventually to change roles with men and make men *their* servants. The usual terms of comparison are Frankenstein's monster and the sorcerer's apprentice. Capek's famous play *RUR* (1920) applied this idea in all seriousness to robots: robots rise (if that is the proper verb) against humanity to claim domination. It is hard to say just what is to be done with this idea except to translate it into the less dramatic assertion that machines may exact the cost of unpleasant alterations in human life in exchange for the immense benefits they bestow, and may at times seem to be leading men to do things that serve no purpose but an endless, useless refinement of mechanical proficiency. Be that as it may, it nevertheless remains true that, as Norbert Wiener has said, the real danger is not that the increasingly subtle and potent machines of modern technology will develop a will of their own (whatever that may mean) but that they are and will continue to be used in the service of evil human wills.[26] One would have thought such a point to be a truism.

A related fancy is that if the whole world became dependent on one immense complex of machinery, either the slightest mechanical failure could disarrange all existence, or, in time of emergency, the intricately interrelated working of the machinery could prove to be irreversible or unchangeable, and therefore

25. Samuel Butler, *Erewhon* (1872), in *Erewhon* and *Erewhon Revisited* (New York: The Modern Library, 1927), Chaps. XXIII-XXV.
26. Norbert Wiener, *The Human Use of Human Beings, op. cit.*, p. 181.

leave men in hopeless bondage to an obsolescent monstrosity, unable to make the adjustments required to meet the new situation.[27] The antiutopian mentality is thus sometimes host to a kind of feverish apocalyptic vision that lacks all but a shred of plausibility.

Then there is the view that machinery transforms men themselves into robots by transforming labor into mere machine-tending that requires a hysterical efficiency and regularity of motion and gesture on the part of the laborer, and by simultaneously eliminating pride of craft and the dignity of skilled labor from the world. The frivolousness of the vision of a completely Taylorized world and the heavy-handed way in which the phrase "alienated labor" is used must not, of course, distract attention from the grave problems raised by this view. Exaggerated as it often is, it promotes speculation as to the kinds of labor, if any, that utopia could have. Automation would seem to promise the end of all routine machine labor and its intolerable psychological effects; and also to guarantee that the world-utopia would not depend for its harmony and stability on a Platonic-Byzantine division of labor that makes all but a few the victims of a horrible stultification. But the next question inevitably is, "Does automation mean a totally laborless world?" If it does, have the psychological consequences of complete leisure been taken into account? If it does not, what labor is left? Would labor be permitted, even though useless; and if useless, would not its savor be lost? The prospect either of complete leisure or of pointless craft is appalling, appalling at least to a preutopian who—it may be claimed—has neither the virtue to manage complete leisure nor the wit to devise a *via media* between drudgery and trifling. St. Augustine, writing about Heaven, thought that the only thing that could be done was to praise God, when "no lassitude shall slacken activity, nor any want stimulate to labor."[28] Utopia is to find other things to do. But these matters are too great to be accommodated in a few sentences in this essay: it must be

---

27. See, for example, E. M. Forster's short story, "The Machine Stops," in *The Eternal Moment and Other Stories* (London: Sidgwick & Jackson, 1928).

28. St. Augustine, *The City of God* (New York: The Modern Library, 1950), XXII, 30 (p. 864).

sufficient to say that utopia does not mean, does not assume, does not require, that men be turned into robots so that the problems of abundance may be resolved with all efficiency and dispatch: the real problem is whether or not labor is needed for mental health (for keeping men in touch with the reality principle, as Freud thought),[29] and if it is needed, how to provide for it in a world that no longer goes round because of it.

Finally, there is the feeling that the machine is hateful because it does better than men what men alone have hitherto been able to do; because it, his own creation, dwarfs him and makes him feel his weakness as nothing else can. Kuno, the hero of E. M. Forster's story, "The Machine Stops," expresses this feeling most touchingly:

> . . . I began by walking up and down the platform of the railway outside my room. Up and down, until I was tired, and so did recapture the meaning of "Near" and "Far." "Near" is a place to which I can get quickly *on my feet*, not a place to which the train or the air-ship will take me quickly. "Far" is a place to which I cannot get quickly on my feet; the vomitory is "far," though I could be there in thirty-eight seconds by summoning the train. Man is the measure. . . . Man's feet are the measure for distance, his hands are the measure for ownership, his body is the measure for all that is lovable and desirable and strong.

---

29. For a discussion of the human need for creative endeavor, as distinguished from mere labor, see Erich Fromm, *The Sane Society* (New York: Rinehart, 1955). For a discussion of the transformation of work into play, of what utopian work could conceivably be, see Herbert Marcuse, *Eros and Civilization* (Boston: Beacon Press, 1955), pp. 187-196, 212-221. For a discussion of various kinds of endeavor, of their respective value, and of the need for endeavor, see Hannah Arendt, *The Human Condition, op. cit.*

Generally, the following proposals could be entertained about the relation between work and play. First, most work could be eliminated, and life turned into one long activity of play. What work remained would simply be an unpleasant but minor necessity. Second, every effort could be made to enhance work, so that it would be loved as if it were play, and consume most of the energy people had. Third, the line between play and work could be blurred, though not erased. There could be elements of play in work, and elements of work in play: there could be playing at work and working at play. The work done would not be fatiguing or exhausting because there is some play in it; and being neither fatigued nor exhausted from work, people would have enough energy left over to make play elaborate.

The natural and the mechanical are placed in implacable opposition. [At times, as in Eugene Zamiatin's *We* (1924), a mindless primitivism is seen as the only possible response to the suffocating automatism of utopia: there the opposition between natural and mechanical operates at its most intense.] To such a feeling, the words of the man of sense who tries to stop Erewhon from destroying its machines make the profoundest reply:

Those mighty organisms . . . our leading bankers and merchants, speak to their congeners through the length and breadth of the land in a second of time; their rich and subtle souls can defy all material impediment, whereas the souls of the poor are clogged and hampered by matter, which sticks fast about them as treacle to the wings of a fly, or as one struggling in a quicksand: their dull ears must take days or weeks to hear what another would tell them from a distance, instead of hearing it in a second as is done by the more highly organized classes. . . . That old philosophic enemy, matter, the inherently and essentially evil, still hangs about the neck of the poor and strangles him: but to the rich, matter is immaterial; the elaborate organization of his extra-corporeal system has freed his soul.

These, then, very briefly, are a few components of the fear and hatred of The Machine.[30] Taken together, they are not a very impressive threat to the peace of mind of one who aspires to utopia. They belong to battles fought and decided long ago; they are mentioned here only because they still make fitful appearances. To understand them is to understand, in part, past aversion to utopia shared by many thinkers, still influential thinkers, who otherwise may have approved of the general humanitarianism that informs utopian thought, and who would therefore have perhaps approved of utopia if it could be had without utilizing industrial technology to the full. But it cannot, and need not.

---

30. For a patient, tolerant, and fair-minded discussion of machine technology, its perils and its rewards, see Yves R. Simon, *Philosophy of Democratic Government* (Chicago: University of Chicago Press, 1951), pp. 274-296, esp. pp. 274-279.

4

Rejection of Utopian Ends:
Against Perpetual Peace

i

It would seem at first sight that no one in his right mind could find perpetual peace an objectionable end. There are, of course, some reasons why political and economic groups have found and continue to find war to be useful in the pursuance of their aims. But a utopian apologist is not interested in these practical, sometimes pernicious designs. What must interest him is the hesitation of those who, not concerned to defend the material utility of war, still find something distasteful in the thought of perpetual peace. They will go with the utopian so far as to acknowledge that there is nothing that makes for war that utopia could not eliminate: gone will be the reign of Thucydide's triad of fear, honor, and interest (Hobbes's gain, safety, and reputation; Harold Lasswell's deference, income, and safety): the world will be one and abundant. They may even be ready to agree that there was no ineradicable need for war inherent in human nature: but is there not something more, they may feel, to be said for war?

Writing before the First World War, in 1910, the year of his death, William James tried to see what more in war there could be. He wrote as a man convinced that perpetual peace was an end worth striving for; but with his usual graciousness of mind he explored in "The Moral Equivalent of War" the opposing views of the war party.[1] The point that worried James the most was that if there were no more wars there would be no more chance for certain qualities of human nature to manifest themselves. James was most responsive to the fear that utopia meant the absence of heroism and exertion, and hence could also mean a slackened manliness. It was not merely that perpetual peace called a halt to the spectacle in which ". . . the destinies of peoples [are] decided quickly, thrillingly, and tragically, by force"; much more than that, "the splendid military aptitudes of men [were] doomed to keep always in a state of latency."[2] No more risks, no more daring, no more discipline and renunciation. The solution proposed by James to the dilemma of wanting to have both peace and manliness was the substitution of Nature for nations as the enemy: by harnessing the energies of men to civilize Nature and remake the face of the world, all the military virtues would continue to have a field for their display, but mankind would be spared the miseries of war.

Whether or not James's solution was appropriate for his own time, it is clear that the advances in technology since James's time, and advances still to come, greatly reduce the impressiveness of Nature as an enemy. It soon will probably be unable to call forth from men the kind of vigorous and self-denying behavior that James had in mind. A time could come when the

1. There are some similarities between James's essay and Ralph Waldo Emerson's essay, "War." See also the very interesting Lecture III, "War," by John Ruskin in his *The Crown of Wild Olive* (1866) in *The Works of John Ruskin,* ed. by E. T. Cook and Alexander Wedderburn (40 Vols., London: G. Allen; New York: Longmans, Green, 1905), Vol. XVIII, pp. 459-493.

2. William James, "The Moral Equivalent of War" in *Essays on Faith and Morals* (New York: Longmans, Green, 1947), p. 320. For a rich and very interesting antiutopian novel that makes use of some of James's points, see Bernard Wolfe, *Limbo* (New York: Random House, 1952). See also Herman Wouk's suggestive story, "The 'Lomokome' Papers," *Collier's Magazine,* Feb. 17, 1956.

world had no enemies left but death. What then would happen to human nature: would it be ingloriously truncated, would men become unfit to meet emergencies that might arise in ways that seem to us now to be only in the province of science fiction? It is, as we have already said, terrible to think of any human capability or characteristic vanishing from sight; worse still to think that utopia would breed a feeble race of men, would produce what H. G. Wells in *The Time Machine* (1895) called "an automatic civilization and a decadent humanity."[3] (No one has written better than Wells the utopian on the advantages of adversity and strife to human nature.[4]) The self-sufficient man, able alone to organize his life around him from meager beginnings, in the image of Robinson Crusoe, is certainly endangered by utopia. It will not do for the utopian to say that if the conditions that made certain human traits desirable were to disappear, then there would be no harm in those traits disappearing as well. No utopian could give absolute assurance that those traits would not one day be needed again; and if the utopian is out to try to make a race of "men like gods" he must surely retain a place for heroism and exertion in the make-up of the new race. If it is too much to liken war to winds that preserve the sea from foulness, as Hegel does[5]; if it is too much to liken war to rain that ends a long drouth, as Robert Frost does,[6] is there not still some threat of moral flaccidity in a safe and harmonious

3. H. G. Wells, *The Time Machine* (1895) (New York: Holt, 1912; paperback edition, New York: Berkley, n.d.), p. 97. Cf. Wells's aversion to a "Utopia of dolls in the likeness of angels," in *A Modern Utopia*, p. 34.

4. Besides *The Time Machine*, see Wells's *Men Like Gods* (New York: Macmillan, 1923), for the speech of Mr. Catskill (pp. 98-103) and the thoughts of Mr. Barnstaple (p. 169). See also *A Modern Utopia*, p. 282. For another, quite powerful expression of worry over the ease of Utopia, by a man of the left, see George Orwell, *The Road to Wigan Pier* (London: V. Gollancz, 1937; New York: Harcourt, Brace and World, 1958), Chap. XII. For an example of the fear that a utopian society would produce a race of amorphous and infantile men, because a utopian society, in theory, lacks struggle and exertion, has abundance, and indulges almost all inclinations, see Herman Fingarette, "Eros and Utopia" (a review of Herbert Marcuse, *Eros and Civilization*), *The Review of Metaphysics*, X (1957), pp. 660-665.

5. G. W. F. Hegel, *Philosophy of Right*, trans. by T. M. Knox (Oxford: Clarendon Press, 1942), par. 324.

6. Robert Frost, "On Looking Up by Chance at the Constellations" in *Complete Poems* (New York: Holt, 1949), p. 346.

utopia? If ". . . the possibility of violent death [is] the soul of
all romance,"[7] the world can do without romance; but can it do
without some of the altruistic qualities of character traditionally
associated with the possibility of violent death? This issue must
give the utopian pause.

ii

But there is another view of the war party that need not give
the utopian pause, the view that society cannot properly endure
without at least an occasional blood-sacrifice on the part of its
members. Hegel is a major intellectual exponent of this view
(though it is common, of course, to many cultures, existing in
various degrees of conscious acceptance). For Hegel, "Sacrifice
on behalf of the individuality of the state is the substantial tie
between the state and all its members and so is a universal
duty."[8] How is a citizen to feel that he is truly a member of a
society unless he either has risked his life for it or lives with the
constant possibility of having to do so? What endears his society
to a man more than the blood he or his kin or his ancestors have
shed in its behalf? Add to that, the blood of the enemy that is
caused to flow, engendering a diffuse guilt. Shared guilt and
shared peril, then, are the tightest bonds a group of men can

7. William James, "The Moral Equivalent of War," p. 316. Compare
what Northrop Frye says in *Anatomy of Criticism* (Princeton: Princeton
University Press, 1957), p. 37. "Romance, therefore, is characterized by
the acceptance of pity and fear, which in ordinary life relate to pain, as
forms of pleasure. It turns fear at a distance, or terror, into the adventur-
ous; fear at contact, or horror, into the marvellous, and fear without an
object, or dread (Angst) into a pensive melancholy. It turns pity at a
distance, or concern, into the theme of chivalrous rescue; pity at contact,
or tenderness, into a languid or relaxed charm, and pity without an object (which has no name but is a kind of animism, or treating everything
in nature as though it had human feelings) into creative fantasy." In idea,
a society dedicated to utopian ends would exclude the usual sources of
fear and some of the reasons for pity, and thus the raw material on which
the spirit of romance works its transmutations. Once again, utopia fails
the nonutopian imagination. This particular failure, however, does not
seem for some reason to be terribly weighty: the spirit of romance seems
too young (perhaps adolescent) and too artificial in its connection to
reality. At its worst, it seems a cheat.
8. G. W. F. Hegel, *Philosophy of Right, op. cit.,* par. 325.

have; and society cannot lightly part with them. If the world were unitary and peaceful the people in it would be atomic individuals. Man needs community, and community needs strife.

The need for the blood-sacrifice informs Robert Frost's "The Gift Outright," and Yeats's "The Rose Tree"; and W. H. Auden's remarkable political poem, "Vespers," concludes with the lines:

> For without a cement of blood (it must be human,
>   it must be innocent)
> no secular wall will safely stand.[9]

(Related to these ideas is the hallucination of Hans Castorp in Thomas Mann's *The Magic Mountain*. In the City of the Sun a beautiful race of people live a beautiful life, but in the heart of its temple hags dismember some of its infants: the darker powers can be appeased only by blood.)

To all this, the utopian could reply that for a clan or a tribe or even a city-state these considerations had a peculiar force. When combat was hand-to-hand, and society in the image of a great family, then what Hegel and others say had full meaning. Hegel himself, however, was led to confine the necessity of sacrifice in modern times to a regular army, except in the direst circumstances. In the world of nation-states the ties between citizens are of a different sort, and the spilling of blood loses its sacrament-like nature. Modern war is, as everyone knows and says, different. So that the world has already reached the stage where these Hegelian reasons cease to work and utopia would resemble preutopia in this respect. In utopia love of place would have other causes than either blood-sacrifice or its modern substitutes. Place will be loved because—to borrow a formulation of Burke's—it will be lovely,[10] so lovely that its loveliness will suffice without the admixture of grief. Blood-mysticism would not seem to have any claim on the utopian.

---

9. W. H. Auden, "Vespers" in *The Shield of Achilles* (New York: Random House, 1955), pp. 77-80. Auden's poem is of great relevance to the general subject of utopianism. Cf. the vulgar hymn to bloodshed sung by Adam Wayne in G. K. Chesterton's *The Napoleon of Notting Hill* (1904) (London: The Bodley Head, 1937; New York: Devin-Adair, 1958), pp. 118-120.

10. Edmund Burke, *Reflections on the Revolution in France* (London: Everyman's Library, 1910), p. 75.

(Another reason Hegel gives in defense of war is that "War is the state of affairs which deals in earnest with the vanity of temporal goods and concerns."[11] Surely if temporal goods and concerns are vain, they are vain only in the face of something eternal. But what could be more temporal—and hence by Hegel's account, more vain—than the enmities of states?)

iii

There is a somewhat blander form of opposition to perpetual peace which is less concerned with blood and sacrifice than with movement and excitement. A fear haunts some antiutopians that utopia means the end of history. Did not Hegel say, "The History of the World is not the theatre of happiness. Periods of happiness are blank pages in it"?[12] Utopia is seen as a place where nothing unplanned or unexpected ever happens; where events (in the sense of dramatic and amazing occurrences) never take place; where there is no surprise; where free and spontaneous behavior is unknown; where anything that could disturb the harmony and equilibrium has been removed; where there are clear and explicit prescriptions to govern conduct of every sort, everything written down, nothing left that is tacit or subtle, no ways of behaving that are acquired only slowly, uncertainly, and with some (beneficial) pain; where waste or gratuitous motion is prevented; where nothing ever goes "unharvested;"[13] where all is known and regulated and predictable; in short, a closed world forever without change. It is not that war itself is desirable; it is rather that peace should not be taken to mean a deathly absence of movement. They would make a desolation and call it peace. A utopian society would be lifeless and immortal.

In highly charged language, Roderick Seidenberg has given the essence of the position:

---

11. G. W. F. Hegel, *Philosophy of Right, op. cit.*, par. 324.
12. G. W. F. Hegel, *The Philosophy of History*, trans. by J. Sibree (New York: Dover Publications, 1956), p. 26.
13. See Robert Frost's poem "Unharvested" in *Complete Poems, op. cit.*, p. 400.

In the ultimate state of crystallization to which the principle of organization leads, consciousness will have accomplished its task, leaving mankind sealed, as it were, within patterns of frigid and unalterable perfection.[14]

and

. . . we may perceive that the trend of events must ultimately approach a condition of stable equilibrium in which the individual will be a rigidly fixed component of the mass in an objective continuum of society and its environment.[15]

(We must be sure to distinguish between the desire for "events" and the desire for change. In a previous section, we discussed the idea of change in utopia, and tried to say that change was to be envisaged as improvement, mostly of a technological sort. We may add here that the only kind of change in accord with utopianism is calculated change, deliberately introduced, and with the greatest possible awareness of consequence. The antiutopian wish for events is a wish for unplanned and disruptive change, for something disturbing and hence memorable.)

It is true that in the utopian sensibility there is generally present some strong predilection for the neat and tidy, for the ordered and arranged. The utopian leaves himself open not only to the charge of finding it painless to impose uniformity (a charge we have already discussed), but also to the related charge of actually preferring a world completely stable and known, where nothing happens that is not supposed to happen, and everything happens in a methodical or routine way. The utopian is thought to carry rationalism very far: he prefers straight lines to curves: he wears a square hat instead of a

14. Roderick Seidenberg, *Post-Historic Man* (1950) (Boston: Beacon Press, 1957), p. 180. See Eugene Zamiatin's important antiutopian novel *We*, trans. by Gregory Zilboorg (New York: Dutton, 1924), p. 28 and p. 179; Joseph Wood Krutch, *The Measure of Man* (New York: Harcourt, Brace, 1954), p. 76; Henry S. Kariel, "Political Science in the United States: Reflections on One of its Trends," *Political Studies*, IV (1956), pp. 113-127; Eugen Weber, "The Anti-Utopia of the Twentieth Century," *The South Atlantic Quarterly*, LVIII (Summer 1959), pp. 440-447; and Lewis Mumford, *The Transformations of Man* (New York: Harper, 1956), Chap. VII ("Post-Historic Man").

15. Roderick Seidenberg, *Post-Historic Man, op. cit.*, p. 236.

sombrero: he lives in a world of formal gardens and intricate time-pieces: he is Prospero subduing his isle. He has no tender sentiment, no *reserve*, when he handles reality; he would rather make things than let them grow; he delights in taking things apart to put them together again in a better way; he desires to know and tell all, to demonstrate how things work rather than shroud their workings in decent obscurity. He hates indirectness, disguises, and ceremonies.[16]

There is concededly a utopian estheticism of order and repose and literal-mindedness (similar, but only in part, to the utopian estheticism attacked by Karl Popper).[17] But it must be said that there is an antiutopian estheticism that answers to it and that may be even more reprehensible.[18] (Recall

---

16. The classic attack on the workings of the rationalist mind in politics is to be found, of course, in Edmund Burke, *Reflections on the Revolution in France*. Burke spoke with scorn of "a geometrical and arithmetical constitution," (p. 52); and of the simplicity of "metaphysic rights" (pp. 58–59); and of "the principles of this [French] mechanic philosophy" (p. 75). For a recent restatement of Burke's position, see Michael Oakeshott's essays: "Rationalism in Politics," *The Cambridge Journal*, I (1947-1948), pp. 81-98, 145-157; "Scientific Politics," *The Cambridge Journal*, I (1947-1948), pp. 247-258; "The Tower of Babel," *The Cambridge Journal*, II (1948-1949), pp. 67-83; "Rational Conduct," *The Cambridge Journal*, IV (1950-1951), pp. 3-27. Cf. Aldous Huxley in *Ape and Essence* (New York: Harper, 1948), Chap. I: "In the field of politics the equivalent of a theorem is a perfectly disciplined army; of a sonnet or picture, a police state under a dictatorship." See also Wallace Stevens's poem "Six Significant Landscapes," VI, in *Harmonium* (1931) (New York: Knopf, 1950), p. 127.

17. Karl Popper, *The Open Society and Its Enemies* (Princeton: Princeton University Press, 1950), pp. 161-164.

18. Popper is concerned with the utopian planner's love for a clean canvas, for a social situation in which the planner can make and unmake as he pleases, and put reality in whatever arrangement that strikes his fancy. It could be said that the utopian wants to *make* life what life seems to be from a mountaintop; the confused scene becomes a nicely patterned carpet, the artifacts of men become toys, men themselves become harmless creatures in motion. But viewed more kindly, utopian estheticism is the outcome of good intentions: the desire to bestow blessings in a godlike way, to make the *right* arrangement, not any arrangement that strikes the fancy. There is doubtless an important element of emotional imperialism in the makeup of the utopian planner. This is illustrated by Rousseau's comment: "Nothing but the pleasure of bestowing happiness on a man can repay me for the cost of making him capable of happiness." [*Émile*, trans. by Barbara Foxley (London and New York: Everyman's Library, 1911), p. 369.] See also Plutarch, "Lycurgus" in *Lives* (New York: The Modern Library, n.d.), p. 71.

the young Nietzsche's claim that ". . . only as an esthetic phenomenon may existence and the world appear justified."[19]) We have already noted the esthetic quality of the conservative complaint about uniformity; the complaint about stability is kindred to it. Both in the understandable but ungoverned delight it takes in observing the flux of events, and in the preference it has, at its extremest, for being at the mercy of chance and the unknown, rather than exercising control, antiutopian estheticism shows its callous disposition. The world is thought to move for its sport: life becomes a succession of scenes and men are taken for characters: to some antiutopians life is to be beheld in the way which the narrator of Tennyson's "The Lotos-Eaters" attributes to the Gods:

> . . . to live and lie reclined
> On the hills like Gods together, careless of mankind.
> For they lie beside their nectar, and the bolts are hurl'd
> Far below them in the valleys, and the clouds are lightly curl'd
> Round their golden houses, girdled with the gleaming world;
> Where they smile in secret, looking over wasted lands,
> Blight and famine, plague and earthquake, roaring deeps and
> fiery sands,
> Clanging fights, and flaming towns, and sinking ships, and
> praying hands.
> But they smile, they find a music centered in a doleful song
> Steaming up, a lamentation and an ancient tale of wrong,
> Like a tale of little meaning tho' the words are strong.[20]

---

19. Friedrich Nietzsche, *The Birth of Tragedy*, trans. by Clifton P. Fadiman in *The Philosophy of Nietzsche* (New York: The Modern Library, 1927), p. 1084. See also p. 974 and pp. 1082–1088. For a related Christian estheticism, see St. Augustine, *The City of God* (New York: The Modern Library, 1950), XI, 18; and Soren Kierkegaard, *Journals*, trans. and ed. by Alexander Dru (London: Oxford University Press, 1938), pp. 467–468 (1260).

20. Lines 154–164. Or, as Emerson put it: ". . . to the tragic imagination, . . . the torments of life become tuneful tragedy, solemn and soft with music, and garnished with rich dark pictures." Note also the verses quoted from an "ancient poet" by William Morris in *News From Nowhere*: "For this the Gods have fashioned man's grief and evil day/ That still for man hereafter might be the tale and the lay." [In *Selected Writings*, ed. by G. D. H. Cole (London: The Nonesuch Press, 1934), p. 54.] Either the mind delights in contemplating suffering, or feels that life, without suffering in it, could not be transformed into worthwhile art. See also the section beginning, "The glorious bards of Massachusetts seem," in Frost's poem, "New Hampshire," in *Complete Poems, op. cit.*, pp. 207-208.

And the luxury of being able to feel that the heart of things is unsearchable is tenaciously defended.[21] (It is, after all, the "Devil" who speaks so warmly of "events" in Ivan Karamazov's hallucination.) Clearly no one wants petrifaction, but the absence of history in all its colorful horror is not petrifaction. Are tastes so coarse that only the dramatic and the spectacular can give pleasure? Are feelings so blunt that "events" can continue to be wanted when it is known that events always involve suffering; and mysteries wanted when they involve submission (of an extravagant costliness) to destructive forces? Is it not a deficiency of the imagination to see interest only in violent movement and vivid contrast?[22] Does not an aversion to peace betray an incapacity to use it profitably and virtuously? Finally, is it not true that there is an element of sheer destructiveness present in this antiutopian attitude?[23]

iv

Lastly, there is a variant of the doctrine of "events" we must briefly consider. It could be said that not only is a utopia a society without events, it is also a society without cycles or rhythms. Utopia tries to secure its basic values permanently; and if there is to be change, it is change only, as it were, on the margin. On the other hand, one of the beauties of the real world is that serious, essential changes have occurred and can occur in

21. For a criticism of those who, for one reason or another, love "the blind play of social forces," see Karl Mannheim, *Man and Society in an Age of Reconstruction*, trans. by Edward Shils (London: K. Paul, 1940), p. 376. See pp. 369–381.

22. See Simone Weil, *Cahiers* I (Paris: Plon, 1951), p. 220: ". . . le mal imaginaire est romantique et varié, le mal réel morne, monotone, désertique, ennuyeux. Pourquoi? Au contraire, le bien imaginaire est ennuyeux."

23. See Eugen Weber, "The Anti-Utopia of the Twentieth Century," *op. cit.*, p. 446: "Again and again . . . the anti-utopian calls on the irrational to disrupt and destroy the planned order." For the same sentiment, though with the coarseness removed, see Yeats's poem "Lapis Lazuli," and part VI of his "Vacillation." See also Granville Hicks's review of Bernard Wolfe's *Limbo* in *The New Leader*, XXXVI (Feb. 16, 1953), pp. 20-21.

it. There can be changes in the whole mode of existence; values can give way to other values; different kinds of sensibility and *Zeitgeist* can succeed each other; different sectors of "the whole arc of human potentialities"[24] can appear, disappear, and re-appear. Let life continue to show a sequence of full-blooded styles of life and thought, each exaggerating certain things and excluding other things altogether, each inherently unstable. Let each style have its day of flowering, push itself to its extreme, and decay from its excess, leaving behind it a permanent contribution to the store of human experience. A world in which none of this happens is a desert,[25] for all the satisfaction it may give to the lower appetites.

And again we see that the spectator's delight has been made to prevail over any other consideration. Of course, the record of an ever-changing world is more interesting than that of a generally stable one. But for the great mass of people who must live immersed in the world, who have only one lifetime, and hence who can experience only one or two "styles," a stable and inclusive excellence is the morally acceptable "style."

v

The subject of war has led us to the subject of stability, and there is one more aspect of stability we must take note of. Though we may allow, in theory, for change in utopia, we nevertheless commit ourselves, as we have already said, to a fundamentally stable world. It could be argued that from the utopian point of view, this very stability is to be deprecated. The reason is that a stable social order may induce in men a terrible sense of enclosure, of finitude, and hence activate what moralists have always thought to be a permanent component of hu-

24. This phrase comes from Margaret Mead's Introduction to her *Sex and Temperament in Three Primitive Societies* (1935) (New York: The New American Library: Mentor Books, 1950), p. 9. The whole introduction, and, indeed, much of the work of Miss Mead, is of the greatest interest to the student of utopianism.

25. See the closing lines of Robert Frost's poem, "The Black Cottage," in *Complete Poems, op. cit.,* pp. 74-77.

man nature, namely restlessness. Unless society can allow its inhabitants to feel that things as they are at any given time can change, and change surprisingly; that things are not once and for all fixed in a pattern, there will grow an appetite for change of any sort. Change will become an end in itself. It is not only the *spectator* of the social scene who may become oppressed by stability or by completely controlled change: those who themselves live in a stable society may become similarly oppressed. Men may come to desire a change from good to bad: evil becomes novelty.[26] This tendency would be especially pronounced in a society in which a high level of technological competence encourages the belief that things can be easily, almost magically, changed. But clearly there would have to be limits to the frequency with which change is introduced into a utopian society, if the cluster of utopian values is not to be seriously jeopardized. If men have a great deal, and know they can have more, they will all the more quickly grow dissatisfied with what they have, though it be a great deal. Furthermore, utopia, in theory, provides men with the blessings of life not as reward, but as due; and when men are given things without any great exertion on their part, they appreciate those things very little. Thus, in utopia, there is no reaching for the horizon; the horizon is not forever receding. There is potentially, then, a double source of turmoil for a utopian society. Utopian order leads, in theory, to frightful disorder.

To this contention, it could be said that given human nature in an unreformed condition—that is, before scientific psychology

---

26. It is bad enough to have to feel that the things bestowed on one, and the general form of one's life, are essentially constant in nature; but also to have to feel that these are the best things and the best form, and there should, in all logic, be no changing them, is even worse. One's restlessness may become yet more aggravated. It is useless to deny that there is something awful about getting in full what one wants, or is supposed to want: no room is left for illusions. The grounds for legitimate complaint are removed. But complaint itself may remain. And in these elementary considerations, a utopian theorist may find still another reason for anxiety over the utopian commitment to stability. Furthermore, there is the idea that reformers should always leave something for the future generations to reform. The desire to improve is as strong as the desire to destroy, and utopia should indulge it.

has been systematically applied in the upbringing of the young —the argument against utopia from human restlessness would seem strong (though not overwhelming). But it would seem reasonable to suppose that the psychological tendencies just described are neither universal nor beyond the power of more careful moral instruction to remedy.

5

Rejection of Utopian Ends:
Against Guaranteed Abundance

It is a notorious fact that a picture of men at ease and in the middle of plenty most often makes people contemplating it both nervous and abusive. Glaucon's epithet for Socrates' favorable description of a rude but comfortable state of nature is "city of pigs."[1] And that epithet sums up quite pungently the hostility that has been felt whenever utopian thinkers have aspired to an untroubled condition of nature as the ultimately desirable condition. The most influential antiutopian book of modern times, Aldous Huxley's *Brave New World* (1932), depends for its most telling effects on the disgust at stupid sensuality it can make its readers feel.

The antiutopians appear to be saying that the world must have pain—deprivation and impairment—in it. At times it seems that the antiutopians favor pain as men would favor it who never felt very much of it and think it may be good for themselves and surely could not be too bad for others; at other times, the antiutopians speak as men who have seen or had so much pain that they have become incapable of imagining that there

---

1. Plato, *The Republic*, 372.

could come a time when pain—at least in its more brutalizing forms—could cease to be. Pain becomes a bad habit. The defenses of pain from such promptings do not touch the utopian apologist very intimately. When, for example, Aldous Huxley's Savage claims the right to have syphilis and cancer and "to be tortured by unspeakable pains of every kind,"[2] the utopian can perhaps take pity on a character driven to such an extreme by the opposite extreme of the Brave New World. But the Savage's sensibility is antiutopianism at its very weakest: the sight of one sick man in the real world turns the words of the Savage to prattle.[3] The Savage's untried fondness for pain cannot be transformed into an inhibiting piece of advice to a utopian idealist. Nor, on the other hand, is the world-weariness of the third chapter of Ecclesiastes, with its bewitched intoned endorsement of eternally recurring woes, to block the utopian's way. From Ecclesiastes, we get the idea that maturity consists in resignation to the fact that life is made up necessarily of alternations of pleasure and pain, woe and joy, good fortune and bad fortune. "Earth-wisdom" accords fullness of being to everything that happens, and finds a place for it in some economy of the universe. There is no idea more lovely in the abstract; there is no idea which better serves the purposes of great art, art aspiring to a Homeric condition. But there is no idea which is more debilitating in its influence on reformist endeavor of any kind, including the utopian kind.

One of the strangest sentiments a utopian apologist can encounter is that pain *is* reality, and pleasure is a deception or illusion.[4] We do not here refer to any religious estimation of the

2. Aldous Huxley, *Brave New World* (New York: Harper, 1932), Chap. 17. A much milder statement of Savage's position can be found in two books by René Dubos: *The Mirage of Health* (New York: Harper, 1954), Chap. 8, and *The Dreams of Reason* (New York: Columbia University Press, 1961), Chap. 4.

3. For almost the best attack ever made on the standard kind of nonsense about the marvelousness of pain, see the great Tory essay of Dr. Johnson, "A Review of Soame Jenyns' *A Free Inquiry into the Nature and Origin of Evil*" in *Works* (2 vols., New York: Harper, n.d.), Vol. II, pp. 604–613. See also the excellent summary by H. J. McCloskey in "God and Evil," *The Philosophical Quarterly*, X (April, 1960), pp. 97-114.

4. Miguel de Unamuno said: "And how do we know that we exist if we do not suffer, little or much? How can we turn upon ourselves, acquire reflective consciousness save by suffering? When we enjoy ourselves we

vanity of human wishes and satisfactions and of the concomitant greatness of divine or eternal things. In several of the essays collected in *The Opposing Self*,[5] Lionel Trilling has spoken of this sentiment, and connected it to the political cruelties of our time, to which men have responded not only with horror but also with fascination. Trilling says, "We are in love, at least in our literature, with the fantasy of death. Death and suffering, when we read, are our only means of conceiving the actuality of life."[6] Trilling also condemns the view that ". . . only by an extremity of pain could we be made to realize that a *being* was actually involved, that a life has been sacrificed—or, indeed has been lived."[7] And any utopian thinker must warmly endorse Trilling's praise of the imagination of joy, and of all those writers —for example, Wordsworth, Keats, and Tolstoy—who can write persuasively of pleasure, joy, happiness, contentment, who can make these things seem real. The point is not to have men close their eyes to the existence of radical evil, but to have them see that there is something in the real world besides radical evil, and that a society, such as utopia, dedicated to the total elimina-

---

forget ourselves, forget that we exist; we pass over into another, an alien being, we alienate ourselves. And we become centered in ourselves again, we return to ourselves, only by suffering." [*The Tragic Sense of Life*, trans. by J. E. Crawford Flitch (London: Macmillan, 1921), p. 140.] See also Hannah Arendt, *The Human Condition* (Chicago: University of Chicago Press, 1958), pp. 120–121; and William Empson's poem, "This Last Pain" in *Collected Poems* (London: Chatto & Windus, 1956), p. 32, for two recent utterances on the unreality of happiness or pleasure. An attack on utopia can also be made by those who say that *pain* is unreal, an illusion. All of life is spectral: it is nothing but one huge game or play, and nothing that happens in it should affect the soul, the inner man. This view goes "beyond tragedy." For a recent discussion of this ancient view see Newton Arvin, "The House of Pain: Emerson and the Tragic Sense," *Hudson Review*, XII (Spring, 1959), pp. 37–53. The utopian must insist on the reality of both pain and pleasure. He must say that the eradication of pain is the eradication of something *really* dreadful; he must also say that the substitution of a life of happiness or joy or satisfaction or contentment or pleasure for a life of pain is the substitution of a better kind of reality for a worse kind.

5. See the following essays: "Anna Karenina," "William Dean Howells and the Roots of Modern Taste," "Wordsworth and the Rabbis" in *The Opposing Self* (1955) (New York: Compass Books, 1959).

6. Trilling, *The Opposing Self*, *op. cit.*, p. 146.

7. *Ibid.*, p. 147.

tion of radical evil is not dedicating itself to nonreality. The tranquillity of a utopian society is not, in theory, the tranquillity given by "tranquilizer pills": the latter is, of course, at its extremest, a species of nonreality, as Huxley has so memorably shown in *Brave New World*.

It is not too much to say that a fear of pleasure can often be detected. This fear has ancient roots in the primal Greek view of ". . . too much success and its punishment by jealous deity."[8] (Recall the story Herodotus tells of Polycrates and his ring.) There is a sense that there is some force at work in the universe which constantly seeks to overturn whatever is too good and ruin anyone who is too happy. Emerson speaks in "Compensation" of "the terror of cloudless noon." Frost has a splendid poem on how "Nothing Gold Can Stay." Hawthorne's narrator of *The Blithedale Romance* welcomes the entrance of a decrepit old man into the utopian community as a kind of counterweight to too much contentment, as a kind of insurance against the displeasure of the darker forces. There is no doubt that one of the most common human feelings is anxiety at good fortune. But utopia is built in defiance of that anxiety: its aim is precisely to accustom men to happiness, and make of happiness the normal condition of life.

But the antiutopian may persist: what about the wisdom which only suffering can give? With all the other things it rules out, does utopia rule out wisdom as well? Placed on the defensive by seeming to be against wisdom, the utopian can reply that if the wisdom that comes from suffering is really only wisdom about the meaning of suffering and how to behold it, account for it, and finally accept it, then wisdom will surely be a casualty of utopia. It is excellent if suffering can bring wisdom, but would one willingly suffer to be wise? (Shall we continue in sin, that grace may abound? God forbid.[9]) And would the wisdom gained by someone who suffered deliberately to gain it

8. See E. R. Dodds, *The Greeks and the Irrational* (1951) (Boston: Beacon Press, 1957), p. 31. See Chap. II, esp. pp. 28–31, and n. 8, p. 51; and M. P. Nilsson, *Greek Piety*, trans. by H. J. Rose (Oxford: Clarendon Press, 1948), pp. 54–59.

9. Romans, VI, 1-2. The implications for utopianism of St. Paul's question and answer are indeed great.

130 UTOPIA AND ITS ENEMIES

be the same as the wisdom gained by someone who had been
violated by suffering, who had suffered against his will?[10] (The
trouble with so many of the blessings of preutopia is that they
are compensations which cannot be deliberately sought, but
must be allowed to come, if they are to come at all, at their
own pleasure and speed. The compensations may be rich, and
we are glad that out of evil a great good sometimes emerges.
But they cannot be planned for; if they are planned for, not
they but illusory substitutes are got. Men must work to the limit
to avoid what makes wisdom, for example, possible, immense
a compensation as it is.) And, finally, does not suffering corrupt
much more often than it ennobles?

Related to the idea that suffering is needed for wisdom is
the idea that culture is inherently bound up with both suffering
and neurosis. The latter idea can be broken down into three
parts: (1) neurosis and suffering are necessary for creating
works of art and engaging in any serious intellectual endeavor;
(2) neurosis or suffering or both are necessary for the comprehension or appreciation of works of art and works of the mind;
(3) suffering is the necessary raw material or subject-matter
on which artists and intellectuals must work. (One recalls the
major contention of Freud's *Civilization and its Discontents:*
suffering in the form of instinctual repression is the foundation
of all the enterprises of civilization. A cynic could say that the
world has produced thought and art by giving leisure to some
and suffering to all.) The really troubling part of the idea is the
first: if that could be taken care of by an utopian apologist, the
other two parts would take care of themselves. In *Walden Two,*
B. F. Skinner assures us that the arts would flourish in his painless community; and one would like to believe him. But there
is not enough to go on. And aside from Lionel Trilling's essay,
"Art and Neurosis" (in *The Liberal Imagination*), one wonders
whether anything sensible has yet been said on the question of
the necessity of suffering and neurosis for creativity. Trilling

10. See Simone Weil, *Cahiers* I (Paris: Plon, 1951), p. 211, and
Cahiers II (Paris: Plon, 1953), pp. 180-181. She reminds us that though
the Christian knows that temptations test virtue, he still prays, "lead us
not into temptation." This attitude is to extend to suffering, most generally.

tries to show that neurosis is not sufficient for creativity: after all, everybody is neurotic (to put the matter crudely), but only a very few create. It may still be the case, however, that neurosis is necessary for creativity. And if that is, in fact, the case, then the utopian has immense cause for worry. Hopefully, it may be an undemonstrable romanticism that neurosis and suffering *are* needed for the production of art and thought. Though some utopians—for example, Morelly and William Morris—can allow the life of the mind to disappear from their utopias (in the name of equality), we surely could not. Modern utopianism must start from the premise that life without learning and scholarship, philosophical speculation and scientific research, imaginative literature and the fine arts, would not be life at all. No amount of general well-being could compensate for their loss.

What must truly trouble the utopian idealist is the general charge that it is precisely by hedonistic standards that utopia falls short: by gratifying all wants so readily and so fully, utopia will in the end produce the most debilitating surfeit and boredom. The picture of men at ease and in the middle of plenty is so awful to contemplate just because everyone knows how soon one tires of what one has been given, rather than taken, and been given before one knew one wanted it. As William James wrote in "The Dilemma of Determinism" (1884):

Everyone must at some time have wondered at that strange paradox of our moral nature, that, though the pursuit of outward good is the breath of its nostrils, the attainment of outward good would seem to be its suffocation and death. Why does the painting of any paradise or utopia, in heaven or on earth, awaken such yawnings for nirvana and escape?[11]

Moral psychology abounds in commonplaces to the effect that something is especially desired or appreciated when one has lost it, or when one has failed after great exertion to get it, or when one is threatened with its possible loss, or when one

---

11. William James, *Essays on Faith and Morals* (New York: Longmans, Green, 1947), p. 165. See also pp. 164–175 of this essay, as well as two other essays by James: "The Gospel of Relaxation" and "What Makes a Life Significant?" both reprinted in *Essays on Faith and Morals*. The latter essay contains a marvelous description of James's feelings about the Chautauqua community, and its lack of human nature *in extremis*.

knows that its loss is sooner or later inevitable, or when one
has worked hard to earn it, or given up something else to get it,
or when one has it only fleetingly or intermittently, or when
one must have it concomitantly with something else one does not
want to have, or when it is forbidden, or when one gets it unex-
pectedly or after having given up hope of ever getting it, or when
one has it and others do not. (The very conditions thought by
some to be needed for pleasure and appreciation are thought by
others to prove the vanity of pleasure and appreciation.) Does
not utopia eliminate all these situations? And if it does, does it
not also eliminate the possibility of ascribing worth to anything
and of having a sensible scale of values, by making all things
instantaneously attainable? Does it not eliminate all true happiness, and leave men with alternations of gluttony and listless-
ness? It is not a question of puritan self-mortification, or of wanting asceticism for its own sake. Rather it is a question of whether
or not utopia kills pleasure by the way and the degree to which
it confers it. If people have everything, they will cherish nothing.
Pleasure to be pleasure must have the accompaniment of pain:
why, St. Augustine in his reflections on eternal felicity insists
that the inhabitants of heaven itself must have a remembrance
of their own earthly ills and a knowledge of the ills of the damned
in hell in order to know the value of their estate.[12] "Pleasure"
can be understood only in relation to "pain," as "life" can be
understood only in relation to "death." Milton, in *Paradise Lost*
(IV, 222) speaks of "Knowledge of Good bought dear by knowing ill." Which is to say that one cannot be constantly well off
and at the same time know that one is well off: paradise to be
known as paradise must be lost (though, hopefully, it is to be
regained). In one of the most gently ironic sentences ever written,
Rousseau said to the citizens of Geneva: ". . . your happiness is
complete, and you have nothing to do but enjoy it; you require
nothing more to be made perfectly happy than to know how to

---

12. St. Augustine, *The City of God* (New York: The Modern Library,
1950), XXII, 30. But in Dante's *Purgatory,* part of the preparation for
Heaven consists of drinking the waters of Lethe and Eunoè. The waters of
the first take away remembrance of sin and suffering; the waters of the
second restore remembrance of earthly goodness. See *Purgatory*, XXVIII,
lines 121-132.

be satisfied with being so."[13] As if those who were content had to be told they were content for them to know it: they could know it without being told only if they had some experience—direct or indirect—of unhappiness. One of the great lessons of Proust is that real pleasure is usually relief from pain, balm for a hurt, or recovery of a loss. Or, to invoke the authority of Freud again: ". . . we are so constituted that we can only intensely enjoy contrasts, much less intensely states in themselves."[14] In sum, pleasure needs difficulty, austerity, contrariety, comparison: and utopians, thinking they enhance pleasure by removing these things, only diminish pleasure. The utopian wants to look on the pleasure of the nonutopian world in the same way in which St. Augustine looked upon the wonders of the fallen world: "And all these are but the solace of the wretched and condemned, not the rewards of the blessed."[15] And yet the utopian is told that rewards to be rewards must be solaces. Want is the mother of Love. And "Death is the mother of beauty." (Sometimes it is the mortality of the beholder, sometimes it is the fragility of the beheld, that is meant to provide the force behind such a sentiment.) Wilderness is paradise enow.

Modern utopianism hopes to give people what people have always said they wanted. Yet there are some who say that such a gift would not truly satisfy the recipients of it. Men, as we know them, could not and would not want to live in a modern utopia. This is enough by itself to demonstrate that the aspirations of modern utopianism have no special urgency. The possibility that

---

13. Jean Jacques Rousseau, *A Discourse on the Origin of Inequality* in *The Social Contract and Discourses,* trans. by G. D. H. Cole, (New York: Everyman's Library, 1950), Dedication, p. 182.

14. Sigmund Freud, *Civilization and Its Discontents* (London: Hogarth Press, 1930), p. 28. This is a major theme in the poetry of Emily Dickinson. Consider, for example, this poem: "Water, is taught by thirst / Land —by the oceans passed. / Transport—by throe—/ Peace—by its battles told—/ Love, by memorial mold—/ Birds, by the snow." [*The Poems of Emily Dickinson,* ed. by Thomas H. Johnson (3 vols., Cambridge, Mass.: Harvard University Press, 1955, Vol. I, p. 96.)] See Richard Wilbur, "Sumptuous Destitution," in *Emily Dickinson: Three Views* (Amherst, Mass.: Amhert College Press, 1960), pp. 35–46.

15. St. Augustine, *The City of God, op. cit.,* XXII, 24 (p. 855). Cf. the fierce remark of Dr. Johnson in his review of Soame Jenyns, *op. cit.,* p. 606: ". . . the transports of recovery only prove the intenseness of the pain."

psychologists in utopia could train people to bear more easily the burdens of prosperity does not go far to save utopianism from embarrassment: psychologists could conceivably train people to bear almost any burden. Why train them for well-being, rather than for something else? Perhaps for something more noble or heroic?

The antiutopian could also press the charge that abundance not only prevented the soul from acquiring certain virtues like humility and perseverence, but also made impossible the exercise of certain other virtues like charity and gratitude, magnanimity and munificence, all of which depend on scarcity and inequality. The utopian apologist would probably be willing to sustain that loss.[16] (Again, the trouble with so many of the virtues and qualities of preutopia is that they are splendid adaptations to conditions of want, turmoil, and travail, and in the face of raging appetites and inclinations; they represent humanity's coming to terms with a world that is in most respects deficient from a hedonist point of view. That men have "pitched the mansion" of their civilized behavior on such an unpromising base is endless cause for marvel. But is it not possible that other virtues and qualities await the birth of utopia?)

It is not simple for the utopian to defend himself against such a line of argument, but he could begin by making one easy point. That is that the economic health of utopia does not have to depend on maintaining any particular level of consumption: production will be governed by need, need will not be excited to sustain production. There will be no economic reason to have any other situation. Hence, planned obsolescence and a neurotic ravenous consumption—things sometimes associated with utopia —need not be found in utopia.

The utopian must then ask himself on what else he can rely to avoid having the gloomy predictions of the antiutopians come true. If it is in the power of utopia to exclude all or most of the things that have caused men pain from the beginning of time, and if the goods are on hand to satisfy the full range of what preutopians would consider normal human wants, could

---

16. See William Blake's poem "The Human Abstract" in *Songs of Experience.*

the utopian leave it to men to gratify those wants in such a way
as to avoid ennui, and the despair of those who never lack? (Dr.
Johnson entitled the third chapter of Rasselas, "The Wants of
Him That Wants Nothing.") Or would the utopian hope that
utopian technology would prove to be so versatile as to be able
indefatigably to arouse and fulfill a continuous succession of
wants and desires? Or would the utopian take the way out that
the controllers of Huxley's *Brave New World* took, that is, employ sophisticated techniques of control over human nature in
order to disable the vast majority of men from ever lamenting
their unrelieved (and low-level) satisfaction? Or would the
utopian, following the example of Burke, place his trust in some
religion to be the opiate of the prosperous?[17] Or would the
utopian take it upon himself to introduce a carefully regulated
amount of pain, mischief, and trouble into his otherwise cloudless utopia in the name of pleasure? Or would the utopian have
to concede that since life in utopia had none of the depths of
life outside it, it would have none of the heights; and strive to
educate men to acceptance of, and accommodation to, a more
temperate world?

Clearly, the answers of Burke and of the controllers of
Huxley's *Brave New World* are unacceptable: utopia disallows
opiates; and the aim of utopia is the welfare of recognizably
human beings, which the bulk of inhabitants of *Brave New
World* are not. As for the suggestion that utopian planners introduce a carefully regulated amount of misfortune into utopia for
pleasure's sake, two things could be said. There is, first, something morally disturbing, on the face of it, about playing with
misfortune, about permitting any evil to exist that could be
gotten rid of, about creating evil where there was none before.
(This may be a superstitious attitude: utopian people, unacquainted with radical evil, would perhaps not take such a
traumatized view of *all* evil, including lesser cares and troubles.)
It could be urged that since utopians already took so much into
their hands when they took the world, there would be no reason

---

17. Edmund Burke, *Reflections on the Revolution in France* (London:
Everyman's Library, 1910), p. 99. The paragraph that begins, "The
English people are satisfied," is amazing.

not to go a few steps further and see to it that the people of
utopia occasionally experienced certain troubles the better to
appreciate their blessings. Let there be periods of scarcity or of
enforced separation from loved ones; invent unpleasant tasks
to be done compulsorily by all; allow minor diseases and ail-
ments to come into the world from time to time; interject some
real danger into the inevitable gymnastic exercises.

It is not merely the irony of such counsel that would dis-
may the utopian. He has dreamt of utopia as a place where
avoidable pain no longer existed: will he have to reintroduce
pain to have true utopia? Where then is the change from, the
gain over, nonutopia? An exchange of unregulated evil for regulated evil, or at best a lessening of evil? That would not be
enough. The utopian must take refuge in our second point,
namely, that though his understanding of the workings of life
in utopia will be great, it will probably be not so great as to
enable him to think that he could confine the consequences of
the evil he introduced. He could not be certain that the measures
he took would not lead to the disruption of the entire system.
He could not safely play in such a way with the passions of
people; and he could not feel morally comfortable in trying to
do so.

The answer to the hedonistic problem of utopia would
perhaps come from a combination of the three remaining suggestions. That is to say, the utopian would look to the fertility
of technology to give life frequent novelty and a marvelous
richness. He would hope, second, that customs and habits would
be encouraged that would work in favor of a (hedonistically)
prudent consumption of the goods of the world.[18] If this prudence seems too gray, if it seems to partake of all the old re-
pressions of a world of scarcity and thus to carry into utopia the
shortcomings of preutopia, the utopian could at least say that
utopian prudence was not, as preutopian prudence often is, a
psychological contrivance for coming to terms with a hostile

18. See Herbert Marcuse, *Eros and Civilization* (Boston: Beacon Press,
1955), pp. 224–237, for a very interesting discussion of this matter. Marcuse speaks of the hope for "a new rationality of gratification" (p. 224).
Also see David Potter, *People of Plenty* (Chicago: University of Chicago
Press, 1954), Chap. IX.

inhuman world always ready to take back what it has given, but rather a way of savoring the perhaps too full measure of happiness achieved through human effort. Third, and most important, the utopian would accept a world where intense pleasures were scarce. If the plenty of utopia does not lead to a life of acutest pleasure for every man in it because want is not present to act as a back-drop for plenty, and if plenty carries with it its own draw-backs of languor, lassitude, and satiety, the utopian could still feel that the net advantage was with utopia and not with what came before it.[19] For utopia means the absence of all the causes of deep suffering that have ever afflicted human beings; and the absence of this suffering is more important than the presence of the intense pleasures that are unseverably joined to it. (Such a condition would satisfy the hedonic calculus, as revised by Popper.) And surely the pains of languor, lassitude, and satiety are far less awful than the pains banished from utopia. It is hard for a preutopian even to think of these utopian pains of plenty as pains at all. But great virtue would seem to be needed if the utopian pains are not to be oppressive.

In any event, it must be clear that modern utopianism cannot conceive of well-being as either a continuous succession of intense sensations, or as a constant state of low-level contentment bought at the price of human rationality or creativity, or as a constant possession of bliss like that had by the souls in St. Augustine's world, at the end of time: "[God] shall be the end of our desires who shall be seen without end, loved without cloy, praised without weariness.[20] Happiness in a modern utopia presupposes not a few simple desires easily satisfied, but complex sensibilities capable of dissatisfaction, and needing the full en-

---

19. Cf. H. G. Wells, *A Modern Utopia* (1905) (London: Nelson, n.d.), p. 229: "It is slowly becoming my dominant thought that the sort of people whose will this Utopia embodies must be people a little heedless of small pleasures. You cannot focus all good things at the same time." See also the distinction between "mixed" and "pure" pleasures made by Socrates in *Philebus* (44–53c), and the discussion in *The Republic* (583–585). Socrates concedes that pleasures mixed with pain are more intense, but still concludes that pure pleasures are to be preferred by the rational man. Of interest, also, is J. S. Mill's discussion of tranquillity and excitement in *Utilitarianism* (New York: Everyman's Library, 1950), p. 16.

20. St. Augustine, *The City of God, op. cit.*, XXII, 30, p. 865.

gagement of the personality for the achievement of well-being.

The goal of utopia, then, is to educate men who are capable of both acting prudently to avoid satiety, and tolerating it when it is not to be avoided; men who, though they have everything, are still happy. Is it not an imputation of our own deficiencies to think that men could not be thus educated and still be at least as human as ourselves?

The last word on the subject must be Aristotle's. He states the problem, provides the hope of a solution, and embarrasses us enough so that we feel we must attain that solution:

> Those then who seem to be the best-off and to be in the possession of every good, have special need of justice and temperance—for example, those (if such there be, as the poets say) who dwell in the Islands of the Blest; they above all will need philosophy and temperance and justice, and all the more the more leisure they have, living in the midst of abundance. . . . If it be disgraceful in men not to be able to use the goods of life, it is peculiarly disgraceful not to be able to use them in time of leisure—to show excellent qualities in action and war, and when they have peace and leisure to be no better than slaves. Wherefore we should not practice virtue after the manner of the Lacedaemonians.[21]

The *only* tolerable life that could be led amidst abundance and leisure is the virtuous life; and the virtuous life is the only life worth living. Abundance and leisure must finally be seen as instrumental to something higher: to the release of creative energies; and as more efficiently instrumental than any other set of conditions.

Virtue in the midst of the abundance, then, is the ultimate utopian answer to the hedonist problem of abundance. And it is to the question of virtue in utopia that we now must turn.

---

21. Aristotle, *Politics,* trans. by Benjamin Jowett (New York: The Modern Library, 1942), 1334a.

6

Rejection of Utopian Ends:
Against Conditioned Virtue

VIRTUE IN UTOPIA

i

Utopian psychology starts from one simple sentiment:
the feeling of waste which can come over an observer when he
sees the great discrepancy between the potentiality for a rich
and happy life that every infant brings with it into the world,
and the actual life lived by most adults. This utopian sentiment
is to be distinguished from two others: first, the informing idea
of, say, Rousseau's *Discourse on the Origins of Inequality;* second, the informing idea of, say, Wordsworth's Immortality Ode.
That is, modern utopian sentiment is to be distinguished from
any sort of primitivism and from any sort of regret for childhood. What animates modern utopian psychology is not the
feeling that civilization is intrinsically degrading, a condition inferior in all respects to the "childhood of the race,"
a dissipation of the native excellence which all men are born
with, and which only early societies preserved intact; nor the

feeling that adulthood is intrinsically degrading, that coming of age necessarily means the loss of early glory, no matter what the society in which a man may grow up. Utopian psychology bemoans loss, indeed; but the loss is that which all societies (unintentionally or not) inflict on most of those born in them: the loss of the chance to become civilized adults, with all powers developed, and all powers exercised in a worthy social milieu. The irony is that one of the most persistent of all antiutopian contentions is that, utopia, in fact, *diminishes* human nature. It is claimed that modern psychological utopianism, far from promising to redeem the loss which it alleges the world inflicts on people, actually substitutes one kind of imprisonment for another; that modern psychological utopianism threatens, even, to impair human nature more radically and more seriously than contemporary civilized societies may already do (to leave aside the case of the backward societies).

Traditionally, of course, utopianism has shown nostalgia for primitivity and the "childhood of the race"; and, traditionally, utopianism has been charged with wishing to keep its inhabitants in a permanent condition of simplicity: the simplicity of innocent childhood or the simplicity of the "natural" savage or the simplicity of the peasant or the shepherd or the simplicity of the soldier or the simplicity of the philosophical man—a higher or a lower simplicity: a simplicity that stops short of civilization or a simplicity that goes beyond civilization. Whether the utopian stress has been placed on individual happiness or on social harmony, whether utopianism has proceeded from an assumption of abundance or an assumption of scarcity, critics have claimed that utopianism has achieved its ends at the cost of the manliness or adulthood or psychological complexity or full self-realization of its intended inhabitants. In the Golden Age or in Sparta, in Socrates' "city of pigs" or in Socrates' ideal Republic, in Rousseau's state of nature or in Rousseau's ideal city-state, human nature is thought to be terribly mutilated. In primitive or pastoral conditions, the people appear to be somewhat like untouched natural growths fresh from their Maker's hand; in organized utopian communities, people are molded by the state. In primitive or pastoral conditions, maturity and morality are sacrificed to uninterrupted repose and sensual gratification; in organized utopian communities, stability requires the death of most of the affections, and, sometimes, of the mind itself. In the former as well as in the latter, the people do not seem to be fully human: their spontaneous or contrived simplicity of character excludes most of the desirable attributes of humanity: they appear to be either Yahoos or Houyhnhnms.

Recently, the antiutopian complaint has been that modern utopianism combines elements from both of its traditions, from both the Golden Age and Sparta. The end is seen to be stability, and stability is achieved through the state's molding of its citizens; but the citizens are not molded into austere and lopsided warriors (or into exclusively public men or into machinelike creatures of reason) but rather into untroubled innocents, preserved in their innocence by an ease and abundance made possible by an utterly nonnatural technology. Aldous Huxley's Brave New World roughly fits this description of automata in pasture. Presumably, the antiutopian desire is for men who develop their own characters rather than endure being "molded," and who develop their characters in a direction different from the one implicitly or explicitly favored by modern utopian psychology.

The most sustained and interesting attempt to relate the advances in modern psychology (such as they are) to utopian aspirations has been made by B. F. Skinner.[1] And this attempt, because of what it says and how it says it, has called forth a

---

1. See the following writings of B. F. Skinner: *Walden Two* (New York: Macmillan, 1948); *Science and Human Behavior* (New York: Macmillan, 1953), esp. Chaps. 1, 2, 12, 19–29; "Freedom and the Control of Men," *The American Scholar*, XXV (Winter 1955–1956), pp. 47–65; B. F. Skinner in Carl R. Rogers and B. F. Skinner, "Some Issues Concerning the Control of Human Behavior," *Science*, CXXIV (1956) pp. 1057–1066. The two last-named essays, together with a number of other interesting essays, some directly related to our concerns, are reprinted in B. F. Skinner, *Cumulative Record* (New York: Appleton-Century-Crofts, 1959): see especially "Current Trends in Experimental Psychology," and "The Flight from the Laboratory." In October, 1959, Skinner delivered the Mead-Swing lectures at Oberlin College, developing the views given in "Freedom and the Control of Men"; in March, 1959, he gave the Page-Barbour lectures at the University of Virginia, on learning-techniques; all these lectures are to be published.

most vigorous and passionate attack. Writers like Joseph Wood Krutch and Carl R. Rogers feel that Skinner's program imperils all that is precious in human nature.[2] It will be our purpose here to try to show that both Skinner's views and the criticism that has been made of them are, in certain notable respects, deficient. We shall undertake to discuss Skinner's views not for their own sake (interesting though they are), but out of a belief that a discussion of them is, perforce, a discussion of some of the matters intrinsic to modern utopianism, generally considered. At the same time, to assess Skinner's strengths and weaknesses—as we hope to do—is, in effect, to urge that anyone who comes to make proposals for utopia avoid certain things and pursue others.

ii

Modern utopia is thought, then, to repose on the molding of character. But the antiutopian is quick to feel that the molding of character promised by scientific psychology is not merely the systematic training in civic virtues that, for example, the Spartans underwent (bad as that was), but rather a remorseless creation of the various psychological types desired by those in control. Education is thought to pass over into "conditioning," and thereby become something altogether different.[3] There would

---

2. For criticisms of Skinner's social views, see Donald C. Williams, "The Social Scientist as Philosopher and King," *Philosophical Review*, LVIII (1949), pp. 345–359; Joseph Wood Krutch, *The Measure of Man* (New York: Harcourt, Brace, 1954); Andrew Hacker, "The Specter of Predictable Man," *The Antioch Review*, XIV (1954), pp. 195–207; Andrew Hacker, "Dostoyevsky's Disciples: Men and Sheep in Political Theory," *The Journal of Politics*, XVII (1955), pp. 590–608; Carl R. Rogers in Carl R. Rogers and B. F. Skinner, "Some Issues Concerning the Control of Human Behavior," *Science*, CXXIV (1956), pp. 1057–1066. For a warning, by a radical sociologist friendly to utopianism, on the potential misuses of prediction in social affairs, see C. Wright Mills, *The Sociological Imagination* (New York: Oxford University Press, 1959), pp. 113–118. For an attack on the "Conditioners," see C. S. Lewis, *The Abolition of Man* (New York: Macmillan, 1947), Chap. III.

3. See Krutch, *The Measure of Man, op. cit.,* pp. 68–69; Hacker,

seem to be no limits on the ability to make people what you want them to be. Not merely is it frightening that people could be made into lesser beings, easy to manipulate and govern; the very fact that people could be said to be *made* into something— actually, made into almost anything at all, good or bad—is frightening by itself. Aside from the terrible possibility that psychological knowledge of the most refined sort could fall into the hands of evil men, it is humiliating to think that human beings can be known through and through and handled as if they were creatures of the utmost plasticity.

It is safe to say that the fiercest antiutopian hostility is reserved for anyone who without hesitation seeks to know ever more about human behavior and then to apply his knowledge in the real world. The exact extent to which advances in the study of human nature should be put to use in the upbringing and education of human beings is a matter of the liveliest controversy. But this much is sure: the critics of Skinner's behaviorist utopianism think that a line can be drawn between guidance and education, on the one hand, and control and conditioning on the other. And when that line is crossed, that is, when

---

"Dostoyevsky's Disciples: Men and Sheep in Political Theory," *op. cit.*, esp. p. 608; Anonymous, "A Hundred Years After," a review of Isaiah Berlin, *Two Concepts of Liberty, The Times* (*London*) *Literary Supplement*, Feb. 20, 1959, pp. 89–90, esp. p. 90. The reasons for distinguishing between education and conditioning are not always made clear. Throughout, we go on the assumption that conditioning is a more effective kind of education; and that the aims of conditioning are those of education. Conditioning would deserve the abuse heaped on it if its critics could show that conditioning, most widely understood, invariably implied either or both of the two following things: first, the creation of behavior which bears no "normal" or "natural" or "usual" relation to the "stimuli" or outside conditions present; second, the creation of behavior which does bear a normal or natural or usual relation, but where the subject, the person, misunderstands or does not perceive the cause of that relation, or does not understand why the behavior is created. Skinner's system seems innocent of the first of the sinister implications of conditioning. In the case of children, however, Skinner's system is not innocent of the second implication. But no kind of education can be, even though Rousseau, in *Émile*, tries desperately to devise a system that is. The important issue is whether or not the adults of Walden Two remain *perpetual* children, ignorant of how it is come about that they act as they act, and ignorant of the reasons why they have been made to act in the ways in which they act. We discuss this issue later in this chapter.

scientific psychology moves to acquire a complete understanding of, and eventually a complete power over, human behavior, then Krutch, Rogers and others feel that men's dignity or morality or rationality is gravely threatened.

iii

In the face of this hostility to Skinner, it is only natural to try to see just where Skinner begins, to see which values guide Skinner in his enterprise of applying psychological knowledge to human affairs. It must first be said that Skinner has the grace to acknowledge in his novel *Walden Two*[4] that one of the ingredients of his "science of human behavior" is the sheer desire to *know*, to understand human nature for the sake of understanding it, irrespective of the beneficial results of that understanding; furthermore, not only to know human nature, but to work one's will on it, to experience the incredible satisfaction of taking the infant and having it grow up to be what one wants it to grow up to be. As Quentin Anderson said, in his book on Henry James, "To compel others to experience life as one conceives it is the greatest imaginable human power."[5] Skinner concedes that his utopian planner, Frazier, delights in this power. But of Frazier, Skinner says, " . . . we do not fear him but only pity him for his weakness."[6] Skinner wishes to take the sting out of the charge that his science is motivated solely by the wish to display godlike powers, by granting that a small part of the motivation is such a wish; the important thing, in any case, is not the motivation, but the results.[7] We can allow Skinner that what matters is the results; but we must also say that the presence of this ingredient is not as free of significance for the whole problem of conditioned virtue as he would have

---

4. Skinner, *Walden Two, op. cit.*, pp. 240–242.

5. Quentin Anderson, *The American Henry James* (New Brunswick, N.J.: Rutgers University Press, 1957), p. 168.

6. Skinner, "Some Issues Concerning the Control of Human Behavior," *op. cit.*, p. 1065.

7. Skinner, *Walden Two, op. cit.*, p. 208. See also Skinner, "A Case History in Scientific Method," *American Psychologist*, 11 (1956), pp. 221–233, at pp. 232–233.

us believe. Perhaps, Frazier is to be feared, after all. Once this has been said, a statement of Skinner's purposes becomes desirable.

In the course of defending his utopia, Skinner makes such a statement:

. . . a world in which there is food, clothing, and shelter for all, where everyone chooses his own work and works on the average only 4 hours a day, where music and the arts flourish, where personal relationships develop under the most favorable circumstances, where education prepares every child for the social and intellectual life which lies before him, where—in short—people are truly happy, secure, productive, creative, and forward-looking.[8]

It becomes clear from Skinner's writings, taken as a whole, that his aim is to produce a society in which happiness is a condition of tranquillity or contentment, not of intensity and the greatest variety of sensation and experience. His grand strategy is to replace the usual methods whereby society elicits the kind of behavior it wants from its members—namely, fear, shame, and punishment, legally, religiously, culturally administered—by a thorough process of conditioning which begins from the minute the child is born. This process is supposed to result in a nearly habitual and quite unreflecting observance of society's standards, and a general disposition to perform one's tasks cheerfully and efficiently. Skinner aims to eliminate the individual's moral struggles with himself; and also to eliminate from the world the usual motivations that drive men to be good and to work well: fear of punishment and deprivation, and passion to compete and excel. At the same time, Skinner is willing to see disappear the very notions of moral choice and political choice: he speaks of the possibility of virtue even where alternative courses of behavior are wanting, even in contemplation; and he favors the rule of planners and managers, co-opted, rather than elected by the members of the community. And standing behind all these preferences and arrangements is Skinner's use of survival as the "ultimate criterion" for the worth of any society, and his belief that the society he advocates would be the society most likely to survive.

---

8. Skinner, "Some Issues Concerning the Control of Human Behavior," *op. cit.*, p. 1059.

iv

Skinner's aspirations disturb two images of man that have been cherished for centuries. The first is of man as an essentially mysterious being, mysterious to himself and surely to others, not fully explicable by his milieu, having at least a small core of unaccountable volition, and capable of some spontaneous (unpredicted, unpredictable) behavior, perhaps even capable of "uncaused" behavior; at the very least, capable of resisting the combined force of his endowment and his milieu in order to determine his own character, his own self; in short, of man possessed of free will. Put negatively, this view denies that in a given set of circumstances, a given person, being what he is, can behave in only one way. The second image is of man as a being who, rationally comprehending the requirements of the moral law, attains, through his own efforts, a measure of moral excellence, using his conscience against his temptations, toughened and refined in the process and therewith granted a full appreciation of what it is to be good, though forever aware of what it is to be bad, forever tempted or impelled to be bad, falling sometimes, and preserving himself upright only through discipline and strength of character. The struggle to be good makes a person's goodness, once attained, hold fast under stress; the desire to do bad, when resisted despite the power to satisfy it, makes a person's goodness meritorious.

Skinner's belief that human nature is fully knowable, predictable, and controllable gives offense to the holders of the first of the two images. Skinner has Frazier say:

I deny that freedom exists at all. I must deny it—or my program would be absurd. You can't have a science about a subject matter which hops capriciously about. Perhaps we can never *prove* that man isn't free; it's an assumption. But the increasing success of a science of behavior makes it more and more plausible.[9]

Skinner's efforts to devise a ". . . moral training which is so adequate to the demands of the culture that men will be good

9. Skinner, *Walden Two, op. cit.*, p. 214.

practically automatically . . ."[10] and ". . . a world in which
people are wise and good without trying, without 'having to
be,' without 'choosing to be' "[11] give offense to the holders of
the second of the two images. In sum, Skinner gives offense by
claiming that it is possible to understand human nature well
enough to allow society to "produce" the type or types of character it wants; and by recommending that society one day
produce a community of people who are effortlessly ("thought-
lessly") virtuous and eagerly productive. We shall contend here
that only the second image of man deserves defense against the
threat posed by Skinner, and that what matters is not some
contracausal notion of freedom but rather some sort of concept
of moral autonomy. That is, we shall contend that modern
utopianism has a vested interest in the advance of scientific
psychology, but that the use to which a utopian society should
put its psychological knowledge is, in some ways, different from
the use urged by Skinner.

Let us take up, in some detail, the two images; Skinner's
attacks on them; and the relevance of the entire subject to
modern utopianism.

v

When we say that modern utopianism has a vested interest
in the advance of scientific psychology, we mean that only as
our understanding of human nature grows, do we become ever
more able to satisfy the utopian longing (to which we have
already referred) to have no man waste his life on earth. (An
atheist utopianism would be all the more feverishly possessed
of this longing.) Only as we come to know how character is
formed, how people acquire their habits and dispositions, how
their temperaments are formed, how their endowments work
with the milieu in which they live to make them what they are,

---

10. Skinner, "Freedom and the Control of Men," *op. cit.*, p. 60.
11. Skinner, "Some Issues Concerning the Control of Human Behavior," *op. cit.*, p. 1059.

can we devise educational procedures which will deliver us from the hit-and-miss methods we now use to instruct and civilize the race. Utopianism is committed to the belief that the ordinary methods are grotesquely inefficient; and, of course, by "methods" is meant not merely schooling but also all the activities undertaken by parents, churches, and whatever. The simple point is that if men are to be better, they must be better raised (in a better milieu); and if they are to be better raised, we must be better informed about human nature.

In his essay, *The Measure of Man,* Joseph Wood Krutch gave voice to what must be a widespread sentiment indeed: the feeling that there is something indecent or unclean about the whole enterprise of studying human nature with an end to employing the fruits of that study in the task of upbringing and education. It is clear that Krutch intends to defend human dignity by shielding humanity from the probings of scientific psychologists. What is not clear is precisely why Krutch thinks that human dignity is necessarily bound up with ignorance of or uncertainty about the facts of human nature. Krutch fears, as all men must fear, the possibility of psychological knowledge coming into the hands of the wicked; but he does not rest satisfied with expressing that fear. In good hands or bad, psychological knowledge, for Krutch, is a danger; is, in fact, poisonous.

There seem to be two divergent theses that Krutch presents in his book. The first is that scientific psychologists are wrong if they think they can learn so much about human nature that they can, one day, do with it what they please, good or bad. The second is that scientific psychologists are bad because they are quickly nearing the point where they will be able to do what they please with human nature, good or bad. That is, Krutch never unambiguously commits himself on the question of whether or not scientific psychology can live up to its claim of understanding and then helping to shape character. He does not say clearly enough whether he believes scientific psychology is doomed to failure, or whether he thinks scientific psychology should stop trying to succeed, even though success is within its grasp. In any event, we shall take Krutch to be primarily interested in defending the second of the two theses: we shall take Krutch to be saying that humanity has a vested interest in self-ignorance. To put Krutch's point of view in this way may sound like tendentious paraphrase, but it is not. Krutch says:

"Democracy," as the West defined it and in contradistinction to the new definition which totalitarianism has attempted to formulate, is meaningless except on the assumption that the individual man's thoughts and desires are to some extent uncontrollable and unpredictable.[12]

It would also seem that Krutch means not only "uncontrollable and unpredictable" by others, but also by the individual man himself. Of course, if knowledge of human nature were a hidden or arcane knowledge, closed to all but a few, or kept closed to all but a few, anxiety would be completely defensible. But one cannot avoid the impression that it would please Krutch to think that human nature is an insoluble mystery; insoluble to all investigators, insoluble to every man.[13] (In chapters seven and nine of his book, Krutch gladly contemplates the possibility that not merely man but the whole physical universe is ulti-

---

12. Krutch, *The Measure of Man, op. cit.*, p. 76. See also Hacker, "The Specter of Predictable Man," *op. cit.*, p. 205.

13. Some of the limits to the predictability of human behavior are usefully discussed by Karl Popper. See, *inter alia*, the Preface to *The Poverty of Historicism* (Boston: Beacon Press, 1957), pp. ix–x. Popper's argument turns on the point that it is logically impossible to predict discoveries or inventions. (We may add artistic creations.) This contention, however, does not prejudice the case for believing in the growth of knowledge of human nature. Skinner's concern, and the utopian concern, is with knowledge of the formation of character. The assumption is that in a given cultural setting, known by psychologists *from the inside,* certain generalizations are possible about the ways in which people become what they are and the ways they can be expected to behave in various circumstances. It is foolish to suppose that the aim of psychological science would be to compile omniscient dossiers on the second-by-second behavior of everybody during the course of his lifetime. There are both logical and practical obstacles to such an enterprise. Perhaps the aversion of Krutch, Hacker, and others to scientific psychology derives in part from the opinion that something like the compilation of these dossiers is, in fact, possible, and sought for by psychologists. It may be that Skinner is guilty of this fantasy; but that is not enough to discredit either his researches or scientific psychology, most generally. See also Ernest Nagel, "Determinism in History," *Philosophy and Phenomenological Research,* XX (March, 1960), pp. 291–317, at pp. 306–308.

mately resistant to the full comprehension of the human intelligence.[14])

Krutch wishes to link dignity and mystery inseparably. He
would have us think of man as quantum physicists are imagined by laymen to think of the atom. But to rest the claim of
human dignity on the mysteriousness of human nature leads to
very curious results. It is to say, in effect, that a man is somehow the more noble the less his actions seem to be consistent
with each other, and the more surprising they seem either to
himself or to those around him. But why should random or
spasmodic behavior be the sign of human dignity? Why should
self-ignorance be a matter for self-congratulation? The appeal
to mysteriousness is not needed to shore up pride in the unusual
courage or resourcefulness or other traits of character that men
often show in defiance of the expectations of the people who
thought they knew them well; nor is it needed to support a
belief in the large range of potential action that a normal human
being is capable of, and which no one wants to deny him.
What the appeal to mysteriousness does betray, rather, is the
same fondness for being at the mercy of chance or the unknown
which we have already noted in the antiutopian mentality. To
say that human behavior is subject to the mastering influence
of sex or economics or the cultural environment is taken as an
affront, while to say that human behavior is subject to unknowable or occult forces is meant to be a compliment. But why is
the latter condition a gain over the former? Is not the latter
condition actually a condition of servitude to a capricious tyranny? Or rather is it not more like the condition of a hypnotist's
subject or ventriloquist's dummy? And if it is said instead that
there simply is no accounting for human behavior, that the
psyche is part of the realm of chance, that the psyche is not
subject either to knowable or unknowable forces, then the
words of A. J. Ayer may be cited:

14. For a statement of the view that it is improper to apply the indeterminacy principle in physics to psychology, see L. Susan Stebbing,
Philosophy and the Physicist (London: Methuen, 1937), pp. 178–182,
211–221.

. . . when a man's actions seem to us quite unpredictable, when as we say, there is no knowledge what he will do, we do not look upon him as a moral agent. We look upon him rather as a lunatic.[15]

Only when it is correct to assume that surrounding circumstances shape character, and when efforts are made to understand how, can freedom be spoken of; for only then is it open to men to become what they want to be, once those circumstances are under their complete governance. And the program of any utopian whose utopia is not an untutored state of nature is to establish that governance. One of the most persistent themes in Skinner's writings is that there is almost no aspect of the cultural environment that is devoid of influence on the formation of character. If this contention is correct—and is there not a *prima facie* case at least for that contention?—does it not become only reasonable to see how the influence is exerted and to try to move into a position where the cultural environment, to the fullest degree possible, is made to stop working in our despite and "behind our backs?" Must not freedom begin with a consciousness of that to which the human being is subject: the prison of endowment and the prison of milieu? The more we know about both, the less we are the dupes of both. It is absurd, of course, to think that freedom could ever be anything but a function of endowment and milieu. But the aim is to understand, and then, if possible, exercise control over both. As Wordsworth wrote:

> In truth the prison, unto which we doom
> Ourselves, no prison is . . .

One would have thought that, by now, such considerations were not merely obvious, but did not even need to be mentioned.

It must also be said that the recent very interesting writing about "reasons" and "causes" does not seem to help shore up

---

15. A. J. Ayer, "Freedom and Necessity," in *Philosophical Essays* (London: Macmillan, 1954), p. 275. See also Charles Frankel, *The Case for Modern Man* (1955) (Boston: Beacon Press, 1959), pp. 96–98; Ernest Nagel, "Science and Society," a review of Joseph Wood Krutch, *The Measure of Man*, in *Logic Without Metaphysics* (Glencoe, Ill.: The Free Press, 1956), pp. 423–427. Also of great interest is A. J. Ayer's "The Concept of Freedom," *Horizon*, IX (April, 1944), pp. 228–237.

contracausal notions of freedom. R. S. Peters[16] and Peter Winch[17] have attacked the view that causal explanations of human behavior are always appropriate. They insist that since man is a rule-following creature, it is often necessary to account for behavior not as the result of certain inner drives or tendencies or inclinations or appetites, but rather as the result of following the rules belonging to patterns of activity (e.g., games). States of mind or bodily conditions are irrelevant to explaining why a person acted as he did, when he made a certain move, or performed a certain act that is part of his role. The considerations Peters and Winch adduce seem very persuasive, though more work is needed to clarify these ideas. What is to our purpose is simply to point out that Peters and Winch are not saying that causal explanations of behavior are sometimes, in principle, impossible; they are only saying that these explanations are often insufficient or beside the point. They do not seem to be suggesting that the phrase "uncaused behavior" has any meaning. It is true that both Peters and Winch are eager to show that a science of human behavior or a science of society, analogous to a natural science, is, in principle, impossible. To understand human behavior in a specific culture, one must first understand the conventions and practices of that culture: human beings are not bodies in motion; the study of human behavior is not like the study of animals and their habits. All the knowledge in the world about the structure and composition of the human organism will never be equivalent to a knowledge of human nature. Indeed, the very notion of a knowledge of human nature is absurd, if the phrase "human nature" is strictly construed. Again, these contentions of Peters and Winch seem very persuasive. But two things can be said. First, in the case of babies, who are as it were "undifferentiated" creatures, a science of behavior, analogous to a natural science, would seem to be possible. The knowledge produced by such a science would be immensely important for any society, like a modern utopia, which is interested

16. R. S. Peters, *The Concept of Motivation* (London: Routledge K. Paul, 1958).

17. Peter Winch, *The Idea of a Social Science* (London: Routledge K. Paul, 1958).

in the systematic training of the young. Second, as Peters acknowledges, it could hardly be said that, in any society whatever, all or most of human behavior is governed by rules or is included within regular patterns. In the setting of a specific culture, where psychologists are "at home," there would be large areas of human behavior where generalizations are surely possible and useful. When we therefore talk of scientific psychology, as we do throughout, we mean to talk of a body of knowledge, capable of greatly increased refinement and scope, which incorporates large numbers of generalizations concerning the behavior of civilized human beings living in a society whose workings are understood. "Knowledge of human nature" is thus only a way of speaking. What is meant by this phrase is, precisely, knowledge of the "nature" of civilized human beings living in a society whose workings are understood.

vi

The wish, then, to know enough to be able to guide the formation of human character does violence to one component of the image of man as a creature possessed of freewill, namely, the mysteriousness of human nature, the unaccountability or indeterminacy of human nature. We should wish to say that this component is not worth defending or even worth the effort of trying to prove it exists. There is one other component of that image, that also deserves consideration: the principle of self-determination. It is undeniable that the phrase "self-determination" carries with it a host of favorable associations; therefore any psychological practice which threatened it, or any psychological theory which denied it, would be bound to arouse hostility.

Now we have seen that the process of conditioning human behavior is held to be an assault on human dignity; those who wish to defend the idea of self-determination would hold that the process of conditioning human behavior is an assault on human freedom. More particularly, conditioning would seem to do nothing but deprive a human being of the ability to form his own character, to determine his own self. Conditioning is looked on as a process which seeks to take away from every man his rightful control over the course of his development and growth, to take away from him the reins by which he guides his "becoming." That is to say, enemies of conditioning represent it as a reprehensible substitution of one kind of direction for another, of outside direction for self-direction: if it were not for the interference of master-psychologists like Skinner's Frazier, men (ideally) would take themselves in hand and freely choose and then govern the way they mature. Carried to its logical conclusion this version of the doctrine of self-determination posits the existence of a self distinct from the biological endowment and unaffected by circumstance, experience, and environment. This doctrine assumes that the self is an entity hidden somewhere in the body, and that from this entity emanate choices that can in no way be conceived as dependent on, or connected with, the life-history of the given individual. Conditioning is thought to crush or incapacitate this self from its free operation.[18]

It is rather late in the day to be confronted by a theory which thinks of the self as able to choose what kind of self it is going to be, to choose its inclinations and dispositions as it pleases; literally to give itself what shape it pleases, as Proteus gave himself the bodily shapes he pleased. Involved in this notion of self-determination is the same tendency (which we discussed above) of trying to detach the human personality from all connection with anything which may be said to influence or affect it; to make it free, that is, from all causal sequence. This, in effect, is to make the self—as all indeterminist theories do—something insanely random or something in bondage to the occult. What this doctrine obscures is what the existentialists call human finitude: the fact that each human being is thrown into the world, the offspring of parents he did not choose; in a time and place he did not choose; surrounded by a culture he had no part

18. See Carl Rogers, "Some Issues Concerning the Control of Human Behavior," *op. cit.*, pp. 1062–1064. Rogers maintains that Skinner's methods are inimical to ". . . the individual human being as a self-actualizing process" (p. 1063).

in making; educated in ways that preceded his birth, formed in his main outlines during the early years of his life, years which are, in no real sense, his own; and coming to consciousness and reason after the world has done to him what, for the most part, he can no longer undo nor even wishes to undo. And by obscuring this, the propounders of this theory of self-determination hinder the exacting business of trying to see just how all of us come to be what we are; by elaborating a false view of freedom, they hinder men from attaining such freedom—freedom from chance, freedom from subjection to blind or unknown forces, freedom from belief in an untenable idea of freedom—as men can attain.

The important thing to insist on, is that conditioning is not a substitution for self-direction or self-determination. The choice is not between making ourselves and being made by a directorate of supervisory psychologists. Conditioning is simply education carried on with more awareness of causes and consequences, and with more care taken to see that certain things happen and certain other things are avoided. From the point of view of a strict theory of self-determination, there could be no qualitative difference between education and conditioning. Even in the world as it is now, how much do we leave of self-determination to the growing child? How could we ever leave it to infants and children to grow up as they please or to form their own characters, whatever that may mean? It is generally true, of course, that we allow children more freedom from superintendence than, say, Skinner thinks desirable: we often "let them be." And it is also true that much of their "acculturation" is imperceptible and unintended by their parents. Then too, when children are chastised, punished, corrected, that is often a result of effusiveness or anger or exasperation, not the result of a detached attitude that always and deliberately looks to the formation of the character of the child. But it nevertheless remains true that parents exercise control over the child, that they are in a position of "superiority" over it; that, in some respects, it is their helpless victim; that the child in no real sense "cooperates with its destiny" for the simple reason that it could not: "it" has not yet come into any but an inchoate existence. By the time the child has something other than an inchoate existence as a character, its character is rough-hewn. We all have a vague idea of how we want our children to grow up, and of the manners, morals, and culture we wish them to have. Conditioning would simply represent a more efficient way of securing these ends: it would simply try to leave less to chance.

vii

To say it again, utopianism has a vested interest in the increase of knowledge of human nature; for the hope to establish a utopian society rests, in part, on improved methods of educating people, and methods can be improved only as we come to know more about human nature. But naturally the question must arise as to what kind of people, specifically, are supposed to be cultivated by the system of education in utopia. One of the refrains of H. G. Wells's *A Modern Utopia* is that people in utopia will be basically like the people of preutopia, only a little bit better. Utopian theorists like Skinner and Herbert Marcuse seem to aim somewhat higher than the Wells of *A Modern Utopia,* the book in which Wells is at his most detailed and practical-minded; though in other writings, such as *Men Like Gods* (1923), Wells aspires to a very high conception of human nature, indeed. But when Wells aspires, he does not, at the same time, indicate the procedures to be relied on to perfect the race: it is almost as if the mere improvement in living conditions has been enough to improve man. Similarly, Marcuse's *Eros and Civilization* contains some marvelously suggestive writing on the changes that would be desirable in the psychic structure of civilized human beings;[19] but there is little attention to what is needed to bring these changes about, aside from the great faith which Marcuse put in an economy of abundance. It is the merit of Skinner's writings that we can find in them both some conception of human

---

19. For other writing of a "left-Freudian" sort (so to speak), see Norman O. Brown, *Life Against Death* (Middletown, Conn.: Wesleyan University Press, 1959), esp. Chaps. 8, 15, 16; and David Riesman's four very suggestive essays on Freud in *Individualism Reconsidered* (Glencoe, Ill.: The Free Press, 1954), Chaps. 21–24.

transformation and some discussion of the preconditions for that transformation. For Skinner, transforming human nature would consist in so educating men as to make it easier for them to be good and to work well. Our concern here is with the former aim, to make it easier for men to be good,[20] to condition them to be virtuous with far less trouble than they now experience.

It seems odd, at first sight, that there could be objections to trying to make it easier for men to be good. To a generation dominated by Freud's work on the misery of repression and the pain of conscience, the promise to lessen the misery and alleviate the pain should be welcome, should it not? And yet there is evident distaste for a condition in which such a promise is redeemed. And it will not do to charge all those who evidence this distaste with chainhugging or Puritan malice, or to assume that they have become so steeped in their psychological travail that they have lost the wish, in their fascinated entanglement with the difficult, to be rescued or to see others rescued. There is surely something more to be said on the subject.

There is no doubt that the utopian impulse has been, for the most part, to reduce as much as possible the tension between individual inclinations and social precept, to make it as easy as possible to be adequate to the requirements of virtue (as virtue is defined in the given utopian society). Traditionally, utopianism has employed three main strategies to achieve this end. First, some utopian theorists have devised a utopia in which the level of virtue that obtains would be considered by the hostile observer to be lower than the level obtaining in the outside world; that

---

20. When we speak of making it easier for men to be good or virtuous, two things are involved. First, making it easier for men to acquire a virtuous disposition, a mature moral attitude which leads one to an acceptance of, and a willingness to abide by, the norms of behavior. The criterion for such a disposition is a general civility (in the broadest sense of that word), expressed in everyday behavior. Second, making it easier for men of generally virtuous disposition to perform the good or virtuous act under conditions of stress, or of conflict with temptation, or of conflict of duties. The first element refers to the nature of the way by which men become moral adults; the second element refers to the quality of the specific moral acts performed by adults. We do not, as Skinner does not, distinguish carefully throughout between these two elements. However, sections VII–IX of this chapter deal mainly with the second element, and sections X–XI deal mainly with the first element.

is, utopia permits more to its inhabitants, it tries to shrink the area of frustration, it expects less of men, and men would therefore, of course, have less to live up to. Being good is easier because fewer things are considered bad. Second, some utopian theorists have devised a utopia in which the level of virtue is the same as that of the outside world, the prohibitions and the allowances remain the same, but it is made easier for men to live up to them. Two things can make it easier: habituation (or "conditioning"); and a simple way of life, an austere mode of consumption: the range of wants and needs felt by the inhabitants is narrowed, men's acquaintance with the material goods of the world is intentionally limited, temptations are removed. Third, some utopian theorists have devised a utopia in which the level of virtue is higher than it is in the outside world, but steps may be taken to compensate for the fact that the level has been raised; and these steps are, again, habituation and austerity. It depends on the hope lodged in the efficacy of habituation or austerity or both, whether the effort to be good will finally be judged by the utopian theorist to be appreciably easier in utopia than it is outside.

Now it is obvious that the major intent of Skinner's psychology is to dispense with punishment and the fear of punishment as means to ensure obedience to society's prescriptions. In his sense of morality as a burden, Skinner is close to Freud's position, especially as expressed in *Civilization and Its Discontents* (1930); though Skinner is certain, as Freud could never be, that the burden can somehow be lifted by perfect habituation. But where Freud found in conscience (and its resulting self-repression and concomitant self-hate) the main source of the painfulness of virtue, Skinner, in the manner of Hobbes, sees fear of punishment as the major source. The picture of society which emerges from Skinner's writings is that of men held in check, with great difficulty, by the constant apprehension of society's retaliation.[21] There are, naturally, inducements to be good: there

---

21. Skinner does, however, talk about feelings of guilt and shame. He puts these words in quotation marks to show his distance from them (*Science and Human Behavior, op. cit.*, p. 337). His most elaborate discussion of the ordinary methods of social control is to be found in *Science and Human Behavior, op. cit.*, Chaps. 22–26. See also "Some Issues Concerning the Control of Human Behavior," *op. cit.*, pp. 1057–1060.

are, that is, rewards. Fear, however—fear of social and legal punishment and chastisement—is the major resource of civil order. And what Skinner sets out to do is to replace the regime of fear with the system of habit. We may say to Skinner that his view of social cohesion is incorrigibly old-fashioned, and that, as a result, he has not discerned the true source of the painfulness of virtue: he has not learned from Freud about the burden of conscience. Be that as it may, the fact remains that Skinner's passion is, in fact, to avoid the association of virtue and toilsomeness. And it is, for our purposes, a matter of indifference that Skinner has perhaps not clearly seen what the real ravages of virtue—aside from sheer sensual frustration—are. What *is* to our purposes is his intent—the traditional utopian intent—to condition men so perfectly that whatever they desire is licit and whatever is required of them they do without strain.

Habituation is the major, although not the only, traditional device that Skinner uses to minimize the separation between what men want to do and what men are supposed to do. Faithful to the utopian past, Skinner makes his ideal society more permissive in some respects, and more austere in other respects. In the matter of sexual behavior and family life, Skinner is more libertarian than the real world: he tries to eliminate some of the usual sources of frustration. In the matter of consumption, Skinner desires a society that is as simple in its tastes and as guarded in its exposure to material variety as possible: he tries to eliminate many of the sources of temptation. Skinner thus plans a mixed utopia, partly ascetic, partly indulgent; but the weight of his ambitions rests, of course, on a radically reformed method of education, on the systematic conditioning of human beings to socially accepted behavior. And it is this advocacy of conditioning, in particular, that has made him the subject of bitter attack.

What then has led, or could lead, to an attack on a man who says he can make it easier for people to be good? (The attack is, or can be, pressed even after it has been settled that human dignity does not depend on ignorance about human nature, and that doctrines of freedom [contracausally understood] and self-determination [literally understood] are untenable. So much can be granted Skinner, and cause remain to criticize him.) When we refer to the second of the two images of man which Skinner's writings threaten, we begin to see the source of some of the trouble Skinner encounters. This second image of man leads those who cherish it to place great value on human effort and human growth. Skinner, on the other hand, speaks as if his methods of education were such as to leave no room for either growth or effort; he speaks as if the individual, by the time he reaches a certain age, will be, morally, all that he will ever have to be, and that the vexatious task of trying to be good will be finally completed before the onset of maturity—when, presumably, the inclination to, and capacity for, wrong-doing begin to be at their strongest. It can be claimed, what is more, that the job of making people good has been so performed as to leave them with little understanding of it, little sense of participation in it, and no real grasp of the import of what has taken place. There are, in short, objections to the way people are made good, and to certain aspects of their goodness. Let us try to see whether these objections are sound.

Skinner gives his warm approval to a comment made by T. H. Huxley, and quoted by Krutch with great displeasure:

. . . if some great Power would agree to make me always think what is true and do what is right, on condition of being turned into a sort of clock and wound up every morning before I got out of bed, I should instantly close with the offer.[22]

This sentence of Huxley's epitomizes, in a rather shockingly abrupt way, Skinner's central design. No one likes to think of being turned into a clock; and, therefore, one must avoid having one's immediate response to Huxley unnecessarily prejudice one's further response to Skinner's argument. The important point is that Skinner does want to make virtue into a habit; he

22. This sentence comes from Huxley's essay, "On Descartes' Discourse Touching the Method of Using One's Reason Rightly and of Seeking Scientific Truth" (1870), published in T. H. Huxley, *Method and Results* (New York: Appleton, 1896), pp. 192–193. In his quotation ("Freedom and the Control of Men," *op. cit.*, p. 61) Skinner omits the words "turned into" which precede "a sort of clock" and transposes "close" and "instantly." Krutch quotes correctly on p. 60 of *The Measure of Man, op. cit.*, but gives no reference. Huxley's next sentence is, "The only freedom I care about is the freedom to do right; the freedom to do wrong I am ready to part with on the cheapest terms to anyone who will take it of me."

does want to make people good without effort and without thought. Would it not, then, be better for the individual man and for society as well, to have virtue a perfect habit? Or do we lose something precious (perhaps many precious things) when we make virtue completely habitual?

Skinner's Frazier says, "All our ethical training is completed by the age of six."[23] And: "All that happens is contained in an original plan, yet at every stage the individual seems to be making choices and determining the outcome."[24] What these remarks call to mind is not so much a community of clocks as a cast of characters performing a play: the actors have learned their lines and their gestures and movements. The world of a stage play is not a world where unexpected events take place to which people must respond according to their lights: it is a world of strictly patterned activity. And of course one wants the actors to say their lines and make their gestures as flawlessly as possible: one wants the play to be performed: one does not want the actors to substitute words of their own or rearrange scenes or follow their whim. The trouble is that life is not a stage play: life is not a matter of going through a fixed pattern of activity: life is improvisation: at least, some of life is improvisation (not in the sense, of course, of "uncaused" behavior). Since that is obviously the case, Skinner cannot so quickly assume that good or virtuous behavior is nothing but a kind of tracing out of a predetermined trajectory in an indifferent medium. Skinner has Frazier say, "You can't foresee all future circumstances, and you can't specify adequate future conduct. You don't know what will be required. Instead you have to set up certain behavioral processes which will lead the individual to design his own 'good' conduct when the time comes."[25] But this disclaimer is untypical. Frazier could not possibly speak throughout the book of effortless virtue, in the way he does, and take these words seriously.

Skinner's utopia is a small and simple community. Its smallness is a presupposition of its simplicity; its simplicity consists in a far greater amount of "routinized" behavior than the real

23. Skinner, *Walden Two, op. cit.*, p. 87.
24. *Ibid.*, p. 247.
25. *Ibid.*, p. 86.

world affords, and in a general lack of civilized intricacy. It is in the nature of the society of Walden Two to be static, for all the piety Frazier has for change.[26] Correspondingly, the chances for moral crises or even moral *frissons* are smaller than we could reasonably expect a larger and more diverse community—a world utopia—to have. Not so small, however, as to allow Skinner to think that even in Walden Two virtue could be as all-heedless as he wishes it to be. Our general moral dispositions and tendencies can be prepared from the earliest age; but that is not the whole story. Life, even in the simplest and most regular community, gives innumerable occasions when moral reflection is demanded, sometimes over small matters, sometimes over large. An articulated moral awareness still remains necessary. And since reflection is demanded, and since one must be constantly prepared to think things through and to put one's standards to work, moral behavior cannot be completely without thought and without effort. At least some of the time, we are called on to engage in the process of moral reasoning; life in even the most harmonious society would continue to present us with choices and decisions to be made. Surely Skinner is right to want to start moral training as early as possible, and to carry it on as effectively as possible. But is he not wrong to think that "all our ethical training (could be) *completed* by the age of six"? Is he not wrong to think that virtue could ever be wholly a matter of habit? Those societies in which socially desired behavior seems most habitual and least conscious are tribal in nature: custom and mute imitation seem to leave nothing to deliberation. No modern society could possibly be such as to accommodate this kind of virtue. It would seem, then, that virtue, in utopia or out-

---

26. *Ibid.*, pp. 173, 241. It would not be unfair to Skinner to say that implied in *Walden Two* is a conception of change not as a prominent feature of the life of an individual person, but rather as something that happens to a society, in stages or jumps, from time to time, and not at frequent intervals. Thus, a generation may differ in its way of life from some preceding generation, thanks to the doings of the controlling psychologists; but changes of any significance which occur in the lifetime of a single generation do not seem to be compatible with the kind of society Skinner has in mind. The people of Walden Two seem scarcely adaptable to the requirements of a society in motion, even regulated motion.

side it, in a harmonious society or in the real world, must be accompanied by much more *consciousness* (although Skinner may scorn this word) than Skinner would have us believe. And once this has been granted, it must then be seen that virtue must still cost some effort, no matter how fine the method of conditioning. At the minimum, there must be the effort of real thought, day after day.

It could nevertheless be asked, in the abstract, whether it is inherently desirable that life present occasions for moral choice. So far, we have only said that even in utopia, it was pretty certain that life would continue to present occasions for moral choice. If Skinner would agree that this were so, he would, one is sure, lament the fact. Is the fact to be lamented? John Stuart Mill said in *On Liberty:*

> The human faculties of perception, judgment, discriminative feeling, mental activity, and even moral preference, are exercised only in making a choice. He who does anything because it is the custom makes no choice. He gains no practice either in discerning or in desiring what is best. The mental and moral, like the muscular powers, are improved only by being used.[27]

(This passage occurs in Mill's discussion of custom; the words could as easily apply to Skinner's proposed methods.) Now, Mill's view does not preclude the answer: the point of developing "moral powers" is to make a person more surely moral; if a person can be good though his moral powers be undeveloped—in fact, be better, because conditioning has taken the strain out of being good—there should be no cause for worry.

It is hard to see the issue clearly. On the one hand, it could be argued that all that mattered was that people did the right thing, behaved in accordance with agreed-upon standards. If, hypothetically, life were such as to leave no scope for moral choice, if life were so simple as to have all activity achieve an automatic harmony, if life were somehow stripped so bare that there clearly was only one thing that ought to be done in any given instance, would not then society gain immeasurably if men

---

27. John Stuart Mill, *On Liberty* in *Utilitarianism, Liberty, and Representative Government* (New York: American Everyman's Edition, 1950), p. 156.

were so brought up as to be inevitably inclined to do only what ought to be done? On the other hand, is it not true that the practice of moral choice has other than moral consequences for character? Is it not a question of a general fullness of *psyche* that is here at stake? Is it not true, that is, that choice—moral or otherwise—is the hallmark of the civilized man, and that it is the ever-present necessity to choose that distinguishes humanity from the rest of creation and the cultivated mind from the primitive mind? A society in which moral choices ceased to be made would be a society permeated by sluggishness and indolence, and possessed of a *vegetable* quality; it would be a return to an Edenic state, and as such would be no mere return, but a regression. That such a condition could satisfy some standard of social efficiency would merely show either the narrowness or the incompleteness of that standard. Within limits, the more choices the better, because choice means thought. And one further point to be mentioned is that Skinner's ambitions, at their extremest, strip human beings of one of the characteristics that separate them from all other creatures: the ability to devise and obey rules. Automatic virtue, if it means activity carried on without conscious awareness of the principle by which one acts and of the reasons for which one acts as one acts, would, then, really consist in going through certain motions, not performing *acts* at all. Automatic virtue would seem to exclude a sense of the purpose for which one is generally virtuous, and also a sense of the moral requirements of a given particular situation, and, as such, is not compatible with what we ordinarily consider to be rational conduct.[28] The very least that

---

28. Skinner's Frazier says, "The code [the basic rules of Walden Two] acts as a memory aid until good behavior becomes habitual" (p. 135). He also says, "But in no case must he [the ordinary inhabitant of Walden Two] argue about the code with the members at large" (p. 136). Skinner's aversion to articulation and discussion of moral and social rules is very much like that of the Spartan Lycurgus; and we do not mean the comparison to be flattering. (See Plutarch's "Lycurgus," in *Lives, op. cit.,* p. 58.) Common to both is a greater desire for flawless performance of acts than for a comprehension of the meaning of those acts. It is the greatest of all utopians, Plato, who supplies the most devastating criticism of this desire. In the Myth of Er, the man who was virtuous only habitually and without a philosophical understanding of his virtue, chooses the life of a

we are entitled to expect from a utopian society is that it not diminish human rationality, whatever the ends may be for which that diminution is effected. Peter Winch makes this point extremely well:

He [Michael Oakeshott] says that moral life is "conduct to which there is an alternative." Now though it is true that this "alternative" need not be consciously before the agent's mind it must be something which *could* be brought before his mind. This condition is fulfilled only if the agent could defend what he has done against the allegation that he ought to have done something different. Or at least he must be able to *understand* what it would have been like to act differently. The dog who balances sugar on its nose in response to its master's command has no conception of what it would be to respond differently (because it has no conception of what it is doing at all). Hence it has no alternative to what it does; it just responds to the appropriate stimulus. An honest man may refrain from stealing money, though he could do so easily and needs it badly; the thought of acting otherwise need never occur to him. Nevertheless, he has the alternative to acting differently because he understands the situation he is in and the nature of what he is doing (or refraining from doing). Understanding something involves understanding the contradictory too: I understand what it is to act honestly just so far and no farther than I understand what it is not to act honestly. That is why conduct which is the product of understanding and only that, is conduct to which there is an alternative.[29]

We cannot resolve this issue; we can only say that if Skinner could show, more imaginatively and persuasively than he has, what energies would be released if morality were made automatic, we would have more cause to lament the necessity for choosing. Efficiency is not enough by itself to make us lament.

Skinner could concede, perhaps, the inevitability of choice, but still feel the basic issue was not the effort of thought but the effort of conscience; that what really mattered was to relieve men of the burden of having to resist temptation. Let it be granted that virtuous behavior must be more than unself-con-

---

tyrant for his next life on earth. Virtue that is only a matter of habit is not virtue at all; or is, at best, a surface virtue. Plato may have thought only a very few men could be truly virtuous; but we do not have to think so. The knowledge we make into a precondition of virtue is not metaphysical or supernatural, but practical—within the reach of all men, at least in utopia.

29. Winch, *The Idea of a Social Science, op. cit.*, p. 65.

scious responses to familiar and recurring situations. Need it be, however, an unremitting contest with the appetites? A permanent war between temptation and conscience? Would it not be desirable if all that a man had to do to be good was to give some thought to where his duty lay and then go on to do his duty free of the torments of wayward impulses and inclinations? Should not the end of conditioning be the creation of the perfect will, of the constant disposition to do what ought to be done, after thought has been taken? What could be wrong with designing a method of education so competent that it trained the passions to the point where, by and large, they remained, as it were, in the proper channels—not extirpated or denied or repressed—but disciplined from an early age?

Now, one of the persistent antiutopian themes is that utopianism shows two opposing (and unacceptable) tendencies in its treatment of the passions: sometimes utopianism tends to indulge all the passions; sometimes utopianism tends to destroy them (not keep them alive and constantly repress them, but condition people in such a way that people are tranquillized or behave as if they had been lobotomized). Huxley's *Brave New World* criticizes the first kind of utopianism; Zamiatin's *We* and Bernard Wolfe's *Limbo* criticize the second. In either case, the discrepancy between what men want to do and what they ought to do is at the smallest conceivable. In the first case, very little "ought" remains; in the second case, very little "want" remains. And there would seem to be something seriously wrong with both cases. The ideal would seem to be to have, oddly enough, some tension between inclination and precept. What matters for us here is not the blend of indulgence and tranquillity for which Skinner strives, but rather the general attempt to make it as easy as possible for people to do the good, whatever "good" may mean in a future society. That is to say, what matters for our discussion is the abstract consideration of the easy performance of virtuous acts, howsoever "virtuous" may be defined, indulgently or tepidly, or in some way altogether different. In the abstract, presumably, it could be claimed that one day psychological knowledge would be so refined as to permit a society to condition men to any species of behavior (specifically, any compound of appetitive satisfaction and appetitive atrophy) it deemed virtuous. But could there be something worth preserving from the ancient devices of hardship (conscience, sense of sin, repression, praise and blame, reward and punishment) which through their very inefficiency and painfulness keep alive the tension, the struggle of virtue? Could it be that this tension, this struggle, is worth preserving?

It is important to be clear as to what is involved in preserving the tension. In *On Liberty*, John Stuart Mill, in effect, defends the continuous existence of this tension in the course of defending the appetites (or desires) themselves.[30] Mill looked to strength of conscience to balance strength of passions, and also looked to the cultivation (or what we should call the "sublimation") of the passions.[31] Out of this psychic economy human excellence would be forthcoming. For Mill an absence of the tension of virtue would mean an absence of energy, an absence of the raw material of human nature. But in Skinner's utopia, an absence of the tension of virtue would not mean an absence of energy; presumably, it would mean, instead, a perfectly disciplined and perfectly employed energy. The alternatives for

---

30. John Stuart Mill, *On Liberty* (New York: American Everyman's Edition, 1950), pp. 157–158.

31. It would seem that Mill is fusing two ideas, rather than distinguishing between them. The first is that conscience checks the passions; the second is that conscience refines and redirects the passions. In the first case, the passions go in the right direction, but tend to go too far; and it is conscience that acts as the brake. In the second case, the passions would naturally go in the wrong direction, and conscience must take the passions in hand and give them direction; that is, it must civilize them. In both cases, the passions are the source of all virtues; though in an ill-governed mind, the passions are, of course, the source of all vices. The conclusion of both ideas is the same: if you eliminate that which makes for vice you simultaneously eliminate that which makes for virtue. A lobotomy is the model for such a procedure. And in two antiutopian novels, Zamiatin's *We*, and Bernard Wolfe's *Limbo*, lobotomization is made to be the last recourse and most characteristic gesture of a utopian society. We may also mention here a related idea that could be made part of an antiutopian argument. That is that every virtue has unseverably joined to it a corresponding vice. Hence if you uproot a vice you will find that you have also uprooted a virtue. You must therefore be satisfied with the mixture in everyone's character; you must therefore not imagine that you can produce a race of men without qualities of any sort. (See Alexander Pope's *An Essay on Man*, Epistle II, lines 161–210.)

Mill were weak passions easily subdued by custom, and strong passions restrained and civilized by conscience. Naturally, Mill would defend the passions, and the accompanying tension, the accompanying struggle to be good. On the other hand, Skinner seems to hold out the possibility of eliminating the tension by eliminating the need for a constantly operative self-discipline, without simultaneously harming or retarding the passions. If it could somehow be shown that the price that Skinner pays for eliminating the tension of virtue is, in fact, the harming or the retarding of the passions; if, that is, it could be shown that the inevitable tendency of Skinner's methods is to produce what D. C. Williams called "zombies,"[32] a lobotomized population, then Mill's argument would apply, with great force, to Skinner's utopia. Let us assume, for the sake of our discussion, however, that the passions need no defense against Skinner; and that, consequently, if there is no tension of virtue in Skinner's utopia it is not because the very source of that tension—namely, the passions—has somehow been made to dry up.

viii

But before we consider whether the tension between precept and inclination is worth preserving we must ask first whether we can, in fact, ever eliminate it, or even reduce it to an insignificant amount, even in utopia, even if the study of human nature were to make enormous gains. This question of desirability is perhaps academic, for the tension may be, after all, a necessary feature of any kind of social life we could find acceptable. Recall that we have already concluded that Skinner cannot cancel the effort of thought and of formulation and of decision from moral activity: as long as a community is removed from meager primitivity, though to the slightest degree, Skinner's aspirations in this direction must meet with a check. Similarly, it is possible that Skinner cannot cancel the effort of resisting temptation and battling with one's appetites.

32. Williams, "The Social Scientist as Philosopher and King," *op. cit.*, p. 348.

And, again, we should wish to say that the great confidence which Skinner reposes in his ability—and in the general ability of scientific psychology—to eliminate (or nearly eliminate) the divergence between what one wants to do and what one is supposed to do presupposes a small and utterly simple and routine society. Skinner's communitarian utopia may seem to allow its planner to think that life could be so plain that appetites remain few and direct, while duties remain few and clear, and moral situations remain few and transparent. Naturally, the task of minimizing the tension between precept and inclination would appear the more easy the less complicated the fabric of society. But even Walden Two is too complicated. And if we take civilization as our *donnée* (whatever Skinner may say), we commit ourselves to a condition in which human desires multiply and, what is more, are constantly being aroused by the very richness of life. Simultaneously, civilization multiplies duties; and not merely duties, but a whole range of other exactions, in manners as well as in morals. Civilization confronts men with countless occasions when duty is unclear or when duties conflict. As the nature of social reality changes, some of the content of moral duty and social obligation must change with it: even in one's life-time. So that it could be said that civilization imposes a double strain: it increases the tension of virtue from both sides: it complicates the passions and it entangles the passions in a maze of duties. Precepts and inclinations abound and increase, and are set at variance with each other. Surprising moral situations constantly present themselves to bedevil the civilized man, who cannot prepare himself, or be prepared by his moral tutors, for all contingencies, well beforehand. That would seem to be the inevitable price to be paid for such fineness as life affords.

If, then, civilization is seen as an inexhaustible source of the tension of morality, and if, at the same time, a modern utopia must be a civilized utopia, we must conclude that it is simply unthinkable for utopianism to include complete psychological repose within its set of hopes. This conclusion does not entail, however, the further conclusion that Skinner is wrong to want to employ the results of psychological inquiry in the upbringing and education of children in the real world or in any hypothetical utopia. All we are saying is that Skinner cannot guarantee an easy and flawless morality to people, inside or outside utopia. Just as social complexity prevents us from believing in the possibility of eliminating thought from moral activity, so the same social complexity prevents us from believing in the possibility of eliminating the struggle with one's wayward inclinations. The aim of utopian psychology must be the traditional aim of all societies: to train as well as possible the dispositions of the young, so that by the time they become adults they possess a general readiness to do the right and the decent. And, presumably, advances in the study of human nature would be incorporated in the educational practices of a utopian society in order to facilitate and enhance moral development. But to suppose, as Skinner does, that ". . . all our ethical training (could be) completed by the age of six," and that adult life would consequently be wholly free of any moral strain, of all tension between precept and inclination, is to suppose wrongly. The only society in which the strain and the tension would be totally missing would be a society so simple or so ascetic or so regimented—or so static—as to defeat the central aims of modern utopianism. Some tension between precept and inclination must be taken for granted, even in utopia: for that matter, even in Skinner's own utopia.

Notice that the mere allowance for change is enough, by itself, to disturb Skinner's dream (and the traditional utopian dream) of a totally effortless virtue (just as allowance for change was enough to disturb the traditional utopian dream of anarchism). We have not so far mentioned what would be, for many, the most obvious and decisive consideration militating against Skinner's (and the utopian) dream: the simple recalcitrance of human nature, the way it would seem to resist all attempts to discipline it completely in the name of any assortment of moral and social values. We have held in abeyance this line of argument against Skinner: a line of argument applicable of course not only to Skinner but to anyone who believes that the development of the study of human nature will permit an ever greater control of human nature. But let us continue to hold this line in abeyance, contenting ourselves with examining the implications of Skinner's thought, and granting him his initial assumption of adequacy to the task he sets himself. Otherwise, the dispute with Skinner would threaten to become simply an exchange of opposed and unverifiable assertions about the redeemability of human nature.

Allowance for change, then, interferes, in theory, with the enterprise of eliminating the tension between precept and inclination. But let us suppose, for the sake of discussion, stability of precepts, stability of moral values and of social expectation in a utopian society. What, on this supposition, should be our attitude towards Skinner's general procedures? Skinner assumes, as we have said, this kind of stability; and then goes on to devote himself to securing an effortless and flawless adherence on the part of the inhabitants of his (and any) utopia to those precepts he takes as worthy of permanent existence. It is obvious that Skinner's general procedures remain a subject of the first importance for any student of utopianism, despite Skinner's seriously questionable assumption that his procedures will serve the purpose of assuring complete fidelity to stable precepts. Whatever doubts it is right for us to have concerning either Skinner's acceptance of stability or his untroubled confidence in the powers of scientific psychology, we must still acknowledge two things: first, allowance for change in precepts in utopia presupposes that, as with all societies, most precepts, anyway, remain fairly constant. Second, our ability to understand and guide behavior *will* increase with time even though it may not increase to the extent desired by Skinner and others. The upshot is that, after allowance for change has been made, and after some of Skinner's pretensions have been discounted, we are still faced with the realization that Skinner does, after all, represent something very important for utopianism. He does, after all, tell us, in effect, that we can do a better job of morally educating the young than the world has ever done before, of roughly (not exhaustively) cultivating their moral sentiments, even though we know that the complexity and changeability of life disallow us from thinking that the moral training can be completely inclusive or completely successful. What then is modern utopianism to do with what Skinner holds out? Scientific psychology cannot perhaps do all it promises; nor can it take fixity of moral and social precepts as a guiding supposition. But Skinner at least offers—whatever else he may think he is offering—the possibility of making it really *easier* to be good: goodness cannot become automatic, but we can assume it *can* become less burdensome. And though adults must continue to feel themselves, throughout their lives, not fully adequate to the demands of morality (and also to the lesser demands of social decency and tact), nor fully prepared for all changes in moral and social expectation, the proper employment of the fruits of psychological research could make a significant difference in the basic social endeavor to make people virtuous. Such a development is, on the face of it, in accord with the traditions of utopianism.

ix

At this point, it may be suggested by the antiutopian that the very concept of virtue is incompatable with ease: not only with Skinner's hypothetically perfect habituation, but, equally, with a condition in which advances in the study in human nature are employed in such a way as to make virtuous behavior, much more than it is now, dependent on the careful and interested instruction of the young. There are those who say that difficulty is intrinsic to virtue, and that therefore the tension between precept and inclination should be preserved so that genuine virtue can be preserved. And notice, they could say, what utopia does to difficulty: utopian psychology is committed to trying to attain a condition in which all things conspire to produce as much comfort as possible; and to remove from the world every kind of adversity, including material adversity and the adversities imposed on one by the deficiencies in one's own character. Utopia seems to tend in the direction of having a totally successful adjustment to a totally painless world. The advocates of utopia want the world marked dominantly by human adequacy, and strive to control reality and to condition men in order, precisely, to remove whatever may detract from everyone's feeling of adequacy,

adequacy to all tasks and demands and expectations. When this utopian aim is examined with particular reference to morality, the scandal of this general arrangement shows itself at its most worrisome, for how could men continue to speak of morality, of virtue, of human excellence, unless we could presuppose that prior to anyone's performance of an act of morality or virtue or excellence there existed obstacles or hindrances to be overcome by the individual in question? To concede, as we have done, that scientific psychology is permanently barred from achieving a complete elimination of the tension between precept and inclination would probably be little consolation to the antiutopian. A significant reduction of that tension is all that is needed to make virtuous behavior a qualitatively different affair from what it is now. And the difference, in the eyes of some, is all to the disadvantage of utopianism: utopianism threatens to banish from the world, together with difficulty, together with most of the tension between precept and inclination, any shred of real virtue. What merit is there in something done with ease?

This line of argument shows the Puritan side of antiutopianism. And it would be fair to this point of view not to take it at its weakest; that is, when it seems to be saying merely that effort and strain are good in themselves, not things which the world must sadly put up with in order to achieve what deserves achieving. But even when this point of view is taken in perhaps a stronger version, that is, as stating that difficulty is intrinsic to meritoriousness, and meritoriousness is (conventionally) and ought to be understood to be inextricably joined to virtuous behavior, the answer which Skinner gives seems unbeatable. Skinner says:

In admiring intellectual and moral heroism and unrewarding labor, and in rejecting a world in which these would be uncommon, we are simply demonstrating our own cultural conditioning. By promoting certain tendencies to admire and censure, the group of which we are a part has arranged for the social reinforcement and punishment needed to assure a high level of intellectual and moral industry. Under other and possibly better controlling systems, the behavior which we now admire would occur, but not under those conditions which make it admirable, and we should have no reason to admire it because the culture would have arranged for its maintenance in other ways. . . .

We may mourn the passing of heroes but not the conditions which make for heroism. We can spare the self-made saint or sage as we spare the laundress on the river's bank struggling against fearful odds to achieve cleanliness.[33]

In short, society is to reserve its praise—if praise it must—for other than moral exploits. Of course, virtuous behavior is meritorious only when it is difficult; and, of course, society sees to it that this behavior is judged meritorious and suitably rewarded. These are fundamental *données*. But if virtuous behavior should become effortless, not only would the wish to judge it meritorious disappear, but, much more important, 'the *need* to judge it meritorious would disappear. It cannot be stressed enough that Skinner is trying to establish, and to get the world to accept, a radically different mode of considering virtuous behavior. And Skinner, in this attempt, is fully in accord with the main tradition of utopianism. When Skinner says that he is untroubled by the thought that virtuous behavior can become easy, and that, therefore, the world can dismantle the whole complex (and inefficient) apparatus it employs to make and keep men good—including the incentives it uses, the prizes it bestows, the feelings of pride in virtuous accomplishment it encourages—he is keeping true to the general spirit of utopian idealism. If the world has always seen virtuous behavior inevitably accompanied by exertion, and has devised its arrangements with the knowledge that virtue is troublesome, repressive, against the grain, the world must now realize that some other way of seeing virtuous behavior and of devising arrangements to secure it is, in theory, possible. And if there are some who would persist in holding that difficulty is intrinsic to virtue, that behavior which did not involve hindrances and obstacles could not qualify for the designation "virtuous," then all that the utopian theorist can do is to allow possession of the word "virtue" to the antiutopian, and rest content with the benefits of the altered situation, howsoever designated[34]—provided, naturally, that nothing done to

---

33. Skinner, "Freedom and the Control of Men," *op. cit.*, pp. 62–63. In *The City of God*, St. Augustine mocks the Stoics by saying that the highest end in life could hardly be waging interminable warfare with one's inclinations to vice. (See *op. cit.*, XIX, 4, p. 677.)

34. Cf. Rousseau's distinction between "goodness" (or "kindliness")

lessen the difficulty connected with virtuous behavior simultaneously jeopardizes human rationality. All difficulty cannot be removed, whatever Skinner may say; but perhaps enough of it can be removed so as to make of virtuous behavior something quite different from what we know it to be today. And the defenders of difficulty for its own sake have not given us cause to mourn its passing (in theory).

X

Skinner's aspiration—the utopian aspiration—of effortless virtue signifies hostility to something else besides the conventional association of difficulty and virtue; and that is the attitude toward virtue epitomized in the parable of the lost sheep (and also in the story of the prodigal son), and expressed by Yeats in the lines from "Crazy Jane talks with the Bishop": "For nothing can be sole or whole / That has not been rent." This attitude towards virtue goes far beyond the ordinary view that behavior cannot really be considered virtuous unless there is some kind of difficulty (in the man or in the situation) connected with that behavior. What we have in mind here is the ancient feeling that the only saint is the redeemed sinner, the only real virtue is virtue issuing from a soul that has known temptation and suc-

and "virtue." Goodness is effortless, but virtue implies effort, the effort of doing what is right despite inclinations to the contrary. Goodness belongs to the savage; virtue to man in society. Rousseau ranks virtue higher than goodness because of the effort required for it: there can be merit only where there is difficulty: and because ". . . kindliness falls to pieces at the shock of human passions." From the latter reason, we see that Rousseau thought that ignorance of self and the world is part of goodness or kindliness. Rousseau did not allow for the possibility of joining self–knowledge and knowledge of the world with ease in resisting temptation. See *Émile, op. cit.,* p. 408 and p. 437; *A Discourse on the Origin of Inequality, op. cit.,* p. 223; and the discussion by Robert Derathé in *Le rationalisme de J.-J. Rousseau* (Paris: Presses Universitaires de France, 1948), pp. 115–116. But elsewhere in *Émile,* Rousseau says, "Happy are those nations where one can be good without effort, and just without conscious virtue" (p. 156). For the view that the ordinary uses of the word "good" imply risks or temptations, see Ninian Smart, "Omnipotence, Evil and Supermen," *Philosophy,* XXXVI (April–July, 1961), pp. 188–195.

cumbed to it, perhaps disastrously, in any event profoundly, and has emerged from its struggle with its own infirmity and corruption chastened, altered, transfigured. Not only Skinner, but utopianism most inclusively, threatens this vision of virtue, this pattern of life-experience. Just as utopian society has little accommodation for the contrast of beauty with ugliness or of pleasure with pain, so it has little accommodation for the contrast of virtue with vice. And if intense pleasure is thereby excluded from utopian society, it would seem that a spiritual kind of virtue is also excluded. In effect, our subject now changes from the consideration of virtuous *behavior*—that is, the way in which anyone in utopia would do what is expected of him, on a given occasion; to the consideration of virtuous *character*—that is, the life-experience by which anyone in utopia would come to possess a general disposition to do what is expected of him, on all occasions.

It must be said that what is involved is not the feeling that all men can or ought to undergo the progression from heedlessness through radical moral *égarement* to conversion and redemption: no one, presumably, would make of this progression a paradigm of all moral experience. Rather, it could be maintained that society must be so arranged as not to preclude the possibility that at least a few men could have this, the highest kind of moral experience open to humanity. But utopia must preclude this possibility, because of its material comfort and its putatively infallible methods of moral training. At the same time, everything in utopia works to discourage the growth of the idea that life is an existentially serious problem requiring a spiritual response. Death, of course remains; but the categories of anxiety, despair, and human corruption wither away. The spirit, without evil, withers away. If utopia eliminates sin, it also eliminates grace. If it eliminates the troubles of the soul, it also eliminates the glories of the soul, which can come only after the troubles. If all possibility of living through the dark night is removed, all possibility of ascending to the highest height is also removed. Utopia cheapens life by excluding sin. Utopia is therefore to be condemned.

Now, this is not the first time in the course of our discussion that we have had occasion to see that the apparent cost of utopia is, in part, the removal of all *circuitousness* from life. It can be truly said that if utopia means the absence of radical evil, misery, deformity, if it means the presence of peace, abundance, and conditioned virtue, it must also mean the loss of that whole range of human experience which presupposes forward movement dialectically. Utopia does not bring good out of evil, it does not bring relief to desperation, it does not soothe pain with pleasure, it does not reward exertion with success, it does not restore losses. What it gives, it gives directly; for the most part, presumably, without prior pain, deprivation, or any sort of insufficiency. There is no doubt that by giving as it does, utopia takes from life one of its most interesting, one of its most thrilling, aspects. For the loss that it thus inflicts on the world, utopia can be immediately and impulsively rejected on esthetic grounds: here is where antiutopianism begins its case. But on the particular question of circuitousness or dialectical progression in virtue, antiutopianism need not remain fixated at the esthetic level in its response. For it is possible for an antiutopian to say that by precluding the possibility that at least a few men can go from heedlessness to redemption, utopian society robs from the store of the world's experience one of its most precious treasures. Furthermore, the average level of virtue would be even lower in utopia than it is now. Though the virtue of the great mass of men in the real world usually betrays few traces of any serious spiritual travail, a certain dim awareness of the gravity of moral issues is often present, a certain manliness sometimes issues from the moral struggle with the world and oneself, a certain maturity forces itself upon those who otherwise have little else to show for themselves as moral creatures. What utopia promises to substitute for all this, is universal innocence; it will send men to their graves bare of any sense of what it means to live an adult life, unacquainted with evil, unacquainted with good.

The charge that utopian society does, in fact, condemn the whole world to perpetual innocence is a long-standing one, and it is not always easy to resist it. This kind of argument would seem to have a greater claim on the utopian theorist than the less sophisticated kind of argument which maintains that difficulty is intrinsic to virtuous behavior. For what we are now concerned with, really, is the overriding question of the *utility* of suffering, pain, and weakness, for human character; not merely the question of whether or not a given act or performance can be meritorious unless first there are impediments to be overcome. The issue is more weighty and it gives prominence to the extraordinary features of moral experience.

A utopian theorist may begin his answer to the foregoing charges by making a simple point which does not, by any means, contain all he has to say to the antiutopian. And that point is that those conditions which the antiutopian holds to be indispensable for the true spirituality of these few men capable of attaining true spirituality are conditions in which the great mass of men attain, if they attain to anything at all, only to a state of dejection or corruption or brutalization. For every man who can transmute his own baser elements into something fine, and do so in conditions of strife or of scarcity or of moral weakness or degeneracy, how many thousands must prove themselves powerless before their own insufficiencies and the moral and material perils of the world? Shall the world be as Nietzsche wished it, or shall it take into account the moral welfare of the overwhelmingly large part of its inhabitants? That is, shall the world be so arranged that in order to prosper (as it were) spiritually and morally, one must be absolutely first-class; and that anyone who is not first-class perishes (or is never born) spiritually and morally? Should a social system be accepted if its highest specimens are superb, though all but the highest are "botched and bungled"? Shall we say with Nietzsche that "A nation is a detour of nature to arrive at six or seven great men"?[35] If the price to be paid for the production of a certain character-type is the abandonment of the many to the ravages

---

35. Friedrich Nietzsche, *Beyond Good and Evil,* trans. by Helen Zimmern, in *The Philosophy of Nietzsche* (New York: Modern Library, 1927), p. 462. Nietzsche is saying, in effect, that a thing is to be judged by its best feature: if its best feature is good enough, the bad features, no matter how bad, are outweighed. A revised utilitarian morality would urge that a thing is to be judged by its worst feature: if its worst feature is bad enough, that thing is to be condemned, no matter how good its best features are. Utopian morality is on the side of revised utilitarianism.

of the nonutopian world and of their own incompetence, then the utopian theorist (and also almost every other kind of moralist) is committed unhesitatingly to the rescue of the many, whatever the consequences to the spiritually capable few. It may be that "sainthood," in the broadest meaning of that term —broad enough to include Nietzsche's ideal of human excellence—is a casualty of utopia. But on balance, the utopian theorist, if forced to this calculation, must decide that a society of a universally high level of happiness that could not accommodate sainthood is preferable to a mottled world that could accommodate it. It would be incumbent on the utopian theorist both to regret the disappearance of sainthood from the world and to approve of those social arrangements which lead to the disappearance of sainthood.

xi

The next task before the utopian theorist would be to try to show that the result of utopian prosperity and utopian methods of education would not be the innocence of the human race. The loss of sainthood aside, is the tendency of utopian society (as we abstractly conceive of it) to lower even further the moral level of the world? If all men in the real world cannot, do not, undergo the dialectical progression from moral heedlessness to moral redemption (luckily for the world: think how uncertain, how precarious, life would be if all took the path to virtue that led through radical sinfulness: the price of Raskolnikov's salvation is the lives of two—albeit "useless"—women), still a large number of men can experience this progression in a minor way. That is, many can go through something resembling a progression in the formation of their moral characters; they can feel some part of the significance of the transition from childhood to adulthood, they can put up some sort of battle with their own inclinations, they can have some feelings of their inadequacies, they can come to have a heightened awareness of the import of moral precepts which they have perhaps taken for granted, they can make and keep new resolves. And, in theory, utopian psychology aspires to the removal of all these situations. (It would be an odd utopia, indeed, in which, say, "feelings of inadequacy" did remain.) Notice, again, that something other than an abstract defense of difficulty is in question here. What is in question is the very quality of the virtue of the ordinary man, the way in which the ordinary man comes into possession of (at least) the core of his fixed adult moral character. In utopia, will that character not be adult at all, but innocent?

Now when we usually think of innocence in the real world, we cannot help associating it with inexperience, immaturity, and perhaps even with real moral inferiority. Adult innocence has been a theme that has attracted a number of writers, especially in America, where abundance and isolation have been thought to contribute a marked lack of worldliness to the American character. The effects of an encounter between American innocence and European worldliness or experience have provided Henry James, for example, with a subject for endless reflection; and American though he was, James consistently (though not unambiguously) suggested in his fiction that a loss of innocence was indispensable, if true moral stature was to be attained, and with it a proper understanding of life itself; and also if the most awful moral consequences were to be avoided: innocence, because it was blind, often worked destructively. James was not the only writer to become fascinated with this theme; but he is probably the most important.[36] And a reader can come away feeling that, of course, James has shown that American innocence provides a splendid commentary on European worldliness, and perhaps an equally splendid criticism of it, as well; but that, after all, in the world as it is, innocence is inadequate, and must give way to something else: if not to European worldliness

---

36. For a recent treatment of the theme of American innocence by an Englishman, see Graham Greene's novel, *The Quiet American* (New York: Viking, 1955). The first third of this novel is crudely anti-American; but thereafter Greene's great talents assert themselves, and a novel of fine moral complexity is the result. Greene's Quiet American is a compound of innocence, self-ignorance, self-righteousness, and intermittent guile. See also Reinhold Niebuhr, *The Irony of American History* (New York: Scribner, 1954), esp. Chap. 2.

tout court, then to some kind of worldliness that is not completely faithless to its innocent origins. It is not sainthood that any of the characters of James achieves; rather, after exposure to the less pretentious morality of Europeans, the conscious and deliberate flexibility of standard and the apparently necessary impurity of behavior of Europeans; and after perhaps becoming implicated in the activities of Europeans, and seeing their (the Americans') innocence being scorned or proved inadequate, or what is worse, inflicting incredible damage; then Americans morally come of age, lose their innocence, but gain in understanding and perception, pity and self-knowledge. (On this subject, James's novel, *The Golden Bowl* is a major text.) Presumably, this pattern of experience is open, to a greater or lesser amount, to large numbers of men in the real world, who receive it in varying degrees of consciousness, and with varying degrees of success. Does utopia, in the abstract, have anything comparable to offer? Does utopia allow its inhabitants to acquire their virtue in this way; indeed, does utopia allow its inhabitants to acquire what could reasonably be called virtue, or does it leave them in a lifelong innocence to which it mistakenly gives the name of "virtue"?

Naturally the immense subject of innocence is not exhausted by some novels of Henry James; and our discussion here does not even sufficiently explore James's own handling of the subject. But for our rough purposes, what we have so far said may give some sense of the issues involved. One has only to go back to the story of the Fall of man, and to the commentaries of philosophers and poets to see all that we are now talking about, in its oldest and most vivid light. It is possible to speak of a tradition within Christianity which sees the Fall of man—his loss of innocence—as a *felix culpa: felix* not, in this instance, because original sin made the coming of the Savior both possible and necessary,[37] not because the forfeiture of Eden allows mankind to come into the greater inheritance of a new heaven and a new

---

37. See Arthur O. Lovejoy, "Milton and the Paradox of the Fortunate Fall" in *Essays in the History of Ideas* (Baltimore: Johns Hopkins Press, 1948); and R. W. B. Lewis, *The American Adam* (Chicago: University of Chicago Press, 1955), Chap. 3.

earth, but rather because this life, here and now, takes on a heightened splendor and meaning from man's acquaintance with, and overcoming of, evil. The exultation of Hegel over mankind's departure from Eden is simply an uninhibited expression of a common (though usually embarrassed) feeling.[38] Especially instructive is Milton's treatment of the subject. In *Paradise Lost,* Milton speaks with magnificent irony of the fruit of that forbidden tree, the knowledge of good and evil, as knowledge of "Good lost, and Evil got"; it is Satan, evil embodied, who impugns the quality of Edenic virtue and equates it with ignorance:

> . . . And do they onely stand
> By ignorance, is that thir happie state,
> The proof of thir obedience and thir faith?[39]

But in *Areopagitica,* when Milton considers the nature of virtue in the real, the fallen world, he can mock the pseudo innocence of those who pretend they can isolate themselves from all acquaintance with evil: he says that now men can know good only by evil, and can be said to be good only after they have resisted the temptation to do evil.[40] Again, in the cases of Hegel and Milton, what is in question is not primarily the sequence of heedlessness, deep sinfulness, and transfiguration; but rather the more prosaic though more central sequence of loss of innocence, acquaintance with evil, and mature morality. Common to both sequences is experience of evil; the evil in oneself and the evil of the great world; common to those who cherish these sequences is the insistence that morality to be morality—no matter the degree of spirituality contained in it—must presuppose some change

---

38. See G. W. F. Hegel, *Encyclopädie,* par. 24, Zusatz 3, in *Werke* (18 Vols., Berlin: Duncker, 1832–1840), Vol. 6, pp. 53–59. This reference is owed to T. M. Knox. See his translation of Hegel's *Philosophy of Right* (Oxford: Clarendon Press, 1942), p. 231.

39. John Milton, *Paradise Lost,* IV, 518–520.

40. John Milton, *Areopagitica* in *Complete Poems and Major Prose,* ed. by Merritt Y. Hughes (New York: Odyssey Press, 1957), pp. 727–729, 733. On Milton's connections with orthodox Christian thought on the Fall, see C. S. Lewis, *A Preface to Paradise Lost* (New York: Oxford University Press, 1942), Chaps. 12 and 18. For a full discussion of Milton's attitude towards innocence and virtue, see Basil Willey, *The Seventeenth Century Background* (London: Chatto & Windus, 1934), Chap. X, Sect. 2, iii–iv.

in perception, some growth, some loss of ease and certainty, some increase in self-consciousness, some increase in scope and force of character. The alternative is infantilism, narrowness, meagerness; in a word, innocence. In this view, there is no fondness for evil: virtue remains the end. But virtue must not proceed by the way of ignorance.

But what of a world in which radical evil is, by definition, missing? What if life has been made materially easy, and virtue has been nearly completely prepared for in the individual soul? The peculiar force of the view of innocence we have been discussing comes from the fact that those who uphold this view had to take for granted a world of contrasts of every sort; but most significantly, contrasts in stations of life, contrasts in the material conditions of life, contrasts in the expectations that each culture establishes, contrasts in style and tone that are indicative of widely divergent *Weltanschauungen.* Thus, innocence must—at least in part—consist in an unawareness of most of the facts of life in a variegated world. Side by side with this unawareness is another unawareness: unawareness of all the tendencies in one's own character. So that when "innocent" Americans, for example, come to foreign countries where life is tough, divisions run deep, and neither peace nor plenty can be assumed, then innocence naturally must blunder, must lack, at the start, an understanding of the possible consequences of its acts in the real world. And it is all to the advantage of innocence to be changed into something else: something that specifically will be able to appreciate the difference between itself and the moral status of others, make allowance for the difference, learn what must be learned, and make adjustments accordingly. And what must be learned is the truth: the truth that life is hard and men are weak—*all* men are weak, including those whom good fortune preserved for a while in a fragile and artificial innocence. Innocence must proceed by the way of experience, as the world— the pitiable world—understands "experience." And in the non-utopian world, the most ardent utopian apologist must side with the world, though he may (like Blake) accord more value to innocence than the world generally does. Innocence is ignorance: it is really deception: deception about the course of

life, and deception about one's own inner tendencies to sinfulness. Innocence must be lost, and can be lost only the hard way.
Abstractly considered, however, utopia does not contain within
itself the raw material out of which "experience" is made. Abstractly considered, utopia does not have contrasts in stations of
life, nor in the material conditions of life, nor in moral expectations; nor does it go on the assumption that its moral education
will leave its inhabitants ignorant of their nature, and at the
mercy of blind forces in their nature. Which is not to say, of
course, that utopia is committed to uniformity: rather it is that
the differences in utopia are not, ideally, supposed to be *inequalities*. The differences are not supposed to issue in tensions,
nor are they supposed to render people mysterious and alien
to each other. Nor is utopia committed to a belief in the absolutely flawless success of its endeavors to make all men good all
the time; rather, it believes that it can make it easier for most men
to be good most of the time. There is to be peace and plenty in
utopia; the causes of suffering are to be removed: that is what
"utopia" means. Consequently, a range of human experience is
removed from utopia; experience that emanates from suffering
and from sinfulness and that is responsive to them. How then
could utopia accommodate the classical pattern of knowing
good only by evil and of being good only after having been bad?
Its desire is to make virtue much less of a problem than it now
is, in the hope of transferring human energies to other concerns:
this is one of the ways in which utopia is to compensate the
world for the losses it imposes on the world. In utopia, the confrontation between innocence and experience, from which innocence emerges altered—stained but redeemed—is excluded in all
its most acute forms. But, on pragmatic grounds, there can be
no occasion for regret: in a world (such as utopia) in which all
are "innocent," innocence cannot be destructive because innocence is not bound up with ignorance of the ways of the world
and of varying human predicaments and of oneself. If evil is
made a necessary part of the definition of virtue, then in a
world from which evil is supposed to be missing there will be
no "virtue." Again, the word may be given to the antiutopian.
But only the word.

Now, it is open, of course, to the antiutopian apologist to feel that though there may be no occasion for regret, on pragmatic grounds, that utopia leaves its inhabitants in a perpetual condition of innocence (as the world now understands "innocence"), there can be occasion for regret on other grounds. It could be maintained that the sheer quantity of experience undergone in the real world makes the real world preferable to any abstract utopian society. The simple fact that a man can trace a pattern of moral *growth;* that he can be acquainted with a *variety* of moral conditions; that he can feel that his capacities in *several* directions (some of them errant) are being developed; and that a *larger* portion of the spectrum of human nature within himself is being brought into play—all this may be enough to lead one to conclude that nonutopian reality is to be chosen over utopian reality (as we are theoretically considering it). The antiutopian can concede to the utopian that in a world in which all are "innocent," innocence is free from ruinous consequences: that is to say, the antiutopian can concede that on pragmatic grounds the case against innocence can be successfully opposed by a defender of utopia, in the abstract. But there remains something besides the pragmatic argument: the desire that on the one hand humanity not be truncated, and that on the other, it not be cut off from a sizeable segment of experience; that neither reality nor the human ability to respond to reality be diminished. And the antiutopian thinker can even strengthen his position with a show of generosity. He can look on the prospect utopia offers with the feeling which William Empsom designates as "pastoral,"[41] the feeling that the innocent man, the simple man, the man unacquainted with radical evil (interior and exterior) is, in certain respects, superior to the more complicated man,

---

41. William Empson, *Some Versions of Pastoral* (New York: New Directions, 1950), pp. 15, 189, 191. Empson's book is of great general usefulness in the study of utopia. See also Derek Traversi's essays on *The Winter's Tale* and *The Tempest* in *Shakespeare: The Last Phase* (New York: Harcourt, Brace, 1955), esp. pp. 111–112, 147, 226–228; and Lionel Trilling's essay on Henry James's novel, *The Princess Casamassima*, in *The Liberal Imagination* (New York: Doubleday Anchor Books, 1950). Traversi contrasts the natural and the civilized; Trilling contrasts the life of security and the life of nobility. Traversi's interest is in pastoral utopianism; Trilling's is in revolutionary utopianism.

the man of troubles and weaknesses, the man who has seen the beast within and the chaos without; but in other respects, in the more important respects, the complex man is superior to the simple man. The complex man has basically more fullness of life. Virtue remains the end, but the virtue is of a broader sweep, a larger scope; it has a more interesting history. The way of sin, the way of experience, the way of loss of innocence, must be the way by which the generally virtuous character is formed. This is the way of the world; this is the way that utopia eschews; but this is the better way.

And there the argument must rest. The antiutopian case applies not merely to Skinner's utopia, but to utopianism, most comprehensively. The antiutopian case is undeniably more romantic than its opposite; it appeals to one's sense of form; it also makes life more absorbing to those who can afford to take a spectator's view of life. Esthetics is, at least to the nonutopian imagination, all on the side of the antiutopian. But whether the antiutopian case is more moral is another question. Naturally, even for the most finicky observer who contemplates what life would be like in utopia, the course of life need not be wholly barren of esthetic pleasure. Though, in the abstract, utopia may eliminate the sequence of deep sinfulness and awakened virtue, and the sequence of innocence, loss of innocence, and mature morality, utopia does not, cannot, eliminate some measure of growth and change: people will change as reality in utopia changes and people will change even without any significant changes in reality, as they experience different things at different ages and from different points of view. All this may sound less interesting in the telling than what we are customarily familiar with. But how much should we grieve on that account?

Lifelong ease in virtue does, of course, presuppose a settled character in a stable environment. But surely the essence of utopianism is stability: not rigidity, not a frozen fixity; but, on the other hand, not volatility, not uncertainty, either. Utopia inevitably lessens the demands made on human adaptiveness: adaptiveness to startling changes in fortune for good; especially to startling changes for bad. The scope for conversion narrows as the chances for being chastened lessen. So that even when it is demonstrated that the hard way of becoming generally virtuous may, as things now are, culminate in richness of character, it would still have to be demonstrated that richness of character can come only by that hard way. Does not stability (with its peace and abundance) have an equally commendable richness of character suitable to it?

xii

The discussion of utopianism and virtue takes a rather curious turn when we come next to consider the question of whether or not a constant disposition to virtue is inherently desirable. What is at issue here is not the proper way to have people attain to a generally virtuous disposition, but rather the simple fact that people do attain to a generally virtuous disposition (by whatever path), and never thereafter deviate significantly into vice. In the name of freedom, voices are raised which condemn the utopian hope to have men stay good throughout their lives *without* deviation into vice. It is, of course, not the utopian hope alone that men be good continuously; it is, presumably, the hope of almost every moralist that ever wrote. This is not the first time, however, that antiutopianism has proved to be surprising: that has been one of our most insistent refrains. But on the question of continuous virtue, antiutopian writers provide even more surprise than usual. They seem to be defending vice itself, not as a necessary preliminary to virtue (that is, not like those who worry over innocence), but as a permanently valuable ingredient of human experience. Perfection in virtue is taken as a cheapening of man's estate; and, what is more, as an abridgment of human freedom. There is a fear of perfection, a revulsion at the thought of it.[42] At times, it may appear that this attitude is

---

42. "Perfection" is specifically disparaged by Nicholas Berdyaev, "Democracy, Socialism and Theocracy," in *The End of Our Time*, trans. by Donald Attwater (London: Sheed, 1933), pp. 187–189; Bernard Wolfe, *Limbo* (New York: Random House, 1952), pp. 399–400; Seidenberg, *Post-Historic Man, op. cit.*, p. 180; Kurt Vonnegut, Jr., in his novel, *Player*

born of petulance or ennui; or a kind of intellectual playfulness carried too far, or a kind of unpleasant dabbling in sin. But at other times, the concern for freedom is evinced with gravity; and from this concern arises an insistence that moral error is the proof of freedom, or that freedom is to be defined as the power to err.

No moral training is to be held acceptable that results in a fairly constant disposition and a usually adequate ability to do the good. What is wanted is a moral training that leaves room for error, that allows human beings sometimes to will the bad and do it, that does not insure that the tension between precept and inclination always be resolved, in fact, in favor of the successful accomplishment of the morally preferable act.

Before we take up this amazing idea, we must make sure that the utopian case does not run afoul of an argument made by John Stuart Mill in *On Liberty*. (It is not to make too great a claim for Mill's essay to say that it deserves to be a permanent companion to any modern utopian thinker. It must not always be allowed to have the last word; but it must always be heard. The essay is relevant at more points in the controversy over utopianism than one would, at first blush, think.) Starting from the premise that any society will contain within itself a variety of opinions on questions of value, Mill goes on to argue that even if a society is assured that its prevailing opinion is correct, it should still permit expression of contrary opinions, and behavior according to contrary precepts (within limits). The opinions and the precepts which a society cherishes may, according to Mill, turn out to be false or dangerous, or merely partial. Or, though they may endure through time, they nevertheless stand to benefit from the trial of competition or from the lesser trial of simple contrast. The upshot of Mill's position is that society should tolerate expression and behavior it thinks to be wrong: freedom should be granted even for error (at least, certain kinds of error). Can an antiutopian theorist use

---

Piano (New York: Scribner's, 1952), p. 262. See also W. H. Auden's poem "New Year Letter" in *Collected Poetry* (New York: Random House, 1945), pp. 292–294: the section beginning "We cannot, then, will Heaven where"; and Wallace Stevens's poem, "The Poems of Our Climate" in *Parts of a World* (1942) (New York: Knopf, 1951), pp. 8–9.

Mill's argument to discredit utopian aspiration? Is Mill saying that error is necessary to freedom?

Several things must be said. First, it is obvious that Mill finds it easier to speak for "error," because he really does not believe that any society is entitled to very much confidence in the eternal and absolute validity of its opinions and precepts.[43] He is certain that what is considered "error" by a society will possess some admixture of truth or plausibility or usefulness. Mill does not love error or vice; rather, he is doubtful that any precept by which some people (though few) consistently guide their lives could be wholly erroneous or conclude in unmixed vice. So that when Mill defends the right to put freedom to the use of error, he means something special by "error."[44] Second, Mill is not urging that people be educated to an imperfect or uncertain adherence to the principles by which they are to live. Of course, Mill is passionately opposed to either a dog-

---

43. Mill looks forward, however, to a time when truth will be dominant in society. He says, "As mankind improves, the number of doctrines which are no longer disputed or doubted will be constantly on the increase: and the well-being of mankind may almost be measured by the number and gravity of the truths which have reached the point of being uncontested." But in the meantime society cannot take for granted that it possesses the truth; and by permitting the free play of opinion it will facilitate the strengthening of what truth it already has, and promote the emergence of new truth. The best condition for society, as Mill knew it, was one in which several moral and religious systems coexisted, stimulating and checking each other, and making their useful but partial contributions to the welfare of society as a whole. (See p. 142.) In the present, ". . . it is not on the impassioned partisan, it is on the calmer and more disinterested bystander, that this collision of opinions works its salutary effect" (p. 148; see also pp. 142–143). It is the bystander who pieces the truth together from various opinions, while society as a whole, made up mostly of men condemned to partiality but prevented from imposing their partiality unsparingly on others, benefits from the compromises opinions force on each other. Presumably in the future, most men would be what only a few bystanders are now.

44. That error is useful to the truth, as inequality is useful to individuality, Mill of course does not deny. But he asks, "Is it necessary that some part of mankind should persist in error to enable any to realise the truth?" (*On Liberty, op. cit.,* p. 137). His answer is an unequivocal "No," though he hopes that when truth reigns, there will be arrangements made for the teaching of error, recognized as useful, but also recognized as error (p. 138). See also Mill's *Autobiography* (New York: The Liberal Arts Press, 1957), p. 107.

matic or mimetic adherence to any principle, moral or other. But Mill would not consider a permanent adherence to a principle that one could rationally articulate, discuss, and defend, to be either dogmatic or mimetic. Mill is interested in championing freedom to behave as one pleases (within limits) when one disagrees with the prevailing principles; he is not interested in championing freedom to behave as one pleases when one pleases to behave in a way felt by one to be wrong. The freedom to err is the freedom to deviate from someone else's standards, not from one's own.

The case against "perfection," however, is not a case for freedom, as a pluralist like Mill would define "freedom." It is a case, actually, for *disobedience;* for freedom defined in such a way as to make its reality recognizable to one only when one has transgressed against a Law one acknowledges as absolutely binding. This position does not allow that a mere abstract understanding of what it means to do other than what one is supposed to do is enough for freedom. There must be first-hand experience of wrongdoing—at least once, in adult life—for us to *feel* our freedom. To remain all our life totally enclosed within the Law, within the system of precepts we accept as worthy of our obedience, is thought to be a kind of servitude. Unless there is a discrepancy—more than that: a chasm—between the Law and the Will, with the Will turning away decisively from the Law, on some significant occasion or occasions, there can be no freedom. As there were those who said that without sin there can be no virtue, so there are those who say that without sin there can be no freedom. Adam's sin is taken as the necessary preliminary to human freedom: *that* Adam disobeyed, not how he disobeyed, or what the peculiar properties of the forbidden fruit were, is the capital consideration.[45] Applied to utopianism, this idea of freedom issues in the claim that utopia condemns its inhabitants to servitude precisely because it aims at making their obedience to its precepts perfect. Apart from the kind of

---

45. See St. Augustine, *The City of God,* XIV, 12–13. But see the way John Milton mocks the idea that Adam should not have had the ability to sin, in *Areopagitica,* p. 733. Without that ability, ". . . he had been else a mere artificial Adam."

precepts that may or may not exist in utopian society, the effort to achieve undeviating obedience to them, if successful, spells the end of human freedom. To whatever ends scientific psychology may be put, as it approaches the point where it can secure full realization of those ends, its threat to human freedom becomes greater and greater.

It is hard to deny that this doctrine has allure. Once again, the antiutopian position seems to be esthetically superior. Then too, the precedent of Adam is always before us. But would it not be fair to say that nearly the whole weight of traditional moral thought is on the side of the utopian cause? There is no doubt that there is a kernel of wisdom in the doctrine we have been discussing. The most fervent utopian apologist would have to agree that if the inhabitants of utopia were bred not only to a faultless (or nearly faultless) obedience to the precepts of their society, but also to a complete lack of awareness of what it means to act differently from the way in which one is supposed to act, then the worst fears of the antiutopians would be justified. Rational morality presupposes an ability to formulate the principles of that morality. And the ability to formulate presupposes, in turn, an ability to say what the morality does not entail, what the morality excludes. Some knowledge of other moral principles, together with the realization that often men have been incapable of living up to the various principles by which the inhabitants of utopia are supposed to live, constitutes a necessary adjunct to the ability to formulate the principles of a rational morality. And if Skinner, for example, or some other utopian theorist, writes as if these requirements of rational morality could lapse without loss, the antiutopian argument keeps its full force. But if a modern utopian corrects Skinner on this matter, what then is left of the antiutopian argument? Why should an intellectual comprehension of vice and deviation be thought insufficient for the purposes of human freedom? Why must there be vice and deviation, in fact as well as in the imagination, for us to be able to say that men are free? The utopian apologist can, in self-defense, point to the words of St. Augustine as a religious expression of his own secular and earthly position. St. Augustine speaks of two kinds of free will, the first kind "consisted in an ability not to sin, but also in an ability to sin; whereas this last freedom of will shall be superior, inasmuch as it shall not be able to sin."[46] Furthermore, not to be able to do wrong is the measure of divine omnipotence. The utopian idea of virtue has kinship to these conceptions. (In several respects, Christian speculation about heaven is a preparation for speculation about utopia. This may sound hateful and treasonous to Christian ears because a Christian could say that a description of heaven is, first and foremost, a description of what cannot ever be on earth.) A secular and modern theory, however, which resembles the utopian theory of virtue is to be found in T. H. Green's writing on "positive freedom," a conception that can be traced back, in modern thought, to Rousseau and Kant. Although there is no need to engage in persuasive definitions of the word "freedom," in order to counter the antiutopian case, it would be well to remember that there have been thinkers, religious and secular—and among them, the greatest writers on ethics—who have maintained the position exactly opposite from the antiperfectionist position on freedom. Freedom has been thought to consist in the ability to do what was worth doing, to do the morally correct; while to do as one pleased, if one pleased to do the wrong, was to be in bondage. These are commonplace ideas which have been refined now one way, now another. Their purport, however, is clear. Given a moral precept which one holds to be right, one could not possibly consider oneself free because one follows that precept only feebly or intermittently.

There is something falsely heroic in this antiperfectionist posture of defiance. One thinks of the romantic satanism which Mario Praz has so graphically described in *The Romantic Agony*[47]: of the shaking of fists at God, and the setting at naught of His commandment. Perhaps in a world composed of Man and God, freedom can be attractively defined only in relation to disobedience: especially if the world of God's creation is,

46. St. Augustine, *The City of God, op. cit.,* XXII, 30 (p. 865).

47. Mario Praz, *The Romantic Agony,* trans. by Angus Davidson (London: Oxford University Press, 1933). See also Albert Camus, *L'homme révolté* (Paris: Gallimard, 1951), *passim.*

in most respects, unsatisfactory to a sensitive man, or if God is made out to be a jealous monopolist of certain moral or intellectual advantages. Also, human dignity can be perversely rested in the peculiar human capacity to act out of accord with natural law; a capacity withheld from all of God's other creatures. However, when the problem is seen away from a theological *décor;* and when, at the same time, the excellence of the precepts to which utopian society instills obedience is acknowledged (if it is acknowledged), then the concern over freedom and obedience would seem unnecessary. Of course, concern would be necessary if men were good in a mechanical or unselfconscious way; that is, if they were ignorant of what they were doing when they were being "good." Then if a citizen of some imaginary utopia suddenly managed to break loose from the fetters of his "virtuous" habituation, if he managed to rouse himself from his "virtuous" sleep-walking, and began to think and to formulate and to question and to disobey, his freedom would be genuinely epitomized by his trangression. But if, on the other hand, his moral training concluded in understanding and rational assent, together with a generally virtuous disposition, then his transgression would be an instance of servitude, which he himself would recognize as such. The aim is usually to have the adult come into an ever more rational possession of what was imparted to him before he was rational. Recall the rhetorical question of Socrates in *Theaetetus:* "Is not learning growing wiser about that which you learn?"[48] Cannot this idea be applied to moral precepts? Who, except for an irrationalist, would take exception? Further, that there would be an underlying moral unanimity in utopia—stronger than anything comparable in the real world—should not be warrant for the claim that utopia is "totalitarian."[49] Unanimity *can* be produced by terror; or by a social system that keeps its people in a condition of mindless contentment, or simply in a condition of mindlessness. But there is, after all, the unanimity on basic principles which men of

---

48. Plato, *Theatetus,* trans. Benjamin Jowett in *The Dialogues of Plato* (2 vols., New York: Random House, 1937), 145.
49. See George Orwell, "Politics vs. Literature: An Examination of *Gulliver's Travels,*" *op. cit.,* p. 66.

rational morality are supposed to come to have. It is this unanimity—neither coerced nor unreflecting—which utopian morality
seeks.

There is a less dramatic kind of antagonism to perfection,
which is summed up in a sentence from George Orwell's essay
on Gandhi: "The essence of being human is that one does not
seek perfection. . . ."[50] At first sight, this viewpoint seems re-
ducible to an identification of humanity with weakness, analogous to the identification of reality with pain or of freedom with
disobedience. The transformation of human beings into machines or robots is conjured up before us, whenever the utopian
aspiration of perfect virtue is mentioned. And the famous formulation of Pascal's is there for reinforcement: " . . . he who would
act the angel acts the brute." But on closer examination, we see
that implicit in Orwell's comment is the assumption that perfection is ascetic in nature, and is to be sought and finally had
only at the cost of renouncing all human relationships and all
human pleasures. In another essay, Orwell condemns with
great eloquence the ideal of perfection set forth in the last book
of *Gulliver's Travels,* stoic aloofness and passionlessness. If
perfection is to be so understood, modern utopianism would
endorse Orwell's censure (though the inhabitants of Walden
Two resemble in some ways, not all ways, the Houyhnhnms).
But there is no modern utopian text in which the ascetic ideal
dominates, not even *Walden Two.* Furthermore, the strain to
be "perfect," involving, as it apparently does, the most callous
disregard or systematic sacrifice of everything we normally think
of as human, is missing from the calculations of modern utopianism. The desire is especially for the avoidance of that strain; the
utopian inclination, the utopian taste, is against saints, and
stoics, and, of course, robots—howsoever a modern utopian may
respect previous utopianisms which idealized either saints or
stoics.

---

50. George Orwell, "Reflections on Gandhi," in *Shooting an Elephant*
(New York: Harcourt, Brace, 1950), p. 98. Cf. Krutch, *The Measure of
Man, op. cit.,* p. 59: "Is it not meaningful to say that whereas Plato's
Republic and More's Utopia are noble absurdities, Walden Two is an
ignoble one; that the first two ask men to be more than human, while
the second urges them to be less?"

xiii

In sum, we have tried to make a rough estimate of the cost that apparently must be paid for effortless virtue. We have assumed that, ideally, utopian thought aims at effortless virtue for three main reasons: first, virtue is painful for the individual man, and utopianism seeks the elimination of as much pain as can be eliminated; second, if virtue becomes effortless, it becomes more certain, and society as a whole will therefore benefit; and third, if virtue becomes effortless, or less difficult than it is now in the real world, human energies can presumably be used more freely in the creative tasks always awaiting them, even in utopia. We have also assumed that there are limits within which the attempt to make virtue effortless must take place: the limits imposed by the very nature of civilized existence, that is, by the intricacy, the complexity, of civilized existence. Virtuous behavior could not become completely routine or automatic; thought about morality must still be taken, choices made, temptations resisted. But we have also tried to defend Skinner when he seemed to be working in behalf of the aims of utopianism. We have concluded that utopia, in the abstract, jeopardizes several of the classic routes by which men come to possess a generally virtuous character; and that the kind of virtuous character which would be produced by Skinner's methods—when Skinner's methods were brought into line with the requirements of rational morality—would be marked by a greater ease in doing good combined with a greater comprehension of what it means to do good. Both the will *and* the understanding would be perfected.

PRACTICAL ASPECTS
OF THE PROBLEM

i

Our discussion, up to this point, has been concerned with effortless virtue in a very abstract way. We have assumed, without examination, that there will be, in the future, great advances in the study of human nature; that these advances betoken an increased ability to guide the process of character formation in a desirable direction; and that these advances can be systematically applied in society, specifically, in a world utopian society. It is now necessary for us to deal briefly with these assumptions.

That there will be advances in the study of human nature there is no good reason to doubt. There is, therefore, no point in staging a debate on a matter on which there seems to be such widespread agreement between those who are pleased by the prospect and those who hate it. We have already taken up the subject of the mystery of human nature as it relates to utopian aspiration, and nothing more need be said in this context. The question that follows naturally in order is, Will an increase in our knowledge of human nature, along familiar lines and also along lines we now only dimly perceive, ever be of such a kind as to make the process of character formation completely controllable?[51] That is, will it ever be safe (or correct) to assume

---

51. Noam Chomsky has said, "Skinner's confidence in recent achievements in the study of animal behavior and their applicability to complex human behavior does not appear to be widely shared." (Review of B. F. Skinner, *Verbal Behavior* in *Language*, 35 (Jan.–March 1959), pp. 26–58, at p. 26, n. 1.) Of especial interest is the critical paper by Sigmund Koch, "Behavior as 'Intrinsically' Regulated: Work Notes towards a Pre-Theory of Phenomena Called 'Motivational' " in *Nebraska Symposium on Motivation*, Vol. IV (Lincoln: University of Nebraska Press, 1956), pp. 42–86. We do not wish to deny that there are serious, and unacceptable, reductionist tendencies in Skinner's writings on human behavior.

that enough can be known about human nature to enable us to think that we can do with it—for the good—just what we please? More particularly, will knowledge of human nature reach the point at which there remains no doubt that man can be conditioned (trained, educated) to a nearly perfect virtuous disposition? Are we to think that vice will wither away (not completely, of course: that would be foolish) when our knowledge of human nature is ample? A specter has always haunted utopianism—the specter of original sin. H. G. Wells defiantly proclaimed in his *A Modern Utopia*—his least fanciful, not most fanciful, utopian work—that modern utopianism rested on one basic denial: a denial of the doctrine of original sin; and Wells was prepared to make the denial.[52] On the other hand, when Skinner's psychologist, Frazier, is told that he seems to have an "unbounded faith in human nature," he replies: "I have none at all . . . if you mean that men are naturally good or naturally prepared to get along with each other. We have no truck with philosophies of innate goodness—or evil, either, for that matter. But we do have faith in our power to change human behavior. We can *make* men adequate for group living—to the satisfaction of everybody."[53] To a man who believes as fully in human malleability as Skinner does, the doctrine of original sin holds no peril; actually, it holds no meaning. Human nature is, in principle, fully understandable; and being fully understandable, it is, in principle, fully controllable, fully governable. This belief informs all of Skinner's writings, and accounts for the certainty he has in the success of his mission.

We have tried to point out some of these tendencies, and Chomsky, with reference to Skinner's writing on language points out others, of at least equal importance. But there still does not seem to be any warrant for saying that Skinner is indifferent to the immeasurably greater obstacles that stand in the way of the study of human behavior. Skinner's *Science and Human Behavior* is full of a sense of complexity. But Skinner does believe that the future of the study of human behavior is immense; and this belief surely has ample plausibility.

52. Wells, *A Modern Utopia, op. cit.*, p. 288. Second in terror to utopianism is the doctrine of innate inequality. In Huxley's *Brave New World*, the science of genetics is thought capable of eliminating inequalities of endowment. Mustapha Mond sardonically explains why all men should not be made "Alphas." See Chap. 16.

53. Skinner, *Walden Two, op. cit.*, p. 163.

It would be absurd if we so much as tried to speak a defini-
tive word about the propriety of Skinner's—and Wells's—and
most utopian theorists'—certainty; and about their dismissal of
the doctrine of original sin. It is clear, however, that the doctrine
of original sin, in one version or another, is the most serious
contradiction of utopian optimism, as it relates to the application of advances in the study of human nature to the education
of men. And this doctrine, owing in part to the persuasiveness
of Reinhold Niebuhr,[54] and owing in greater part to the political
atrocities of our time, pervades men's ideas, and has become,
almost, one of the criteria of mature reflection. What Irving
Howe said of Hawthorne could be said of many of our most
influential intelligences: "He felt that no matter how questionable the notion of 'original sin' might be as doctrine or how
distasteful if allowed to become the substance of a practical
morality, it nonetheless touched upon a fundamental truth concerning human beings. This truth he reduced from a dogma to
an insight, defending it on empirical grounds rather than as
revelation."[55] The doctrine of original sin can be made secular,
supported by quotations from the archsecularist, Freud (e.g.,
". . . the tendency to aggression is an innate, independent, instinctual disposition in man"),[56] and made to issue in the assertion that there is something depraved at the very center of man's
being that neither is caused by even the worst social milieu and
social training nor is to be cured by even the best. The core

54. See, for example, Reinhold Niebuhr, *An Interpretation of Chris-
tian Ethics* (New York and London: Harper, 1935), esp. Chap. III.
Niebuhr distinguishes between the "metaphysical" connotations of the
Fall and the "psychological and moral ones" (p. 76). For criticisms of
Niebuhr, see Charles Frankel, *The Case for Modern Man* (Boston:
Beacon Press, 1959), Chap. VI, esp. pp. 99–100, 106–111, 221–223; and
Morton White, "Original Sin, Natural Law, and Politics" in *Social
Thought in America* (1949) (Boston: Beacon Press, 1957), pp. 247–280,
esp. pp. 247–259.

55. Irving Howe, *Politics and the Novel* (New York: Horizon Press,
1957), p. 164.

56. Sigmund Freud, *Civilization and Its Discontents*, p. 102. See also
Freud's *The Future of An Illusion*, trans. by W. D. Robson-Scott (London: Hogarth Press, 1934), Chap. 1. For St. Augustine, not aggressiveness but pride is the key: "And what is the origin of our evil will but
pride? For 'pride is the beginning of sin.' And what is pride but the
craving for undue exaltation?" (*The City of God, op. cit.*, XIV, 13, p. 460).

of man is unreachable by even the most learned and well-intentioned students of human nature; and naturally emanating from that core are tendencies to cruel or selfish or wanton or overweening or vain or restless behavior. We can be reminded of the supreme utopian recantation, that of Plato in the Myth of Er at the end of *The Republic,* in which the man who had behaved well because he lived in a society with good regulations, chooses for his next life the life of a tyrant, as if to show that deep down inside himself the beast remained all the time, yearning for release, and never getting it, thanks only to the power of social constraint.[57] We can keep in mind Dostoyevsky's Underground Man who will go berserk (with Dostoyevsky's approval) just to upset the established harmony; and Dostoyevsky's Ridiculous Fellow who cannot avoid corrupting the utopia of his dream. We can be sobered by the criminal behavior of the earthlings when placed in utopia in H. G. Wells's *Men Like Gods.* It would seem that men itch to smash, especially to smash the perfect; to put it as generously as it can be put, they crave excitement, especially forbidden excitement; they cannot be tamed.

Hopefully, we in this essay have done our duty by the doctrine of original sin, by including it among the large number of doctrines (and ideas, moods, feelings, attitudes, dispositions) that can be described as antiutopian. The doctrine of original sin, anyway, does not lend itself to any precise formulation, nor to anything resembling strict verification or falsification. It is, however, there, precise or not, and perhaps the more effective for not being precise. It also could be the last antiutopian defense, if all other antiutopian defenses yield. One does not mean to be cavalier; but this is the only way in which the matter can be accommodated here.

We now come to the last of our hitherto unexamined as-

---

57. Plato, *The Republic,* 619. We must remember, however, that the virtue of the man in the Myth of Er ". . . was a matter of habit only, and he had no philosophy." The discipline of suffering in the afterlife, from which this "good" man was exempt, leads other souls to make more sensible choices. But better than the discipline of suffering is wisdom: the wise man will choose well: ". . . he might . . . be happy here, and also his journey to another life and return to this, instead of being rough and underground, would be smooth and heavenly."

sumptions; namely, the assumption that the advances in our knowledge of human nature can be systematically applied in society; specifically, in a world-utopian society. And it is at this point that, once again, an apparently insuperable obstacle is placed in the way of the modern utopian hope. Just as the use of violence was declared to be incompatible with the full and true realization of utopian ends in general; and just as the allowance for change in utopia was declared to be incompatible with the specific utopian end of vanished authority; so it now seems that the very size of the utopian society and the nature of the life to be lived in it are incompatible with the systematic application of psychological knowledge, and hence with realization of the specific utopian end of effortless virtue. For the fact is that Skinner's methods—and any methods we can now imagine—are unseverably tied to the form of a small community. The close supervision of the upbringing of children, which is so essential to Skinner's—and utopia's—aims, would seem to be possible only when a small number of children are involved: even a small number of children require a comparatively large number of supervisors who possess the requisite knowledge of psychology for the onerous tasks implicit in the upbringing of children. Perhaps a large enough number of such people could be found today who could proceed to establish a Walden Two; and in the future, there may perhaps be enough to establish more Waldens. But when we come to think of the whole world with its billions—and a modern utopian idealist must think of the whole world, and nothing less—we may be forced to conclude that close supervision is a practical impossibility.

It would be easier to have a definite opinion on this subject, if Skinner had been clearer in *Walden Two* on the precise way supervision is carried out, and by whom. Are we to assume that any adult is capable of taking part in the education of the young? Are we to assume that though the planning for the raising of the young can be undertaken only by trained psychologists, the actual implementation can be carried on by the lay citizens of a society? It is clear that for Skinner's hopes to materialize—and this point is obvious—much more care must be expended on the raising of the young than is expended, in most instances, in the real world today. Not only is a great increase in our understanding of human nature necessary for the purposes of modern utopianism; also necessary is a society so arranged as to permit the systematic application of our increased understanding. We may, in all reason, assume that there will in fact be a great increase in our understanding of human nature; but that is not enough to give full plausibility to the utopian dream of effortless virtue for the vast number of inhabitants of a *world* community. The demands of practice, of practicality, constantly intrude into the deliberations of a utopian theorist; and in no other case is the intrusion more rough than it is in the case before us. Must the raising of the young be in the hands of technicians? If so, how can there ever be enough of them? If not, how much must the layman know in order to do what must be done? How much time would the layman have to give to this endeavor? What answers are forthcoming to these questions? Are we to conclude, unhappily, that Skinner has given us, at least in theory, a way of achieving a small communitarian utopia, of truly achieving a small communitarian utopia, at just the time when a small communitarian utopia is hopelessly irrelevant to the problems of the world? There was a time, as Arthur E. Bestor, Jr., has shown, when those who planned and lived in communitarian utopias in the United States from 1800-1850 believed that their example could convert the rest of American society to their way of life.[58] This belief was shored up by the further belief that American society, as a whole, was fluid in its institutional structure, and that, therefore, social change by means of conversion could take place. But surely such a cheerful view is not in accord with reality at the present time: it probably was never in accord with reality. There is no doubt that Skinner could, as he suggests, do a better job of devising a successful communitarian utopia than the idealists of the early nineteenth century.[59] But is the small and manageable community, which does not demand

58. Arthur E. Bestor, Jr., "Patent-Office Models of the Good Society: Some Relationships between Social Reform and Westward Expansion," *The American Historical Review*, LVIII (April 1953), pp. 505–526.

59. Skinner, *Walden Two, op. cit.*, pp. 128-129.

large numbers of trained psychologists, the scope of Skinner's potency? Are we to feel grateful to Skinner for having so carefully considered the presuppositions of an improved life on a small scale, and then give up the idea of anything more ambitious? That is, give up modern utopianism? If both ease in virtue and a high level of common virtue are central to modern utopia, considered as an ideal-type—are, in fact, the presuppositions for much else in utopia—how can we continue to think seriously about utopia, when practical difficulties of an insuperable sort present themselves? We have already said that the practical difficulties inherent in going from the real world to utopia by way of a violent revolution are overpowering; but we nevertheless have proceeded to speculate about utopianism anyway, out of the belief that there is some value in being clear about what is desirable, even though there is next to no chance for the desirable to become actual. Now, however, there would seem to be something fantastical not merely in the enterprise of attaining utopia, but also, and more alarmingly, in the essence of utopia itself. It would seem to be incontrovertible that an improved milieu and a higher standard of living, by themselves, are not enough to assure certain and effortless virtue. William Morris, H. G. Wells, Lenin, Herbert Marcuse all say or imply that these things, by themselves, would be enough. But the doctrine of original sin, or, really, any sort of pessimistic common sense, can provide the needed corrective to this terribly sanguine view. Skinner does not share this view, as we have said: he is certain that people cannot be left to themselves and still turn out to be good, as a utopian would conceive of "good," howsoever peaceful, abundant, and decent society may become. Care is required; scrupulous and constant attention is required. Education in virtue, in the utopian manner, rests on the application of special knowledge, knowledge of human nature. The question remains: How can this knowledge be applied to vast populations? We cannot answer this question; that is beyond us. We can only ask it, in perplexity and alarm.

Not daunted, we shall assume, for the purposes of this essay, that the difficulty we have just mentioned did not exist. Let us consider the matter, as is our wont, in the abstract; let us assume that the study of human nature will one day be so refined as to permit the belief that the process of character formation can be guided faultlessly; and let us disregard the problems connected with putting into effect the results of the study of human nature. The reason for our pursuing this theme further, even after we have confessed ourselves undone by practicalities, is that it raises still another question, the answer to which may be as disheartening as the answer to the prior question, Can psychological knowledge be systematically applied in the upbringing of a vast population? The question we now raise is, Can psychological knowledge be applied and yet *manipulation* still be avoided? Is there a moral obstacle to go with the practical one we have already considered?

ii

There would be a moral obstacle if the process of character formation involved a body of knowledge that was inaccessible to the lay intelligence and that remained the preserve of a segment of society—the preserve of trained psychologists. If such were the case, the character of any man in utopian society would be a secret closed to that man, the reasons for his behavior, the reasons why he is as he is, the possibilities for becoming different from what he is, the influence of his conditioning on his behavior, the *rationale* of the procedures constituting his education, the *rationale* of the habits he has acquired and the forms and practices of his life, would all be unknown to him. That most men in the real world live and die in this kind of ignorance does not provide an excuse for theorists who would perpetuate this ignorance in utopia. In fact, this ignorance is even worse in utopia. It is worse not only because any deficiency becomes magnified when there is an expectation of perfection; but also and primarily because modern utopia, considered as an ideal-type, rests on an advanced understanding of human nature: if that knowledge is confined to a few and denied to the many, a gulf between the few and the many would exist which is of greater *moral* significance than any in the real world. The gulf would be greater, in effect, than that between priest (most broadly understood) and laity: the few psychologists would possess the keys to human nature, not to the imaginary realms of heaven and hell. Also, the gulf would be greater—again, in moral consequence—than that between men learned in natural science or the humanistic disciplines and the ordinary man. Those who guide the process of character formation wield, in truth, godlike powers. And unless psychological knowledge can be understood by all, and applied, to some degree, by all, the worst charges made by Skinner's critics would seem valid. Specifically, the charge of manipulation would seem valid: Skinner's people would indeed seem like marionettes or wind-up toys. It may be that not all men can understand the science of human behavior; it may be that the citizens of utopia simply cannot comprehend that which has gone into their "making." But if that is so, then, aside from the practical difficulties, the moral difficulties inherent in the systematic application of psychological knowledge are fatal to the utopian dream. It is possible that, on balance, a society in the image of Walden Two, manipulation and all, would be superior to a society that got on without the systematic application of psychological knowledge; but it would not be utopia precisely because of the manipulation in it.

It is important to note that the mere existence of conditioning does not entail the existence of manipulation. If by "conditioning" we only mean a way of educating men that is more certain to produce a rational morality, and that is also less painful than the usual methods of the world, we are entitled to feel that manipulation represents something fundamentally different. We should wish to say that manipulation was characteristic of a social system if the methods of education used therein reposed on a body of knowledge beyond the comprehension of most, or that was kept secret by a few, and that tended to produce a group of men who did what was expected of them without question, without understanding, without even so much as an articulated awareness of what was expected of them, possessed of a sense that what is had to be, could not be otherwise, has never been otherwise here or elsewhere; while, on the part of a few men in society, there was reason and understanding. We should have manipulation even if the governors were benevolent. The aim of conditioning is to liberate reason, and, by making virtue less difficult, perhaps to liberate other sources of energy and talent as well; the aim of manipulation, when it is benevolent, is to keep people ignorantly contented and, consequently, barely adult. But it must be insisted that the mere application by society of increased psychological knowledge is not intrinsically antirational and debasing to the citizens of that society; and those who defend conditioning as a more sophisticated kind of education are not, simultaneously, committed to defending manipulation. The trouble is that it is undeniable that Skinner's views are not free from manipulative tendencies. And these tendencies do not manifest themselves in the course of self-control that Skinner puts the six-year-olds through, or in the complete supervision he wishes to have exercised over children, generally; children are everywhere, and necessarily, the subjects of treatment that is, in a very obvious sense, manipulative. Rather, these tendencies manifest themselves in the relationship which subsists between the adults of Skinner's utopia and the governing elite. What is especially troubling is that perhaps no other kind of relationship could subsist in any society in which there was the systematic application of psychological knowledge. We should wish to say that Skinner is not sensitive to this problem.

Of a piece with Skinner's disregard of the manipulative tendencies in his utopia are his views on democracy. Present throughout Skinner's writings is a scorn of democratic politics, which derives from some crude and falsely tough-minded beliefs about the way democracy works and what it is supposed to accomplish. Armed with this easy cynicism, Skinner proceeds to dismiss democracy as an anachronism that once served a purpose but is now inadequate to cope with the requirements of a new social order. From this attitude to democracy Skinner easily passes over into an advocacy of a social system in which all decision-making is vested in a few Planners and Managers, and in which the very idea of citizenship is missing. The substance of Skinner's political theory is contained in this utterance of Frazier's:

In Walden Two no one worries about the government except the rew to whom that worry has been assigned. To suggest that everyone should take an interest would seem as fantastic as to suggest that everyone should become familiar with our Diesel engines. Even the constitutional rights of the members are seldom thought about, I'm sure. The only thing that matters is one's day-to-day happiness and a secure future. Any infringement there would undoubtedly "arouse the electorate."[60]

A more refined political understanding would have saved Skinner from the folly of thinking that the political function could ever be conceived of as just one function among many in a community. The moral weight of the political function never enters into Skinner's purview. The relation between moral autonomy and the political realm is never considered by Skinner. That there could be reasons to justify democracy other than the pragmatic ones connected with the abuse of power never occurs to Skinner.

In effect, the inhabitants of Walden Two are the wards of a few men possessed of a special knowledge and entrusted with all political function and power. The mass of people lead their lives, have their pleasures, do their work; at the same time, they are in the dark about how the system works: they are not even permitted to discuss the Code by which they live. There is no residual aspect of a public life allowed to the people of Walden Two; they are creatures of the planners. And that they feel no resentment, and no sense of loss, does not mitigate the situation. Of course, it would be absurd to say that the governors of Walden Two are just like Dostoyevsky's Grand Inquisitor: there are naturally tremendous differences between the kind of human being produced in the respective social orders. And the most significant difference of all is that, as Skinner

---

60. *Ibid.*, p. 225. See also "Freedom and the Control of Men," *op. cit.*, pp. 53–54, 63–65. In that essay, Skinner says, "No matter how effective we judge current democratic practices to be, how highly we value them or how long we expect them to survive, they are almost certainly not the *final* form of government" (p. 53).

proudly points out, there is no gratitude felt by the people of Walden Two towards those set above them. Besides, all the outward markings of authority and superiority are absent. But for all that, it nevertheless remains true that, whatever the psychology of the situation, there is a great gulf between the ordinary people and those responsible for the operation of Walden Two and the initiation of changes in it. A more complicated political and moral outlook would have saved Skinner from his rather casual handling of the problem of manipulation, would have saved him (or his surrogate, Frazier) from this sort of statement:

When we ask what Man can make of Man, we don't mean the same thing by "Man" in both instances. We mean to ask what a few men can make of mankind. And that's the all-absorbing question of the twentieth century.[61]

And it is no extenuation that the adults of the real world, as it is, suffer even worse manipulation than they would suffer in Walden Two. Utopia, by definition, is supposed to be better than the real world; it is supposed to correct its worst qualities. But despite certain advantages which Walden Two has over the world in the area of social relations, it still has not managed to eliminate *mystery* from society, it still has not done away with the opacity or (to switch the figure) the viscosity of social life, nor replaced them with clarity; it has failed to produce a race of men both able and eager to understand the medium in which they live, and interested in taking a direct or indirect part in controlling that medium. Skinner has failed to feel the *moral* urgency at the heart of Rousseau's defense of popular sovereignty and Mill's defense of representative government: the defense of popular government is not exhausted by pragmatic considerations. To repeat, the issue is not predicting, shaping, controlling human behavior; the issue is the nature of the relationship between the formed adult and the society around him. The moral loss sustained by humanity in a community where governance and change are in the hands of a few, wise and good as they may be, is irreparable. We can grant to Skin-

---

61. *Ibid.*, p. 247.

ner that the ideal community must be designed and set in motion by a few; but after that, the many must share in something' resembling citizenship. Their very rationality depends on it. We have dwelt on this issue because it is bound to loom large in any discussion of utopianism and bound to be an important part of the antiutopian case.

It must be stressed that we intend to say no final word on the question of the inevitability of manipulation in a society in which psychological knowledge is systematically applied, or on the question of the inevitability of some kind of elite in such a society. We only wish to point out what perhaps is only too obvious to those who do not look very kindly on utopianism from the start; namely, that the idea of utopia is often prone to come to grief, and never more pitiably than when the means needed to assure effortless virtue are discussed with any candor. We here can only hope that difficulties that now appear to be insuperable may turn out, after others give their attention to these matters, to be not insuperable, after all. This may be more utopian delusion, but it may not.

iii

One last point must be made in connection with the subject of the sytematic application of psychological knowledge. And that is that the family is threatened by such application. If we assumed that close supervision of the process of character formation were free, or could be made free, of the moral and practical difficulties we have so far taken up, there would still remain (at least) one more cause for worry: the fate of the family in a society in which there is close supervision. In Walden Two, parents know who their children are, and husband and wife live together, and stay married with the presumption of permanent union. But husband and wife do not raise their children in the home; the children are raised in common. In effect, the family as we know it is eliminated. Skinner is fully aware of the consequences of his system for the family; and in an excellent chapter of *Walden Two* (Chapter 17), he gives some reasons (some his own, some taken from Plato's *Republic*, some taken from Freud) for his refusal to regret the attenuation of family life. For instance, he (Frazier) says: "By balancing the sexes we eliminate all the Freudian problems which arise from the asymmetrical relation to the female parent"; and: "In the family, identification is usually confined to one parent or the other, but neither one may have characteristics suitable to the child's developing personality. It's a sort of coerced identification, which we are glad to avoid."[62] These reasons may have much to recommend them; though naturally Skinner's few comments do not dispose of so immense and profound a subject. We do not mean to deal with this subject in this essay. We only mean to notice that a close supervision of the upbringing of children which involves the use of technical psychological knowledge may not be compatible with the preservation of the family as we know it. For some, conceivably, this threat to the family is sufficient to discredit the whole enterprise of careful conditioning, inside or outside utopia. For some, the family would be worth preserving despite all the illness that could be held to emanate from it: not merely illness emanates from it. In any event, we must acknowledge its gravity: a sufficient antiutopian case could be made to rest on the sanctity of the family.

---

62. *Ibid.,* p. 120.

7

Character in Utopia:
A Few General Considerations

i

The subject-matter of the previous chapter has been conditioned virtue—effortless virtue—in utopia. Yet, it is clear that there is a larger subject than virtue which must dominate the thought of anyone interested in utopianism; and that subject is, of course, the totality of human character, the kind (or kinds) of man that would be formed in a modern utopian society. We have given our attention to the question of virtue, and placed this question at the center of our discussion of utopian ends, because virtue has always been at the center of discussion of ends, most generally. In the course of our discussion on virtue we have inevitably touched on the larger subject of human character from time to time. It may not be amiss, however, to introduce a few more considerations, at this point, on the subject of human character in a modern utopia, in order to identify some other sources of antiutopian feeling. The question of effortless virtue probably calls forth most of the important antiutopian ideas on character in utopia; but there are still some additional antiutopian ideas which deserve treatment (if only sketchily), and which manifest themselves as we extend the discussion from virtue to related matters. The subject of virtue will, however, continue to figure in this discussion.

We have already noted that a persistent antiutopian theme is the diminishment which human nature is supposed to suffer in utopia; we have seen that the utopian handling of virtuous behavior and of virtuous disposition as exemplified, for instance, by B. F. Skinner's writings, feeds antiutopian wrath. Some of that wrath is naturally to be explained not just by a preference for one kind of education rather than another, nor even by a preference for one kind of path to virtue rather than another. Always in the background is the overriding concern for the fullness or richness of human nature: utopian virtue is simply the most telling and the most decisive illustration of how utopia diminishes human nature. And the charge that utopia does diminish human nature is an old one, and not one peculiar to critics of Skinner or of modern utopianism. And when we turn to some of the major modern utopian texts, we may find that the antiutopian charge has some plausibility. Or we may find, contrarily, that though human nature is not diminished, it has not been significantly enhanced, either. The people of William Morris' Nowhere are charming and sane; but they do not seem complicated: they do not seem *interesting*. The people of Wells's Modern Utopia, arranged as they are in several broad strata, are meant to be like people in the real world, only a little bit better: is that enough to satisfy utopian longing, though it may have satisfied Wells's longing (at least in 1905)? The people of Edward Bellamy's Boston are, again, like people as we know them, only a little bit better. Lenin's few sentences in *State and Revolution* on human nature in the classless society are unfortunately uselessly vague; they do not seem even to possess much imagination. There is some eloquent writing in Herbert Marcuse's *Eros and Civilization* on the need for the liberation of human energies and the gratification of human appetites.[1] And Marcuse directs

---

1. The heart of Marcuse's position is in these words: ". . . Orpheus and Narcissus reveal a new reality . . . The Orphic Eros transforms being: he masters cruelty and death through liberation. His language is

.r attention back to Schiller's astonishing work, *On the Aesthetic Education of Man*.[2] But the same unreality that surrounds Schiller's ideals also surrounds Marcuse's. And we seem driven to conclude that the utopian imagination either depends too heavily on reality or severs itself too completely from it. It is easy to become petulant about these lacks, or alleged lacks, in the utopian imagination. After all, what could be harder than to describe a new kind of human nature? Is it not certain that whenever such a description is attempted, the result will be too close to reality or too far from it? All the difficulties the human mind has had in its picturing of God, gods, angels, and devils must beset the human mind when it tries to picture a humanity better than the one it knows. God, gods, angels and devils turn out to be indescribable; or very much like human beings, though exaggerated now in one respect and now in another. Add to that the scandalous fact that it is easier to speak of vice and wretchedness with passion, beauty, and credibility than it is to speak of virtue and happiness. In the words of Yeats's "Vacillation":

> The Soul.   Seek out reality, leave things that seem.
> The Heart.   What, be a singer born and lack a theme?
> The Soul.   Isaiah's coal, what more can man desire?
> The Heart.   Struck dumb in the simplicity of fire!
> The Soul.   Look on that fire, salvation walks within.
> The Heart.   What theme had Homer but original sin?

These lines apply to descriptions of all human situations.[3]

And yet after these concessions have been made to utopian writers—pretentious though it must sound to talk of making

---

song, and his work is *play*. Narcissus' life is that of *beauty*, and his existence is contemplation. These images refer to the *aesthetic dimension* as the one in which their reality principle must be sought and validated." [*Eros and Civilization* (Boston: Beacon Press, 1955), p. 171. See Chaps. 8–10.] In Hannah Arendt's *The Human Condition* (Chicago: University of Chicago Press, 1958), which prizes endeavor above everything, we have a book that contrasts nicely with *Eros and Civilization*. See also Lewis Mumford, *The Transformations of Man* (New York: Harper, 1956), a book of great beauty and suggestiveness.

2. Friedrich Schiller, *On the Aesthetic Education of Man*, trans. by Reginald Snell (London: Routledge, Kegan Paul, 1954). See esp. Letters 13–15, 22–23, 26–27.

3. In Book X of *The Republic*, Plato memorably discusses the dependence of art on vice. See 604-606.

concessions, when one is not oneself prepared to essay the task
of speculating about a new humanity—though there is nothing
more pretentious than to essay this task—we still must feel
cheated. What, finally, are men to be in the ideal society? Who
are the Good Men and what are the Good Lives?

We turn, once more, to Skinner for help. We turn with the
following questions in mind: Are Skinner's descriptions of human
character in Walden Two premonitory of some new image of
man? Are the descriptions neither too close to reality, nor too far
from it? Do the descriptions compose an image of man which is
not open to the charge that utopianism diminishes human nature?
We do not expect miracles; we do have a right to expect something full-blooded.

It is apparent from a reading of *Walden Two* and from some
of Skinner's other writings (already referred to) that Skinner's
imagination does not soar. Skinner says, "Let us agree, to start
with, that health is better than illness, wisdom better than ignorance, love better than hate, and productive energy better than
neurotic sloth."[4] "Let men be happy, informed, skillful, well-
behaved and productive."[5] And the society of Walden Two is
devoted to the securing of these ends. There are two places in
Skinner's novel in which Skinner gives a rather more elaborate
articulation of his ends. These ends are unexceptionable, though
they seem primarily to be the opposites of the prevailing conditions in real life, not ends that, taken together, would constitute a
transformation of life. They are the ends of the welfare state
consolidated and made more certain of attainment. Skinner's
Frazier explains his purposes in this way: ". . . what they [the
inhabitants of Walden Two] get is escape from the petty emotions which eat the heart out of the unprepared. They get the
satisfaction of pleasant and profitable social relations on a scale
almost undreamed of in the world at large. They get immeasurably increased efficiency, because they can stick to a job without

---

4. B. F. Skinner, "Freedom and the Control of Men," *The American
Scholar*, XXV (Winter 1955-56), p. 51. On Skinner and the subject of
values, see the critical comments by Joseph Wood Krutch, *The Measure
of Man* (New York: Harcourt, Brace, 1954), pp. 83–95.

5. Skinner, "Freedom and the Control of Men," *op. cit.*, p. 47.

suffering the aches and pains which beset most of us. They get new horizons, for they are spared the emotions characteristic of frustration and failure." Later in the book, Frazier rises a little higher:

The Good Life also means a chance to exercise talents and abilities. And we have let it be so. We have time for sports, hobbies, arts and crafts, and most important of all, the expression of that interest in the world which is *science* in the deepest sense. . . . And we need intimate and satisfying personal contacts. We must have the best possible chance of finding congenial spirits. . . . And we don't restrict personal relations to conform to outmoded customs. We discourage attitudes of domination and criticism. Our goal is a general tolerance and affection.⁶

It would be ridiculous to belittle these goals. At face value, they surely represent a life which would be, in most ways, better than that led by most people. We can even say that Skinner promises to do, at small cost, what the elite of Aldous Huxley's Brave New World do at infinite cost: make all people *adequate* to their vocation and to all the demands imposed on them by their society. Brave New World solves the problem of human adequacy by condemning the great mass of men to incompleteness, and, simultaneously, diluting reality intolerably. On the other hand, Skinner's Frazier does not sacrifice intelligence or human capacities, though he may make the texture of life a good deal less rich and various than is desirable, and though he may not give full due to the requirements of civilized mentality. But, in all fairness, it must be said that Frazier does not take the principle of human adequacy to its logical and absurd hedonist conclusion: he tries to achieve human happiness on a uniform level, and that level a fairly high one. (We must make one serious qualification: Skinner is not sufficiently attentive to the moral gap which exists between his planners and managers, on the one hand, and the rest of the society in Walden Two, on the other.) When this has been said, however, it must also be said that, on the whole, Skinner's sights are set low. Frazier is made to scorn a static conception of man; he is made to speak of the "potentialities of

---

6. B. F. Skinner, *Walden Two* (New York: Macmillan, 1948), p. 91, p. 133.

man."[7] But it may be that what Frazier really scorns is a static science of human behavior: he may be more interested in perfecting the means for his ends than in changing or expanding those ends. Frazier says, "Oh, our efforts will seem pretty crude a hundred years hence . . . My hunch is—and when I feel this way about a hunch, it's never wrong—that we shall eventually find out, not only what makes a child mathematical, but how to make better mathematicians! If we can't solve a problem, we can create men who can! And better artists! And better craftsmen!"[8] Could it not be said, though in caricature, that Skinner is more concerned to improve functions than to improve men?[9] Frazier goes on to envisage the possibility of communal science, communal authorship, communal art, communal music: "We can construct groups of artists and scientists who will act as smoothly and efficiently as champion football teams."[10] After a certain point is reached, Skinner's enthusiasm is channeled from the perfection of the individual man to the order and efficiency of the collectivity. He is aware that the old antiutopian charge of "anthill" can also be made of his utopia;[11] but he is not aware enough. His final passion is for smooth operations; his greatest regret is our present inefficiency: "Does it seem to you unreasonable to estimate that the present efficiency of society is of the order of a fraction of one per cent? *A fraction of one per cent!* And you ask what remains to be done!"[12] What remains to

7. *Ibid.*, pp. 173, 241.

8. *Ibid.*, p. 243.

9. Skinner's stress on function, on performance, is evidence of the hyperscientism of his mind. The fact that he is an uncompromising *behaviorist* psychologist also takes its toll. He has a tendency to reduce the study of human behavior to the study of "bodies in motion." He disregards human intention or purpose almost completely. His doctrine prevents him from caring about the "inside" of human activity. As a result, he is oblivious to the claims of any kind of *personalism*, and is therefore incapacitated from developing any novel idea of human character and what expectations we can, in theory, have of it. If there is one sentence any utopian theorist must always keep in mind, it is Mill's: "It really is of importance, not only what men do, but also what manner of men they are that do it." (*On Liberty, op. cit.*, p. 156.) Utopian theory must think not only of function, but of character; and when it thinks of character, it must think with boldness.

10. Skinner, *Walden Two, op. cit.*, pp. 243–244.

11. *Ibid.*, p. 210.

12. *Ibid.*, p. 244.

be done is, unfortunately, the building of the "Superorganism."

Thus we should‹ wish to say that Skinner's imagination is finally circumscribed by the deficiencies of the real world, the world in which first, welfare, and second, efficiency, are, for the most part, still to seek. And when we return to the questions we were to keep in mind as we read Skinner, we find that the answers are quite disappointing. Skinner's descriptions are not premonitory of some new image of man: they are, in fact, too close to reality: they correct reality in ways that one would have guessed only too easily. The three most notorious human passions—lust for power, prestige, and possessions—are effaced; human aggressiveness is tamed. The level of moral goodness is slightly raised; and it is made fairly easy for people to reach that level. But not much else is done (though to say that must sound ungrateful). Then, as far as the charge that Skinner's model of human nature diminishes human nature is concerned, we can only say that apart from Skinner's terrible disregard of the requirements of rational morality (a disregard that was one of our major interests in the chapter on conditioned virtue), the adult of Walden Two does not deserve most of the abuse that has been heaped on him. It is certainly true that he is not very interesting to contemplate; but, as we have said too many times, human contentment is not usually very interesting to contemplate. The trouble is that though Skinner is guided—one should say "driven" —by the idea of human waste, the primal utopian idea, the idea of preventing human beings from coming into the world and dying, never having lived, the idea of liberating human energies and talents and of exploiting the full range of human capacity for the good, he still does not remove himself far enough from the intimidating effect of the deficiencies in the real world that beg for reform. In some respects, as we have tried to show, Skinner does diminish human nature in the abstract; in many respects he improves on it and enhances it. But he enhances it only to a small degree. Really, it is not so much that he diminishes it, as that he does not, given the bent of his mind and the nature of his purposes and the certainty he has in his own eventual success, truly enhance it. His greatest lack is a vision; his greatest need a philosophical anthropology.[13] And this criticism is to be made of modern utopianism, most inclusively; it cannot be confined to Skinner. We require images of human greatness. We say "images," not "an image": there can be varieties of excellence for which perpetual peace, guaranteed abundance, and effortless virtue prepare the way. The marvelous technique of human conditioning which Skinner promises must first be corrected by the canons of rational morality, and then employed in the creation of types of human beings higher than Skinner has any intimation of.

ii

At this point in our discussion, we must take note of some sober advice that could be given. We have been urging on utopian theorists a new and imaginative conception of humanity; we have been finding fault with the conceptions already put forth by several utopian writers. It could be asked of us what we really expected or wanted. Human nature can be changed only a little; some improvements in human behavior can be "engineered." But

---

13. We must distinguish between three kinds of speculation about "human potentialities." First, there is speculation about ways in which feelings, sensations, and states of mind can be induced in people (as we know them), apart from what we would normally consider to be experience. By means of pills, drugs, "wires in the brain," and whatnot, various kinds of pseudo experience are made possible: we say "pseudo experience," because the usual connections between experience and response (of one sort or another) to experience are missing. Presumably, the utopian idealist, being a rationalist, would not stand to benefit very much from this kind of speculation. Second, there is speculation about ways in which the science of genetics can be used to bring about major organic changes in human beings, and thus transform the race. We in this essay can only mention this subject, and acknowledge its potential significance for utopian thought. See, for example, H. J. Muller, *Out of the Night* (New York: Vanguard Press, 1935); and Jean Rostand, *Can Man Be Modified?* trans. by Jonathan Griffin (London: Secker & Warburg, 1959). (Genetics plays a large part, of course, in Aldous Huxley's *Brave New World*.) Third, there is speculation about ways in which the human race, more or less as it is now endowed by nature, can be improved. For the time being, the third kind of speculation would be the most profitable. The hope is that for the race *as it is now endowed by nature* more is possible than utopian thinkers have so far suggested.

men must be men, even in utopia. Wells and Skinner have, with
good reason, stayed close to reality in their depiction of utopian
man. There are inescapable facts about people: there are limits
which a sensible imagination will respect. As Lionel Trilling says:

It was the *just people* aspect of life that Arnold could never get; he
missed the right perception of that world which has always existed,
and perhaps always will exist, which no Utopia, no State, no culture,
no rule of superior intelligence, no progress, will—or should—ever get
rid of: life warm, mistaken, silly, but the "dirt" out of which things
grow.[14]

The bulk of life must be ordinary; the bulk of men must be
ordinary; the bulk of the experience of even extraordinary men
must be ordinary. And any deviation in thought from this fact
must be to the detriment of the thinker. The utopian sense of
the waste in human lives is fine; the utopian passion to improve
the species and make a better, higher, race of men is fine. But
fine only as an inspiriting beginning for speculation: it is useful
that thinkers aim higher than they expect, in all seriousness, to
reach. Let there be no disappointment, however, when their attainment falls short of their aims; as it inevitably must.

And to this, we can concede that howsoever grand our ambitions for life in utopia, we must bear in mind that it would be
men who live that life. We can even add that for life to be tolerable, most men most of the time must be inert or in repose, and
that life cannot be a constant exercise of individuality on the
part of every person in society. We must recognize that though
the aim of utopian idealism is to liberate human energies, these
energies can be liberated only in the framework of a settled
society; and that as liberation is heightened, the problem of control becomes intensified. And if that is true, there would come a
time when numerous undesirable social practices of an insid-
iously repressive sort would be necessitated, if society were not
to explode. No, life even in the perfect society must be nine-
tenths dross or "dirt" (to use Trilling's word). Yet, for all that,
two things must still be said. First, the point has not been reached
which would allow us to conclude that the most that can be

---

14. Lionel Trilling, *Matthew Arnold* (1939) (New York: Meridian
Books, 1955), pp. 361-362.

"made" of man had already been announced in the works of
the major modern utopian writers. If there must be limits to our
aspirations, those limits have not been reached. We can hope
that in utopia, people would be just people on a higher plane.
Second, and perhaps more important, utopian psychology—if it
is to be true to its most ancient traditions—must be devoted to
the liberation of all men, not just a few. It must answer Trilling's
sentences by a counterassertion: namely, that the great mass of
people, in utopia, can not be thought of as "just people" from
whom emerge a few brilliant souls. Rather, the wish is to produce
a mass of men, all of whom are perforce (and perhaps not unfortunately) "just people" most of the time, but all of whom are
some of the time, and in different ways, more than "just people."
One of the great benefits of conditioned virtue is that it would
seem to permit, in the abstract, a universal individualism, so to
speak. By raising the general level of virtue, and making virtue
more certain, scientific psychology changes the nature of the
presuppositions of individualism. As the new psychology is used
to liberate human energies, it simultaneously provides the needed
corrective to that liberation: it assures, or tries to assure, that
human energies always remain in moral channels. And when it
is remembered that utopia, in the abstract, is a place of abundance, and hence is a place in which the material resources are
on hand for the exercise of the talents of all and the satisfaction
of the tastes of all—then we can say that a utopian society is the
one society that affords a genuine haven for individualism, for
the special "individuality" (to use the word of Mill) of every
man. Thus, it is only in a world-wide utopian society, in which
human productivity is rationally organized and distributed and
human ingenuity expended on the raising of the young that the
presuppositions of thoroughgoing individualism are met. In short,
we maintain that the task of utopian speculation is to refine our
understanding of what the individual should be, and that the
task of a utopian society would be to insure that every man in it
were given the chance to be an individual, to promote—in the
great words of Marx—"an association in which the free development of each is the condition for the free development of all."

iii

Now it may be thought that our stress on individualism hardly comports with any utopianism, ancient or modern. Naturally, one can find exceptions to the usual utopian hostility to personal differences, to human variety, but is it not true that human sameness, not variety, prevails in utopian speculation? H. G. Wells built his Modern Utopia on personal differences; but he was conscious that the uniqueness of his utopia lay in the accommodation it gave to liberty, privacy, and personality:

To the classical Utopists freedom was relatively trivial. Clearly they considered virtue and happiness as entirely separable from liberty, and as being altogether more important things. But the modern view, with its deepening insistence upon individuality, and upon the significance of its uniqueness, steadily intensifies the value of freedom, until at last we begin to see liberty as the very substance of life, that it is indeed life, and that only the dead things, the choiceless things, live in absolute obedience to law. To have free play for one's individuality is, in the modern view, the subjective triumph of existence, as survival in creative work and offspring is its objective triumph.[15]

Surely this is untypical of utopianism, and just as surely, to follow Wells is simply to perpetuate a utopian eccentricity. Is not Wells's position on individuality solely attributable to the fact that his modern utopia is not really a utopia, in the fullest sense, at all, but merely a society which corrects the most awful absurdities of the real world, and then leaves things pretty much alone? Could it not be said that an absolutely consistent utopian thinker could not possibly make individualism one of his main ambitions or, *a fortiori*, the center of his ambition?

The reason for having these forementioned suspicions of utopianism is, in a word, equality. One of the oldest and most plausible charges against utopian thinkers is that they level, bring everything down to the same dreary lowness, make everything uniform, in the name of equality. And it could reasonably be thought that where there was equality—for whatever cause

---

15. H. G. Wells, *A Modern Utopia* (1905) (London: Nelson, n.d.), p. 41.

or causes—there could not be, at the same time, individuality. (Indeed, Wells's Modern Utopia pays little attention to the question of equality; it assures to all citizens a decent minimum, but within the framework of a class system; and a class system seems the only one in which Wells·could guarantee the retention of individuality.) The question to be asked is whether, in the abstract, a commitment to equality—and it is not open to doubt that utopianism has some kind of commitment to equality—is reconcilable with a full flowering of individuality. (We have already said that there are some for whom *liberty* and equality are not reconcilable.) Obviously, equality carried to its conclusion *is* uniformity: if all men wanted and were given the same things, there would be perfect equality. Only it would be, at least to the outside observer, a nightmare, a situation worse to contemplate than one in which there were the most unjust inequalities.[16] But need uniformity be the conclusion of utopian equality?

We do not here pretend to deal with the great (and neglected) subject of equality. But there are a few things we must say, in order to show still another side of antiutopianism: that is our only purpose. And it is natural that the hostility to the idea of an equalitarian society should grow, as the ability to control

---

16. It is necessary, when thinking about a utopian society, to remember that the response to utopia of one brought up in it would be different from the response of an outside observer or of one who had direct experience of both utopia and a preutopian society. (See, for example, p. 124 and p. 134 of *Walden Two, op. cit.*) Acceptance of a utopian society by someone ignorant of an alternative is suspect; rejection of utopian society by someone already formed in some other society may also be suspect. How fine it would be if it made sense to conceive of an "unconditioned" choice among ways of life. (Not even the choices in Plato's Myth of Er are unconditioned.) It would even be fine if any man were of such a kind as to be able to appreciate to the full all ways of life and then to choose one of them as the best. But we are all finite; no man is open to everything. We must trust, then, to a vague consensus, in the hope that that consensus represents, to some degree, the wishes of men who, like J. S. Mill's ideal Utilitarian, have experience of many things, if not of everything, and rank their preferences. The utopian claim is that a utopian society would commit its inhabitants to a way of life which incorporated the values generally favored by men who rejected competing values; and that the inhabitants of utopia would not become incapable at least of imagining other values than their own. For an argument like Mill's, see Plato, *The Republic,* 581–583.

human behavior grows; for the new psychological knowledge could be used to cancel human differences, in the name of equality, or in whatever name.

Equality can exist as uniformity, in an imaginary utopia, for a number of reasons. A perverse esthetics can be at work: a passion for neatness or tidiness or regularity can issue in a society in which uniform men lead uniform lives, and all the rich confusion attendant on different men leading different lives has been gladly given up: surface monotony and individual similarity are thus added to technical fixity and historical immobility to form a frozen utopia. Or, there can be too great a regard for the ease of utopian governors; and in the name of efficiency or order, life is made uniform, and equality given as the justification for that uniformity. Or, scarcity can be assumed, and a passion for justice can decree that the scarcity be equally distributed, with the result that, again, uniformity prevails, though for a purer reason. Or, it can be thought that everything has to be sacrificed to the task of removing the vices of pride or envy or avarice: these vices can be supposed to be excited by small or large differences between men and to be cured by equalitarian sameness.[17] Or, it can be thought that for justice

---

17. Indeed, there are some who say that the more equality there is, the more important seem the inequalities that remain. See, for example, Alexis de Tocqueville, *Democracy in America*, Vol. II, Book II, Chap. XIII, and Book IV, Chap. III; and George Orwell, *1984* (New York: Harcourt, Brace, 1949), p. 192. Tocqueville has in mind a society of abundance and Orwell a society of scarcity.

On the general subject of equality, there are two recent essays of great interest: Isaiah Berlin, "Equality," *Proceedings of the Aristotelian Society*, LVI (1955-56), pp. 301-326; and John Rawls, "Justice as Fairness," *The Philosophical Review*, LXVII (1958), pp. 164-194. A recent novel by Michael Young, *The Rise of the Meritocracy, 1870–2033* (New York: Random House, 1959), deals with the clash between the claims of merit and equality. In Young's novel, see pp. 87-98 for the ways in which inequality can be justified in an elitist society; p. 124 for a listing of puzzles about equality; and pp. 135-136 for the manifesto of the unequals, the lower orders. For an interesting discussion by a man of the left, of the question of equality, with the view that rewarded only according to merit is inferior to one that mixed merit with irrational considerations (such as birth), see Roy Jenkins, "Equality," in *New Fabian Essays*, ed. by R. H. S. Crossman (London: Turnstile Press, 1952), pp. 69-90. There is some very useful writing on equality in George Santayana, *Reason in Society* in *The*

to exist, all men have to be treated exactly alike: equality has to be manifest in every detail of life: everyone is raised in the same way and given the same things: nothing is allowed that all cannot do, and everything allowed is done by all.

Obviously, certain of these reasons do not have a place in modern utopianism. Perverse estheticism is not intrinsic to modern utopianism, or to utopianism, most generally, whatever aberrations could be found in the literature; this vice of the mind is, in theory, avoidable. Modern technology presumably diminishes the problem of rule, and hence can also diminish the concern for efficiency. Abundance is taken for granted in the speculations of modern utopian writers: scarcity is not what is to be distributed. There remain, then, two reasons for having equality exist as uniformity: differences between men cause pride, envy, or avarice; and differences between men are inherently unjust. We assume that equality is a necessary part of a modern utopian society. But need that equality be the equality of uniformity? That is, need the imperative of equality be so taken as to mean the death of individuality, as the active discouragement of different kinds of human beings leading different kinds of lives?[18]

Let us assume for the sake of this discussion (something which we probably should not be allowed to assume) that the techniques of conditioned virtue are so good that the argument to equalitarian uniformity from consideration of the vices of

---

Life of Reason (New York: Scribner, 1905), Vol. II, Chap. IV. See Yves R. Simon, *Philosophy of Democratic Government* (Chicago: University of Chicago Press, 1951) for a discussion of the inevitability of functional inequalities, even in democratic societies. See also C. A. R. Crosland, *The Future of Socialism* (London: Cape, 1956), Pt. 4. The perils of equality are memorably specified by David Hume in *An Enquiry Concerning the Principles of Morals* (New York: Hafner, 1948), Sect. III, Part II, pp. 193-194. Finally, there is the classic writing on equality throughout the second volume of Tocqueville's *Democracy in America*.

18. In the words of J. S. Mill, "To give any fair play to the nature of each, it is essential that different persons should be allowed to lead different lives." (*On Liberty, op. cit.*, p. 162.) Mill later elaborates, ". . . the unlikeness of one person to another is generally the first thing which draws the attention of either to the imperfection of his own type, and the superiority of another, or the possibility, by combining the advantages of both, of producing something better than either" (p. 173).

pride, envy, and avarice no longer holds. This would confine our discussion to the relation of justice to equalitarian uniformity.

In a few very suggestive pages on the subject of equality in his *The Good Society*,[19] Walter Lippmann distinguishes between "objective equality" and "subjective equality."[20] The heart of the distinction is simply this: since men are satisfied by different things or satisfied in different ways by the same thing, a policy of distributing uniform things to an entire population must result in unequal satisfaction. (Probably, this will always be true, no matter how men are educated or conditioned.) This idea has two consequences (which we, not Lippmann, draw out of the idea): first, if the principle of equality is taken to entail the construction of a society in which men are given the same things and induced to live in the same way, there would result a society of men who are happy in unequal "amounts" (if that is the word to use); second, if on the other hand, the principle of equality is taken to entail the construction of a society in which men are given different things in order that they may be made equally happy, there would result a society in which some men, at any rate, are made happy in a way unbefitting the expectations we hold out for rational creatures. Thus, uniformity can produce a society with much unhappiness; variety could produce a society with much inferiority. The fact that a uniform society would produce unhappiness is enough to discredit the notion that justice can be served only by uniformity. The fact that the criterion of happiness could lead to the indulgence of unworthy (though not necessarily illegal or immoral) appetites means that the criterion of happiness is not, by itself, a sufficient criterion.

We can therefore say that, in the abstract, though a modern utopian thinker would have no commitment to a literal uni-

19. Walter Lippmann, *The Good Society* (1937) (New York: Grosset's Universal Library, n.d.), pp. 75–77.

20. Cf. Lenin's distinction between socialism and communism; and Tawney's distinction between "identity of provision" and "equality of provision" in *Equality*, (fourth edition revised, London: Allen and Unwin, 1952), p. 39. In Bellamy's *Looking Backward* (1888) (New York: World, 1946), everyone has equal purchasing power, but can spend his money as he sees fit.

formity, this would not allow him to have a commitment to a promiscuous variety, either. The aim must be—and this is obvious —to construct a society in which there is an assortment of excellent things that prove satisfying to the various tastes and talents existing at any given time, and in which these things—goods, artifacts, situations—provide the setting, or the raw material, or the source of contemplation or use or adornment or delight for the human beings alive at any given time. The aim must be to construct a society in which individuality flourishes, but within the limits of excellence. That is the ideal, no matter that in a world-community of billions of people that ideal could not conceivably be reached. Skinner asks, "Should we reject such a system on the grounds that in making all students excellent it has made them all alike?"[21] We may substitute "people" for "students" and may answer No and then go on to say what Skinner elsewhere[22] recognizes: the wish is to have all men alike in that they are excellent, not to have all men excellent in the same way. This, ideally, is the nature of utopian equality, an equality which is not the equality of uniformity, and an equality which is compatible with individuality. And to say it again, the combination of abundance and improved methods of assuring virtuous conduct permits the hope that equality can be various and that individuality can be wholly moral.

All that we have been saying may sound unconvincing; it may sound as if we are trying to squeeze into utopia two things —equality and individuality—that really cannot coexist; worse than that, it could be thought that the (abstract) omission from utopia of anything that is not excellent is deplorable. It could be thought that to desire many kinds of excellence is not to go far enough to meet the requirements of individuality and variety. What is wanted is a world which continues to display the full range of human nature; and for that to be the case, not only must there be excellence (of ability, temperament, cultivation, performance), but mediocrity, deviation, folly, triviality, vice, and criminality, as well. For the human comedy to be played well, many more character-types are called for than the utopian pas-

---

21. Skinner, "Freedom and the Control of Men," *op. cit.*, p. 59.
22. Skinner, *Walden Two, op. cit.*, pp. 103-104.

sion for excellence would seem to allow. And for there to be all
the character-types, the very conditions of existence must be
much more varied than the utopian passion for welfare and
justice would seem to allow. By bending every effort to insure
peace and abundance, to eliminate suffering and radical pain, to
habituate men to a more certain virtue: in short, both by making life's path more smooth and men more able to walk it,
utopian society eliminates numerous kinds of individuality from
the world and also impoverishes the kinds of individuality that
manage to remain. The utopian world would not be a world
crowded with a huge array of full-blooded types. It would be
a world with a small number of differing kinds of excellence;
and those kinds would not differ very much from each other.
It is not only that life would be less interesting from the spectator's point of view; this is an esthetic consideration, to be
taken seriously, but not too seriously if one wants to avoid the
charge of immorality. Rather, it is that only in a society in which
there are great differences in styles of life and methods of upbringing and levels of culture and standards of well-being can
there be full individuals representative of any one style, method,
level, or standard. Contrast is needed for any kind of character
to define itself; and it is unthinkable that there could be contrasts sharp or numerous enough within excellence: there are,
after all, a comparatively few ways in which men can be good;
there is only a comparatively small range of human nature that
goodness brings into being. There may be no reason why utopian
society must be a society in which there is a literal uniformity;
but given its passion for universal excellence, *and* the methods
it promises to use to assure that excellence and the conditions in
which that excellence is to be cultivated, something resembling
uniformity is inescapable. And when it is remembered that
utopian society embraces the world, it is seen that still one more
factor making for individuality—that is, cultural diversity—is
weakened, and the peril of uniformity consequently heightened.

To this line of argument, we can only reiterate a thesis which
has appeared several times in our essay; and that is that, in the
abstract, it is undeniable that some of life's sharper contrasts
would be missing from a utopian society. The elimination of

radical evil from social life exacts a cost: one of the costs may very well be the disappearance—or at least, the attenuation—of sharp contrasts of individuality. One of the devices of self-definition—namely, one's pronounced dissimilitude of background, rank, quality, expectation as compared with other people—disappears or is at least weakened. Furthermore, certain kinds of individuality, certain character-types, are, in essence, incongruous with the idea of a utopian society: beggar, soldier, tyrant, benefactor, and others, too. Certain gestures, certain acts, certain traits, go, if a utopian society comes. From the point of view of one who cherishes *every* part of the spectrum of human nature—its light colors and its dark—utopia is a net loss. But one can feel contrarily that, on balance, a world without radical evil is better than one in which the full spectrum of human nature does show itself; and also that the possibilities for exploiting the capacities of human beings for right-doing and for morally acceptable creativity are much greater than the worldly imagination would concede. This may be misplaced piety or wishful thinking; but whatever it is, it is the one answer to the anti-utopian concern for individuality that can be given.

iv

Let our final word on virtue and character in utopia be an admonition to any utopian idealist. We should wish to say that utopian psychology cannot allow itself to grant happiness to people at the cost of limiting their aspirations or narrowing their capacity for experience; it cannot settle for the contentedness of unformed, uncomplicated people. Nor can it allow itself to rest satisfied with the naïve acceptance of its arrangements by people ignorant of contrast and left unable to live any way but the way they live or even to imagine that another way could be possible. The following conversation from Huxley's *Brave New World* must never take place in a modern utopia:

"I suppose Epsilons don't really mind being Epsilons," she said aloud.

"Of course they don't. How can they? They don't know what it's like being anything else. We'd mind, of course. But then we've been differently conditioned. Besides, we start with a different heredity."

"I'm glad I'm not an Epsilon," said Lenina, with conviction.

"And if you were an Epsilon," said Henry, "your conditioning would have made you no less thankful that you weren't a Beta or an Alpha."[23]

Planning must be done with these things in mind, if antiutopian argumentation is to be put down.

---

23. Chap. 5. This is a grotesque version of the sublime moment in *The Divine Comedy* when Piccarda explains why the lower ranks in heaven do not envy the greater fortune of the higher ranks. See *Paradise*, III, lines 64–90.

8

Conclusion

When we come to take a summary view of our whole subject, we see that the surprise we felt at the fact that well-intentioned men could be made despondent by the prospect of a utopian society can give way to a more sober emotion. As we have tried to show, there are a large number of considerations, taken singly or together, that tend to dampen utopian ardor, or that can reinforce an initial skepticism concerning the utopian endeavor. But we want to insist that though these considerations weigh heavily, they should still not be enough to shake the mind completely free from the hold modern utopianism may have on it; nor enough to let us feel that modern antiutopianism is, in most of its tenets, impregnable. We should wish to say that each of the various arguments we have reviewed which are used or can be used to discredit utopianism is, at the least, plausible; and is, sometimes, genuinely compelling. We also must say, however, that, in the end, it is plain common sense which proves to be so fierce to utopianism, rather than the larger and more formal antiutopian arguments. And after common sense has done its damage, we must say, finally, that remorse for the weakened condition of utopianism is the proper feeling to have.

No utopian thinker can deny the value of the antiutopian

critique. To be sure, the common-sense elements of that critique can appear fatal to utopianism, and we hardly expect a utopian thinker to be grateful for being shown the reasons why his fondest dreams seem assigned inevitable failure. But if the voice of common sense is temporarily and conveniently drowned out, and the rest of the antiutopian case listened to, the utopian thinker stands to gain from some of the arguments we have retailed in this essay.

One of the benefits accruing to the utopian thinker from the hostility he meets or can meet is the strong reminder that not everything in the real world is besmirched and must be given up in some world in the future. The sum of human experience cannot be dismissed as evil, or as a mere preparation for some later stage of human development. Certain of the values which both conservatism and liberalism have fought for and achieved, precariously and only with great effort, are to find a place in utopian schemes. These are values which have a permanent force, for they are a part of any definition of civilization or of community or of manliness or of rational morality that can be reasonably suggested.

Another contribution that the antiutopian critique makes to the utopian thinker is to make him realize what he is naturally inclined to overlook or take lightly; and that is that there is a price to be paid for a utopian society—a world society of peace, abundance, and effortless virtue. The price we have in mind is not the price of revolutionary violence, but rather the price in values, situations, responses, attitudes, and accomplishments. It is unavoidably the case that a society of peace, abundance and effortless virtue would seem to have no room for a number of things we in the real world now cherish or respect. The struggle against great odds, against scarcity, against infirmity of will, the chance to do a great deal with very little, the occasion to display certain virtues or habits or characteristics which only a dark world gives, are all, in theory, eliminated from a utopian society. Utopia may seem to confine human nature and to dilute human experience, and offer compensations that are not readily seen to be, in fact, compensations (let alone, more than compensations). (Though we must insist yet again that the price to be paid for a modern utopian society is different in many respects from the price exacted by utopian thinkers in the past.)

Still another favor bestowed by antiutopianism on utopianism is to show the dangers inherent in carrying any utopian value too far. There is one text or another on hand to demonstrate the logical conclusion of each part of the utopian program. Virtue can become automatism, painlessness can become animality, equality can become uniformity or truncation, stability can become stagnation, efficiency can become compulsive routine, social rationality can become social texturelessness, harmony can become lifelessness. Lastly, antiutopian thinkers establish the point that even in utopia it is not possible to have all utopian ends satisfied at the same time. A choice, for example, between anarchism and technological advance would perhaps have to be made; or a choice between bland contentment and intense pleasures.

In short, utopianism must borrow some of the values of the real world; it deprives itself of some of the values of the real world; it tends to be relentless in the pursuit of some of its own values; it may not be able to see all its values coexist. And antiutopian thinkers, and thinkers who are not explicitly antiutopian but whose writing can be employed in attacking utopianism, are always there, ready to sound their warnings; and from these warnings, utopian thinkers have much to take to heart.

And there is one last service various explicit or implicit antiutopian thinkers have to perform. That is to keep constantly before us the awareness that peace, abundance, and effortless virtue do not constitute all there is to man's existence. One can feel that even if all possible social questions be answered, the problems of life have still not been touched at all. There are realms of experience—moral, spiritual, esthetic, intellectual— toward which critics of utopia are more likely to feel protective than utopian thinkers. The latter are generally more interested in relieving pain and correcting social absurdity than in sending the spirit upward. Such an apportionment of sensibility is, in the long run, all to the good. The utopian thinker, however, must give the spirit its due; and the views of Wells in *A Modern Utopia* are, on this matter, admirable. The utopian thinker is left with two questions which are to be found in antiutopian writing in varying degrees of consciousness and in varying intensity: What in the utopian ideal threatens the spirit? How can utopian psychology contrive to promote the workings of the spirit?

These, then, are a few of the ways in which the contact of utopianism with antiutopianism may enrich utopianism. But at this point in our essay, we surely do not wish to imply that there is a parity between utopian idealism and antiutopianism. The common-sense elements in antiutopianism may ultimately cripple utopianism; but before we come to this conclusion—a conclusion pertaining to the practicalities of the matter—we see that there is a good deal that is morally or intellectually suspect in the cluster of antiutopian arguments. If there are terrible oversights and exaggerations in the utopian position (or positions), there are sometimes even worse oversights and exaggerations in the antiutopian positions. For all the strengths in antiutopianism, for all the reasons it can give us to change our surprise that there is antiutopianism (in the first place) into a grudging acknowledgment of its right to exist and be heeded, it nevertheless remains true that there are strange ideas, indeed, at work in it. We have tried to show that, in a number of instances, a contention that is supposed to be, by itself, sufficient to discredit the utopian enterprise is marked with some kind of peculiarity or eccentricity. In our discussion of the antiutopian positions on the use of violence for idealistic ends, we tried to demonstrate that the arguments put forward were disabling for all political action; or were inconsistent; or tended to a parasitic attitude; or could result in consequences more bloody than the competing contention. In our discussion of the antiutopian positions on the nature of government in a modern utopian society—in the period of transition, and afterwards—we tried to demonstrate that the arguments put forward were shrill; or out of touch even with what had already become part of the political life of the United States, the British Commonwealth, and Scandinavia (that is, responsible bureaucracy and intelligent planning); or oblivious to the potentialities of modern technology; or prone to sacrifice moral considerations to esthetic ones. In our discussion of the antiutopian positions on utopian ends, we tried to demonstrate that the arguments put forward were (again) prone to sacrifice moral considerations to esthetic ones; or allowed the delight of the observer to prevail over all other considerations; or showed too timid an attachment to the real world and a reluctance to envisage the rewards of an altered social order;[1] or displayed some dubious philosophical presuppositions; or were world-weary; or tended to make means into ends; or took for ends what were only compensations; or made into ends what no one in the past would have thought could be made into ends. Naturally, not all the antiutopian arguments had one or more of the above shortcomings; and good intentions were almost always in evidence. But too often, an antiutopian attitude has finally to be called immoral, because of what it indicates can be given up in order to preserve something else. The scrupulousness of the antiutopian positions on means is matched by the ruthlessness of the antiutopian positions on ends. Judged by the standard of human welfare, numerous antiutopian arguments are inimical; and real scandal is avoided only because the debate between utopianism and antiutopianism is academic; no antiutopian man is in a position to prevent, by an act of will, a utopian order from coming into being. The course of world affairs will spare him that exertion.

We should say that the model for the antiutopian thinker to imitate is Tocqueville. Though he did not speak directly on the subject of utopianism, Tocqueville spoke on something in

---

1. At one point in *Within a Budding Grove,* Proust tells how Elstir, the painter, had begun by fearing solitude, but had grown to love it "as happens with every big thing which we have begun by fearing, because we know it to be incompatible with smaller things to which we cling, and of which it does not so much deprive us as it detaches us from them. Before we experience it, our whole preoccupation is to know to what extent we can reconcile it with certain pleasures which cease to be pleasures as soon as we have experienced it." [Marcel Proust, *Remembrance of Things Past,* trans. by C. K. Scott Moncrief (2 vols., New York: Random House, 1934), Vol. I, pp. 623–624.] May it be that these words of the master-hedonist can be used to still the fears that the image of utopia seems to arouse in the hearts of well-intentioned men? The tendency of the antiutopian to lock himself fast in the real world is analogous to the tendency of the utopian to lock his imaginary utopia fast in a pre-established pattern. The antiutopian does not allow for the emergence of new excellence; the utopian does not care to allow for the emergence of anything.

some ways similar: the emergence of a democratic and equalitarian society. The importance of the words we are about to quote comes first, from their closeness to our substantive interests; and second, and more important, from the frame of mind they disclose. He who would be both antiutopian and unimpeachably moral must have an attitude analogous to Tocqueville's. Tocqueville said:

When the world was full of men of great importance and extreme insignificance, of great wealth and extreme poverty, of great learning and extreme ignorance, I turned aside from the latter to fix my observation on the former alone, who gratified my sympathies. But I admit that this gratification arose from my own weakness: it is because I am unable to see at once all that is around me, that I am allowed thus to select and separate the objects of my predilection from among so many others. Such is not the case with that Almighty and Eternal Being, whose gaze necessarily includes the whole of created things, and who surveys distinctly, though at once, mankind and man. We may naturally believe that it is not the singular prosperity of the few, but the greater well-being of all, which is most pleasing in the sight of the Creator and Preserver of men. What appears to me to be man's decline is, to His eye, advancement; what afflicts me is acceptable to Him. A state of equality is perhaps less elevated, but it is more just: and its justice constitutes its greatness and its beauty. I would strive, then, to raise myself to this point of the Divine contemplation, and thence to view and to judge the concerns of men.[2]

For clarity, for generosity, for a profound comprehension of all the implications of the position adopted, for the courage both to proclaim an attachment to a position and yet concede that this position may have to be given up, though with aversion, in the name of something higher, Tocqueville's utterance is matchless. That this utterance also expresses a most serious opposition to values that are related to, though not identical with, utopian values, adds to its weight. If antiutopian writers showed, more than they do, the same qualities that Tocqueville showed, the utopian apologist, and perhaps the ordinary moralist as well, would be compelled to have a greater respect for antiutopian arguments.

---

2. Alexis de Tocqueville, *Democracy in America, op. cit.,* Vol. II, p. 410.

Appendix:

A Note on George Orwell and 1984

This essay has been concerned exclusively with benevolent opposition to benevolent utopias. Works like George Orwell's *1984* and Virgil Gheorghiu's *The Twenty-Fifth Hour* (1950) are excluded from the antiutopian category. The fact that a book is about what the future may be, or about a society with total *Gleichschaltung*, or about the sinister uses to which machines can be put does not necessarily make that book antiutopian. Good intentions must be taken for granted if "utopian" and hence "antiutopian" are to have any meaning. The temptation is common to speak about *1984* especially as if it were an antiutopian book, a variation on the themes of Aldous Huxley's *Brave New World*. Huxley's book is clearly an example of benevolent opposition to a benevolent utopia. But the society of 1984 is one in which complete malevolence reigns, a society existing consciously to prevent the consummation of a utopian order, and Orwell is not, of course, endorsing that society. If *Brave New World* is a hell of pleasure, *1984* is a hell of pain; if *Brave New World* is a false heaven, *1984* is a real hell.

Fred L. Polak has used the term "de-utopianizing." [*The Image of the Future*, trans. by Elise Boulding, 2 Vols. (Leyden: 1961), Vol. II, Chap. XVI.] Polak also distinguishes between disutopia, pseudo utopia, semiutopia, and negative utopia. In his book on H. G. Wells, W. Warren Wagar talks about "inverted utopias," but does not distinguish between novels which paint an awfully benevolent future, novels which paint a malevolent one, and futurist novels which paint neither. [*H. G. Wells and the World State* (New Haven: Yale University Press, 1961), pp. 252-253.] We could, with George Woodcock ["Utopias in

Negative," *The Sewanee Review,* LXIV (1956), pp. 81-97],
speak of the society of 1984 as a negative utopia, in which
the contrary of every utopian end prevails in order to satisfy
the power-sadism of the Inner Party, and in full realization
that the technical means are on hand to produce a social
order ". . . in which men should live together in a state
of brotherhood, without laws and without brute labor," the
idea of which had ". . . haunted the human imagination for
thousands of years." (*1984, op. cit.,* p. 205.) O'Brien, a member
of the Inner Party of one of the three superstates, describes
the political system of 1984 as ". . . the exact opposite of the
stupid hedonistic utopias that the old reformers imagined" (p.
270).

To be sure, some of the features, some of the institutional
arrangements of life in 1984 bear some resemblance to those of
past utopias. Hence it appears as if Orwell were saying that past
utopias were evil as Oceania is evil. But these are debased resemblances: Oceania stands to past utopias as Dante's Hell of
many circles stands to Dante's Heaven of many circles; as Dante's
three-headed Satan stands to Dante's triune God. Nor does
Orwell imply that Oceania is the logical conclusion, the fully-
developed embodiment, of past utopias or utopian thought.

In his essay on Arthur Koestler (1944), Orwell says: "It
is the dream of a just society which seems to haunt the human
imagination ineradicably and in all ages, whether it is called
the Kingdom of Heaven or the classless society, or whether it
is thought of as a Golden Age which once existed in the past
and from which we have degenerated." (Orwell, *Critical Essays,
op. cit.,* p. 133.) But, adds Orwell, "Perhaps, however, whether
desirable or not, it [the Earthly Paradise] isn't possible. Perhaps
some degree of suffering is ineradicable from human life, perhaps the choice before man is always a choice of evils, perhaps
even the aim of socialism is not to make the world perfect but
to make it better." And, "Men can only be happy when they do
not assume that the object of life is happiness." However, in
"Politics vs. Literature: an Examination of *Gulliver's Travels,*"
Orwell wrote the "Utopian" words quoted on page vi of this book.

Index

Acculturation, 155
Acton, Lord, 96n
Adam, 190-191
Adams, Henry, 96n
Adaptivity, 186
American character, 180-181
American society, 201
Anarchism, 70, 72, 82, 83
    and democracy, 88
Anderson, Quentin, 144
Animal Farm, 45
Anthropology, 217
Anti-Soviet feeling, 45
Antiutopianism, 2-3
    benefits of, 232-233
    imperatives of, 18
    modern, 3, 4, 14
Aquinas, St. Thomas, 72n
Arcadia, 7n, 72
Arendt, Hannah, 4n, 29n, 98, 111,
    128n, 212
Aristocracy, 70, 83-87
Aristotle, 4, 55, 71, 88, 138
Art and neurosis, 130
Arvin, Newton, 128n
Auden, W. H., 11n, 117, 188n
Authority, 72, 76
Automatic virtue, *see* Conditioned
    virtue
Automation, 76, 110
Autonomy in utopia, 93
Ayer, A. J., 150, 151n

Bagehot, W., 60n
Bakunin, M. A., 54
Banfield, E. C., 61n
Bauer, R. A., 51n
Behaviorist theory, 143-144, 215
Bellamy, Edward, 10, 95, 211, 224
Benn, S. I., 56n
Berdyaev, N. A., 13, 14, 187n

Berlin, Isaiah, 51n, 62, 222n
Bernstein, Eduard, 74
Bestor, A. E., 201
Blake, William, 134n, 183
Blood sacrifice, 116
Brave New World, 13, 20, 86, 104,
    126, 129, 135, 141, 166, 217n,
    227, 235
Brinton, Crane, 48n, 49
Brothers Karamazov, The, 36
Brown, N. O., 156n
Brzezinski, Z., 51n
Büchner, Georg, 54
Bureaucracy, 16, 59, 61, 65, 102
    and bureaucrats, 60n, 61
    "permanent," 103
Burke, Edmund, 48n, 55, 117, 120n,
    135
Butler, Samuel, 109

Cadoux, C. J., 30n, 31n
Calvin, John, 26, 28
Camus, Albert, 38, 44, 192n
Capek, Karel, 109
Capital punishment, 40
Capitalism, 74
Carlyle, A. J., 6
Censorship, 78
Character
    American, 180-181
    psychological, 142
    in utopia, 210-227
    and virtue, 210-211, 227-228
Character formation, 142, 147, **149,**
    153, 178, 203, 226
    control of, 196
    cultural effects on, 151
Character structure, 142
Character-types, 225-227
Chesterton, G. K., 117n
Child training, 155, 162, 169, **171,**
    200, 205